MEN'S TRADITIONS REVISED

BY

ESTHER SPRADLING

Order this book online at www.trafford.com
or email orders@trafford.com

Most Trafford titles are also available at major online book retailers.

Printed in the United States of America.

ISBN: 978-1-4269-7954-5 (sc)
ISBN: 978-1-4269-7955-2 (e)

Library of Congress Control Number: 2011912834

Trafford rev. 06/28/2012

www.trafford.com

North America & international
toll-free: 1 888 232 4444 (USA & Canada)
phone: 250 383 6864 • fax: 812 355 4082

Our Heavenly Father,
Help us to be worthy of your only
begotten Son, Jesus Christ. Open the minds
and hearts of those who read this book, and give
them full understanding of your pure word and may
every word engulf them with joy and a peace of mind as
you set them free from bondage's of men's traditions.
May the living God fill us all with His Holy Spirit and
bring lost souls into the light of your truth.
In Jesus Christ's name I pray.
Amen

TWO MOST IMPORTANT REFERENCES

* "*The Companion Bible*" and * "The Strong's Concordance Dictionary": are the two most compatible books on the market, to obtain for our in depth study. "*The Companion Bible*" provides marginal notes that gave us all of the translations of the ancient "*Massoretic-Critical Text*" of the Hebrew language recorded in the "*Old Testament", by* Dr. C. D. Ginsburg and His team. They not only provided the translations of the *"Great Massorah Text" in their* foot notes, but also the 198 Appendixes that provides us with additional in-depth understanding of the subject, time, place, additional scriptures and information that apply to each verse in the "*King James Bible*", also located within "The Companion Bible". We are brought into light with facts and phenomena that were hidden within the "*Great Massorah*". We have become more aware of many astonishing facts recorded in God's Word as we studied the foot notes. Our understanding gives us renewed hope, reassurance and determination to seek the hidden truth of God's word as we grow. The truth amplifies it's self and becomes more exciting, adventurous, dynamic, and intriguing as it brings forth new questions and answers that thrill our souls.

The Marginal Notes in * "*The Companion Bible"* were given by Dr. C. D. Ginsburg, who also collected the "*Massorah Critical Text"* of the *Hebrew Bible,* from all over the world. The 198 Appendixes provides a wealth of information regarding the Hebrew "*Sacred Massorah Text"* that comes alive to those who want to study to show ourselves approved unto God. The Bible is full of idioms, that are pointed out in our Bible. Its order is determined by knowing, when and where the subjects were written, according to the original Text. "*The Companion Bible"* contains the "*King James version",* that allows us to translate and judge whether our understanding is correct or not, according to what the words in the Bible teaches us, whereby we know that the Bible always proves its self when we rightly divide the word of truth.

* The "*Strong's Concordance Dictionary*", with numbers, has the *Hebrew, Greek,* and *Chilean* languages as well as other valuable information. These two books work together, to bring us full understanding of this dynamic, exciting, and rewarding venture into God's living Word. We see clearly the world that once was; where Our Heavenly Father's domain is, where we go when we die, and the complete history of this world we live in, as well as eternity. You will discover that the Bible stands alone, without errors. It gives us hope, covers our sin, builds us into a person worthy of His Kingdom because the Bible proves it's self. The Holy Bible is full of amazing and astonishing truths that fills us with pure joy, if only we will try to study to show ourselves approved. It's truths These are the two books we must use to study so we can know for ourselves, just as God's pure word has revealed them to us in this book.

These references were created in London England at Oxford University by authors from different parts of the world from 1840 into the early 1900's. Their books were designed to help students obtain complete understanding of God's word. Each author had their own team of men working under them. They all knew the languages necessary to translate the ancient languages into English. They researched the ancient, "*Massorah Text*" that Ezra and Nehemiah preserved in Hebrew and Chadian languages. They have revealed the hidden meaning of God's words so that we can know His truth today.

The authors listed below worked together at Oxford University for eight years, translating and preserving the ancient text that Ezra and Nehemiah spent their lives protecting. This text is called "*The fenced to the Scripture*", and also known as the "*Great Massorah Text".* Not one jot nor tittle could be changed, because the fenced Scriptures locked in every letter of every word just as Ezra and Nehemiah wrote them centuries ago. This fenced Massorah Text is spoken of in the New Testament in Mat. 5:18 and Luke16:17, and in the *"Old Testament"*, recorded in Neh. 8:1-8 This informa-tion comes from, Appendixes 30 in "*The Companion Bible*".

Detailed Instruction of how to use, the Strong's Dictionary is found within it. Every word written in the "*King James Bible*" can be found within "*Strong's Concordance_Dictionary*", with numbers we can find the root word, written by James Strong. This Dictionary provides us with numbers written in K.J.B. From these numbers, we can find the root word to obtain the meaning of the original word of the "*Great Massorah Text*" that Ezra, Nehemiah, and the Levities, has preserved for us. They were known as the high priests. These two books coincide with one other which give us a deeper under-standing of various key words within a sentence that determines the exact meaning of the ancient Hebrew or Greek & Chadian words. You will fully understand the ancient languages and learn how the meaning of words have changed from the Hebrew of the *Old Testament* and the Greek in the *New Testament*. It's the most rewarding and thrilling adventure anyone could ever want to pursue.

After choosing a word, look it up in the "*Strong's Concordance Dictionary*". Then go to your strong's Concordance and locate the chapter and verse where your word is recorded. Notice that it lists all of the places that your word is written in through out the entire Bible, both in the Old and New Testament. Find the exact scripture in the list. By determining where your word came from, the Old or New Testament, you will know the exact meaning of your word by the reference number. After you find your Scripture listed, go to the left to find its reference number. This number is the key in finding our root word so be sure to write it down on a piece of paper because it may change several times before you find your root word. When you find the number of your root word, circle it to make sure you know which one it was later on. If your scripture was found in the Old Testament, you will go to the Hebrew Dictionary to find your number. You may be given several different numbers, so be sure to write each new number down and continue on until you find the number of your "*root word*". This will give you the exact meaning of what that word meant in ancient times.

Go through the same process in the New Testament, when Jesus lived, using the Greek Dictionary. The Old and New Testaments have different meanings, because they were written in different periods of time and at different locations. For example in Hebrew, the word "*mountain*" really means "mountain", where as in Greek it means, "*Nations*", depending on what period of time it was written, and in what language it was spoken. The word "cloud*," means* a cloud in the sky, yet this same word "cloud" in a different verse means a "*crowd of people*" depending on whether it was written in the Old or New Testament. This sample shows us why it's important to learn how to use the "*Strong's Concordance"* so we will know what the words meant when it was written. We have used this method of study for the past twenty five years. This is how we can say that God's word proves it's self. Because God's word has recorded the same stories throughout the Bible in many different places by different prophets of the Lord. The Bible proves it's self through out the entire both New and Old Testaments Bible. He has spoken His word and it will come to pass exactly as it is written because, He is the eternal God, Jesus Christ, King of Kings, who is the only one worthy to be called God! We know Him as the triune God, the Father, Son and Holy Spirit.

Index

RAPTURE
Chapter 1

Most denominations today are built on "Men's *Traditions*" that goes against God's Holy Bible, such as Easter being mixed with Passover. Their religious customs are so grounded in their traditions that people have lost sight of the truth that's recorded in the Bible. They have established their own laws and customs, which have been in their families for many generations, and if anyone departs from their traditions it causes stress among them. Although their traditions have perverted God's pure word, they continue preaching them.

The first tradition that God has warned us about in our final generation, is the Rapture Theory, which was mixed with Passover, and people today don't know the difference between them. Passover was one of God's most Holy Days; it was when the children of Israel had been in Egypt for the past 400 years, every since Joseph was carried down into Egypt, and was sold by his brother's into slavery. God told Moses to go to the Pharaoh and tell him to, "*Let My people go.*" The Pharaoh had a hardened heart against Israel and refused God's request. That night was the fourteenth day after the Spring Vernal Equinox, when the death angel passed over Egypt and claimed the lives of the first born of both mankind and animals. Passover was given to us by God as a reminder of His wrath upon the Pharaoh, and those who refused to do as He had said in Exodus 11:1.

Exodus 11:1 "*The Lord said unto Moses, "Yet will I bring one plague more upon Pharaoh, and upon Egypt; afterwards he will let you go hence: when he shall let you go, he shall surely thrust you out hence altogether.*"

Moses listens to God's instruction, and prepared the people for the final plague that would come upon Egypt.

Exodus 11:4,5 And Moses said, "*Thus said the Lord, about midnight will I go out into the midst of Egypt:" "And all the firstborn in the land of Egypt shall die, from the firstborn of Pharaoh that sets upon his throne, even unto the firstborn of the maid servant that is behind the mill and all the firstborn of the beast.*"

Remember, the followers of Jesus Christ had to take the blood of an innocent lamb and spread it on the door posts of their front door, and over the top of the door, to prevent the death angel from entering their home.

Just like the Pharisees of Jesus day, many pastors today are spiritual blind and have closed their minds to the instructions recorded in God's word. Their heart is like the Pharaoh's heart was, so hardened that he couldn't see why God was so angry. People today are just like the Pharaoh was back then. The night of the fourteenth day after the first day of the year, God established the Spring Vernal Equinox; That was when the Death Angel passed over Egypt. The next day when Pharaoh arose, all the first born, of both animal's and people were dead, even his own son. That's when the Pharaoh's heart was changed, and he forced the Israelites to get out of his land that same day. This established the first tradition in the scripture that God put upon His people, known through out the nation of Israel which included all ten tribes of Israel.

Exodus 12:14,15 "*And this day shall be unto you for a memorial; and ye shall keep it a feast to the Lord throughout your generations; ye shall keep it a feast by an ordinance for ever." "Seven days shall ye eat unleavened bread; even the first day ye shall put away leaven out of your houses: for whosoever eateth leavened bread from the first day until the seventh day, that soul shall be cut off from Israel.*"

This feast day is called Passover, not Easter. When the death angel passed over the Israelites, they were under the Law and also those who prepared the blood of the lamb for their homes. We are to keep it, "*for ever*" until the end of this earth age which comes with the return of the true Jesus Christ. Today we use olive oil, prayer and faith in the Lord God who will keep us safe in these end times.

When we read I Corinthians 5:5-8 we see that Paul is reminding us to keep the time of Passover, not as they did under the law, but as required in the New Testament.

I Corinthians 5:7,8 "*Purge out therefore the old leaven, that ye may be a new lump, as ye are unleavened, For even Christ our Passover is sacrificed for us:*" "*Therefore let us keep the feast, not with old leaven, neither with the leaven of malice and wickedness; but with the unleavened bread of sincerity and truth.*"

Under the traditions of the Old Testament, the Passover was when they sacrificed animals, however when Jesus Christ died on the cross, the animal sacrifice stopped. Today this feast time is celebrated in our churches, and is called, "*The Communion Table of the Lord.*"

Today we take wine and unleavened bread at the Communion table worthily. We think only about Jesus Christ. Because of the shed blood of Jesus Christ we can take the bread and wine which is symbolic of the body and blood of Jesus Christ, as we focus on His Sacrifice for our sins. The reason this tradition is first, is that so many denominations have already accepted their Rapture doctrine. Their doctrine believe that their church will be taken out of this world, in these end times, before the sixth trumpet sounds. Millions of Christians will follow their false Christ, because they believe that Satan will free them from bondage. They will cover the earth during the final five months of this earth age. of mankind. Revelation 9:4,5 tells us clearly that only the Elect will be ready for Satan's arrival at the sixth trumpet, and those who are not sealed in their mind with the truth, will be taken in by Satan, in ignorance. If people knew these words are the gospel truth, wouldn't they want to tell everyone so they can have their eyes opened to God's pure word? The word Revelation means, revealed in Greek.

Daniel 9:27 tells us about the, *"Abomination of Desolation"*. The desolator Satan, will eliminate *"The Communion Table"* known as taking bread and wine in the churches, because most Christians will believe that Satan is the true Christ that has returned. However the Elect of God know that's a lie, they will not follow them. Most Christians today don't know what they should believe, because their pastors has told them that the book of Revelation and the Old Testament is not to be understood, yet the word Revelations mean's to be revealed. Jesus warned us in Matthew 24:15,16.

Matthew 24:15,16 *"When ye therefore shall see the abomination of desolation, spoken of by Daniel the prophet, stand in the holy place, whoso readeth, let him understand:" "Then let them which be in Judaea flee into the mountains:" "Let him which is on the housetop not come down to take anything out of his house:"*

If you believe in the Rapture theory that came from a vision of a mentally disturbed fifteen year old girl named Margaret MacDonald, from Scotland, in May 30,1830, rather than what the scripture tells us. That's your choice, but remember that the word of God always proves it self. Even if the word of God proves that it's a lie, there will be thousands of souls who will follow their pastors, yet some will change their minds. If the truth is not allowed in the churches and it's taken from the earth like Amos warned us about in Amos 8:11-12. We learn that the Rapture doesn't fit into the scriptures, there are millions of people who are deceived by believing in this deadly doctrine. It destroys the souls of mankind and will lead souls into Satan's camp when he arrives. Even today pastors are killing themselves because they fear the wrath of God is down upon them for teaching the Rapture Theory. Yet, all they have to do is repent and tell their followers the truth, then get out of the "*World Council of Churches*" before it's too late. Pastors may loose their retirement, but not their souls, if they repent before the *"Great Tribulations"* takes place. When Satan arrives to lead mankind into all sorts of evil activities that will take people into darkness and despair, it will be too late to repent.

Matthew 24:21,22 "*For then shall be great tribulation, such as was not since the beginning of the world [flesh age] to this time, no, nor ever shall be." "And except those days should be shortened, there should no flesh be saved: but for the elect's sake those days shall be shortened.*"

The reason the Elect of God are so special at the time of the sixth trumpet, when all the other Christians are not mentioned by Jesus in Revelation 9:4. It tells us that the Elect of God will know the entire Plan of God and that it's "*sealed in their* minds, so when the sixth trumpet sounds they will know that Satan is not the true Jesus Christ nor the Messiah. They are the only ones that knows God's Plan, the rest of the Christian world will believe in Satan as their savior, in ignorance. They will become, *The Great Harlot* of Revelation 17 that goes whoring after the kings of this earth, with Satan in command. This is revealed to us, to set us free in the true Jesus Christ our Savior.

Revelation 17:1,2 "*And there came one of the seven angels which had the seven vials, and talked with me, saying unto me, "Come hither; I will shew unto thee the judgment of the great whore that sitteth upon many waters:" "With whom the kings of the earth have committed fornication, and the inhabitants of the earth have been made drunk with the wine of her fornication."*

Remember John was taken into heaven in this chapter and he looked forward into the end of this flesh age, then he was told to write down the things that Jesus Christ revealed to him. These events are stored in the minds of the Elect that's why Satan can't tempt the Elect of God, because they know who he is. Those that have been listening to the Kenite's lies will see Satan in all his splendor, they will receive his free gifts and believe in his supernatural powers. Satan's followers will believe that he is the true Jesus Christ, who has come to carry them away in a Rapture, but that will never take place.

The *"Judgment"* of *"the Great Whore"* are the Christian Churches *"that setteth upon many waters."* which are Christian nations that have been taken in by Satan and his army of fallen angels when they are booted out of heaven upon the earth with him.

They are multitudes of peoples, nations and tongues that this old whore has turned into a spiritual wilderness, today it's known as the *"One World Government,"* which is the United Nations of today. Their whorish churches will rule the world, and Satan will give them their power, through their *"World Council of Churches". They* will be deceived as they bow to Satan as their god. This is also referred to as the *"Abomination of Desolation"* that Jesus was speaking of in Matthew 24:15.

Revelation 17:8 *"The beast that thou sawest was, and is not; and shall ascend out of the bottomless pit, and go into perdition: and they that dwell on the earth shall wonder, whose names were not written in the book of life from the foundation of the world, when they behold the beast that was, and is not, and yet is."*

The son of perdition is Satan, also known as the dragon or the beast, is the *"Great Deceiver"* of this earth age. Satan will not be in the Millennium Age because he and all of his fallen angels will be cast into the bottomless pit for a thousand years. All the people on the entire earth, except for the Elect of God, will "wonder" and be amazed by Satan's supernatural powers that he holds over them as they willingly bow to him as their savior. Most churches that claim the name of Christ are all part of the "*Great Whore*", "*The Mystery of Babylon The Great*", "The *Mother of Harlots*" and known as "*Abominations of the Earth*", in verse five. Remember those Christians who bowed to Satan are from the five churches of Rev. ch. 2-3 that did not know who the Kenites were. They will accept Satan in ignorance. However they are saved by their works at the end of the Millennium Age. It's time to get out of those churches, and confess your sins that go against God's word before it's too late. These are God's warnings to the modern churches, from Jesus Christ's pure living word from our "*King James Bible*" before it's too late.

Revelation 2:26,27 "*He that overcometh, and keepeth My works unto the end, to him will I give power over the nations:*" "*And he shall rule them with a rod of iron; as the vessels of a potter shall they be broken to shivers: even as I received of My Father.*"

Christian denominations who say that the church is not mentioned after Revelation 1, are correct. However they don't understand when God took Apostle John into heaven in his Spirit. The truth was shown to Paul rather than the churches. God revealed these things to Paul, so that we can know and fully understand what these events mean to us in these end times. It was written so that the Elect of God will be sealed in their minds with God's truth when the true Jesus Christ returns at the sounding of the seventh trumpet in the end times.

These events are recorded in Rev. 4-20, it gives us the description of the 1000 years of Millennium, where as Rev. 21-22 gives us the description of the Eternal age and the entire Godhead when all of mankind will be changed into their spirit bodies. The moment Christ returns we will be changed into our spirit bodies instantly, and our world as we know it will be completely destroyed. Every living soul is in their spirit bodies, and we're in the *New Heaven* and *New Earth* when it comes down to earth and settles in Jerusalem, God's favorite place on earth.

Those who bowed to Satan in ignorance have to wait until after the 1000 years of the Millennium age is over and then their judgment will be according to their works. They won't know whether or not their names will be written in the Lamb's book of life until after the Millennium age is over. That's when God's final judgment takes place. Its also known as the, "*Great White Throne of God.*"

Revelation 20:12,13 "*And I saw the dead, small and great, stand before God; and the books were opened: and another book was opened, which is the book of life; and the dead were judged out of those things that were written in the books, according to their works." "And the sea gave up the dead which were in it; and death and hell delivered up the dead which were in them: and they were judged every man according to their works.*"

Those souls who chose not to follow God's warnings will be judged by their works in the Millennium age. They will not receive grace from our Lord Jesus Christ because they rejected Christ in this second earth age of mankind. These spiritual dead souls are the ones who followed Satan, even after they had said a prayer to accept the Lord Jesus Christ as their savior. In their ignorance they believed in the Rapture Theory their churches taught them, therefore they will be led into Satan's camp, as a lamb is lead to slaughter.

This is why the rapture doctrine is so dangerous, it gives a false sense of security, and takes away the desire to study the Bible and prepares people to follow Satan in the sixth trumpet when he arrives. This is from the Holy word of God not what I think, The Bible records it.

Revelation 20:14,15 "*And death and hell were cast into the lake of fire. This is the second death." "And whosoever was not found written in the book of life was cast into the lake of fire.*"

God warned us through the Prophet Ezekiel regarding, what He thinks about those who teach His people to fly.

Ezekiel 13:20,21 *"Wherefore thus saith the Lord God; `Behold, I am against your pillows, wherewith ye there hunt the souls to make them fly, and I will tear them from your arms, and will let the souls go, even the souls that ye hunt to make them fly." "Your kerchiefs also will I tear, and deliver My People out of your hand, and they shall be no more in your hand to be hunted; and ye shall know that I am the Lord."*

The "*pillows*" and "*kerchiefs*" means, man made promises and false doctrines, designed to give people a false sense of security. This is exactly what Nimrod was teaching the people in Genesis 11. They were trying to build their own way back into heaven to be in the presence of God. All traditions are created by people who try to reason a way into eternal life, and avoid the death of their physical bodies. God has a master plan and He has told us how to find our way back to Him, it is all written in the "*King James Bible.*" We are not to change one "*jot nor tittle*" of the "*Massorah Text.*" However we can translate every word with the tools the Lord has preserved for us. *See the list of References in the back of this book.

When the Thessalonians were in doubt as to the location of their loved ones that died and went to be with the Lord, Paul wrote to them telling them exactly where the souls of their loved ones went. The modern day church world has taken this verse and twisted it to make an escape for them to avoid facing Satan the Antichrist. They call it the Rapture Theory. It made a way for them to avoid going through the Great Tribulation that Jesus has told us about in Matthew 24, Mark 13, and Luke 21. The pillar of their false doctrine comes from I Thessalonians 4:13,14-17, and by looking deeper into their doctrines and comparing them with what the Bible actually tells us we learn that, it's vital that we fully understand the truths recorded in God's word. The subject in these verses are all in verse 13.

I Thessalonians 4:13 "*But I would not have you to be ignorant, brethren, concerning them which are asleep, that ye sorrow not, even as other which have no hope.*"

To understand these verses, set aside all your preconceived ideas about the rapture theory, then decide if you're willing to accept it as truth once you have studied these verses. Paul told the Thessalonians to live right in their community, and search their own souls for sin in their lives and then repent of their sins. Then Paul spoke about the subject of what happens when death comes to the human body. This topic was important to Paul, for it is the stabilizing factor in the lives of all Christians because it removes the fear that comes from not knowing about death. Paul is giving us this information so that we will not be ignorant like the heathens concerning death.

The subject is about those "*which are asleep*". They were concerned about their loved ones that had died. Paul tells us not to be sorry for those Christians that have died and gone to be with the Lord, because they have the hope of salvation. The heathen have no hope because they believe life is over at the time of burial. People even go to the grave site and talk to the dead souls but they are not there because their soul lives on, they are with God in heaven. Remember God created every living soul in the first earth age, and all living souls belong to the creator.

I Thessalonians 4:14 "*For if we believe that Jesus died and rose again, even so them also which sleep in Jesus will God bring with him.*"

Christians believe that Jesus Christ set the example for us, and we will follow after Him. Jesus died and rose again into His eternal body, therefore we will do the same in like manner. To sleep means to die, in their flesh bodies. The Greek text is very clear about it. The subject in this text is; "*that ye not be ignorant as to where the dead are.*" This is talking about Christians who know the Word of God and were under the teaching of Paul.

If you claim to be a Christian you know and believe that Jesus Christ died, was buried and after the third day rose from the dead. He came out of the tomb victorious. If you don't believe this, Paul classifies you as being ignorant and a heathen which is an unbeliever. Solomon wrote in Ecclesiastes.

Ecclesiastes 12:7; *"To be absent from the body [flesh body] is to be present with the Lord."*

When the flesh body has died, the soul body instantly leaves, and the flesh is left to rot back into the dust of the earth from which it was made of, and our soul body is in heaven in the presence of the Lord; all living souls that have passed away were either saved or unsaved: Some will receive rewards and other will be judged.

I Thessalonians 4:15 *"For we say unto you, by the word of our Lord, that we which are alive and remain unto the coming of the Lord shall not prevent in no wise [precede] them which are asleep."*

"The coming of the Lord" is at the sounding of the seventh and last trumpet. This is the time when all saints are gathered back to the Lord. The Lord has given His warnings to all those who are saved, and it's time for the Elect to be alert and watch for His coming. Many that call themselves Christians will be ignorant, and blind regarding the warnings of God's word. God has revealed to us all of the things that would happen before His return. One of them is in Matthew 24:15, *"the Abomination of Desolation spoken of by Daniel."* This happens after the sixth trumpet when Satan is on his throne in Jerusalem here on this earth, playing the role of the false Christ.

Jesus expects us to know all the meanings of these seals. We are told to know the truths of God's word because they will be sealed in our minds before Satan's arrival so we won't be deceived. Satan will look just like what we expect the true Jesus Christ to look like, he will talk and perform supernatural acts just like Jesus did when He walked on this earth. Jesus doesn't want us to be deceived by Satan, nor his children the Kenites, who are already living among us, as well as his army of fallen angels who have had their offspring with women. Notice the extremely tall and very large people living today.

Paul told us in I Corinthians 15:50-52 that we will not see the true Jesus Christ's return while we are still living in our flesh corruptible bodies. If you think you are seeing Jesus Christ pinch yourself and if you feel it, you will know it's Satan disguised as Jesus Christ. Because we will only see the true Jesus Christ if we're living in our spiritual bodies, at the sounding of the seventh trumpet, when all living souls on earth will be changed instantly. All of mankind will be changed from their corruptible flesh bodies, into their incorruptible bodies like the angels have. For the next thousand years those souls who followed Satan will have to prove themselves by their works, in order to have their names put into the Lambs book of life. That's "*the mystery*" Paul told us about. "*We shall not sleep [die] but we shall all be changed.*" There is no Rapture Doctrine nor any hiding place from Satan, we either make a stand against him, or we are ready at the coming of our Lord at the seventh trumpet, if not we will stand in shame still looking for the fly away doctrine to be saved.

This fifteenth chapter is written to the end generation, and those still alive at the sounding of the seventh and last trumpet. We all are living today in the sixth trumpet, we are waiting for the seventh trumpet to occur. You are either going to be a faithful servant when the Lord Jesus Christ comes at the seventh trumpet, or you are going to be a pregnant bride of Satan standing before the Lord in shame. This will occur right here on this earth when the millennium begins. It's your choice. God loves you no matter which way you chose because He died on the cross for your sins and He created you.

I Thessalonians 4:16 "*For the Lord himself shall descend from heaven* [at the seventh trump] *with a shout, with a voice* *of the archangel, and with the trump of God: and the dead in Christ shall rise first;"*

Once again the subject of these verses is, *Where are the dead in Christ* ? The dead in Christ have gone into heaven to be with Him and at the seventh trumpet when Jesus returns, those dead souls are all ready with the Lord. They went into heaven instantly when they died. It doesn't matter if it happened in Paul's day or a thousand years later in our generation. At death our spirit body goes directly to the Lord instantly, and every living soul that He has ever created is with Him. By this time we have already lived through, The Great Tribulation and will face Satan.

If you were sealed with the truth of God's Word in our mind, and we stand fast in His word and we know our soul is preserved in Christ for eternity. However, if anyone is not sealed in their mind with the truth, they will become Satan's bride. This is why the Rapture theory is so dangerous. It makes people ignorant of the things we're talking about in this book.

If your hope of salvation is in the Rapture Doctrine, then you will be rejoicing with Satan when he kills the two witnesses of God, and you will spend that last three and a half days of this earth age, rejoicing with Satan, while he is claiming himself to be God. Revelation 11:1-12 is telling us all about it. Read it for yourself.

I Thessalonians 4:17 "*Then we which are alive and remain shall be caught up together with them in the clouds, to meet the Lord in the air: and so shall we ever be with the Lord.*"

It's time to pay attention to these verses. The word "*clouds*" spoken of here, are in reference to a large gathering of people, in fact this refers to all the people that are living upon the face of the earth at the sounding of the seventh trumpet because it's the last trumpet. No one is going anywhere, because the seventh trumpet is the start of Jesus' Millennium Kingdom right here on earth in Jerusalem. This time is spoken of in Ezekiel 40-48, when all souls will be changed from their flesh bodies into their spiritual bodies just as the angels have. There is No Fly Away Doctrine, and no way to escape the tribulation of the Antichrist, which is Satan's deceptions. The true Jesus Christ will return and end Satan's Tribulation and we will all be changed instantly, faster than you can blink an eye as we inter into the *New Millennium age*. The "*Air*" spoken of here is the "the breath of air we take while living in our flesh bodies", after we're changed into our spiritual body known as our incorruptible bodies, we will never get sick, nor die again because we're in our spirit bodies at this time.

The whole idea of the rapture doctrine started in May of 1830 in Scotland by a mentally ill teen age girl. She was having strange visions and her visions were written down by her pastor. This entire story is in the book titled, "*The Incredible Cover-up*", by Dave MacPherson & Margarette MacDonald. By her own admission, she said that, "when this vision came to her, it was evil" because it was a doctrine of demons given to her from the Devil. Satan gives this same kind of vision to any Christian that is looking for an easy way out of this life. They say the repentance prayer at a meeting, and now they think it is up to the Lord to protect them. He will but only if we search His word for our selves, in prayer. The Holy Spirit will teach us truth if we are sincere.

This doctrine has spread like wild fire throughout the Christian world while the events of the end times are happening today all around us. The trumpets started many years ago, when the United Nations were formed and Israel became a nation. There is not much time left to prepare. Remember that the Rapture Doctrine is so deadly it could destroy those souls who believe in it.

Paul said the damage of his first letter caused much confusion by the Pharisee's who twisted the truth so much that

Paul was compelled to write his second letter to the Christians in the Thessalonians church because of perdition.

II Thessalonians 2:2,3 "*That ye be not soon shaken in mind, or be troubled, neither by spirit, nor by word, nor by letter as from us, as that the day of Christ is at hand.*" "*Let no man deceive you by any means: for that day shall not come, except there come a falling away first, and that man of sin be revealed, the son of perdition;*"

Satan is the *"man of sin"*, known as the "*son of perdition*". The day that Paul is talking about is at the coming of our Lord Jesus Christ. That day is at the sounding of the seventh trumpet, when this flesh age is done away with. The Great Tribulation is over, and Satan will be locked away in the pit. Remember that the falling away or Apostasy of Satan comes first. Today we're living in that time of Apostasy.

II Thessalonians 2:4 "*Who opposeth and exalteth himself above all that is called God, or that is worshipped; so that he as God sitteth in the temple of God, shewing himself that he is God.*"

Satan is the one that opposes and exalts himself above God. His pride caused his fall in the first earth age, and he will demonstrate His wickedness at the sounding of the sixth trumpet. When Satan sits in Jerusalem telling the world that he is God and if you believe in the Rapture, you will think that Satan is God. Because Revelation 9:5 tells us that God the Father will turn your soul over to him, and you will worship him in ignorance if you choose to follow traditions of men. Also recorded in II Thessalonians 2:5-13. It's your choice, we were all given a free will, to chose who we will serve. God Almighty is our only judge.

PARABLE OF THE FIG TREE
Chapter 2

For centuries Christians have tried to keep sexual matters from their small children, and the best way was to create a lie that was believable. Eve's sin was not eating an apple then sharing it with Adam. Understanding the truth makes it clear and helps us to know the other mysteries in the scriptures such as all the parables that Jesus taught. One of the final warnings that Jesus gave us before He went to the cross was, "*Learn the Parable of the Fig tree*". Today, most Christians including pastors have no idea what the, "*Parable of the Fig tree*" is all about.

Paul gave us a glimpse of what happened in the Garden of Eden when he wrote about how Eve was beguiled in II Corinthians 11:1-3.

II Corinthians 11:1-3 "*Would to God ye could bear with me a little in my folly: and indeed bear with me.*" "*For I am jealous over you with godly jealousy: for I have espoused you to one husband, that I may present you as a chaste virgin to Christ.*" "*But I fear, lest by any means, as the serpent beguiled Eve through his subtlety* (cunning-crafty), *so your minds should be corrupted from the simplicity that is in Christ.*"

Paul established the Corinthian Church and after he finished teaching there, he moved to another location to start another church. Paul begins to warn his people about, allowing false doctrine to come into their churches and trying to change the meaning of God's pure word. Paul had righteous jealousy toward his converts. He had nurtured those Christians at the very beginning in Jesus Christ, they were taught to become a virgin "*bride of Jesus Christ*", and were known as the anointed ones.

Paul is telling these Christians that he wants to present them as "*chased virgins to Christ*", symbolically; was a virgin bride that has not been exposed to preachers and their false doctrines. Paul is using a physical event of what happened to Eve in the Garden of Eden. The early church knew the truth about Eve, but they taught them a false story about eating an apple in the garden, where by the people chose to believe their lies. To day we know that when a young woman is espoused to her husband, and if she gives herself to another man before their marriage vows are exchanged. That woman is carrying another man's child in her womb, and she is not a virgin, she is an unfaithful bride just like Eve was.

Child bearing is caused by the conception between a man and a woman without them both, there would be no children. The life of a child grows within the woman until it is born. Every child is born in the likeness of both parents. This gift of life is from God our Father who breathed the first breath of life into every new born baby. People have taken this truth and covered it up with a story of an apple where by, they created a tradition that has been accepted without question for centuries. The truth is that through Eve's conception in the Garden of Eden with Satan, caused her to sin and she was no longer a virgin. On that same day she conceived Adam's seed. That caused Eve to giving birth to twins, her first son was Cain whose father was Satan and her second son was Able, who's father was Adam. The churches don't tell you this truth.

Eve's sin in the Garden of Eden was when she become pregnant by Satan, who had transformed himself into a man. Don't spiritualize this physical act. When the fallen angels came to earth in Genesis 6 these "*Niphilim*", were known as fallen angels who married the daughter of men, and their children were known as giants. At that time only Noah's family was saved, along with two of each race which were the only ones left with pure seeds which were not contaminated. That's why God sent a flood to kill all of those Giant's God called, misfits. All of this activity was performed physically, because the women of that day were marrying the fallen angels that were transformed into flesh bodies, just as it will be at the end of this flesh age. Today we can see evidence of the fallen angels among us because people are becoming more like giants every day. It's given to us as a sign of the times we're living in today.

Christians today should know that the "*serpent*" in the Garden of Eden was a man, not a snake. The serpent is called Satan, He "*beguiled Eve*" who was transformed into a handsome man that lured his prey. He will be doing the same thing in these end times. He is active today in the Christian Churches, all over the world because people have not been taught these truths.

Jesus told John in **Revelation 12:9** exactly who the serpent was; the great dragon was cast out, that old serpent was called the Devil known as Satan, which deceived the whole world: he was cast out of heaven upon the earth, and his angels were cast out with him. Satan played the role of the "*dragon*" in the first earth age, as the deceiver; he was also called the "serpent and Devil". Shortly at the sound of the Sixth trumpet, Satan is booted out of heaven, and will play the role of Antichrist and the entire world will believe him just as they believed that Eve ate an apple. Satan will transform himself into a man with supernatural powers just as he did before, because God created him in "*the full pattern of beauty and wisdom*" to fulfill a purpose. Remember, originally Satan was created to protect the mercy seat of God, who said to Satan, *"thou art the anointed cherub that covers and I have set thee so; thou was upon the Holy Mountain of God; thou hast walked up and down in the midst of the stones of fire." "Thou was perfect in thy ways from the day that thou hast created, till iniquity was found in thee".* Ezekiel 28:14,15.

When God creates a person, He places certain gifts in our physical bodies, and gives us gifts to use to His glorify Him. When we take those gifts and take the glory for ourselves, we're doing the same thing that Satan did in that first earth age. Satan made a profit from his beauty and neglected to give the credit to God who placed them within him, he took all of the glory and honor for himself which grew into pride that rightfully belong to God. He wanted people to worship himself, rather than the living God.

Ezekiel 28:16,17 *"By the multitude of thy merchandise they have filled the midst of thee with violence, and thou hast sinned: therefore I will cast thee as profane out of the mountain of God: and I will destroy thee, O covering cherub, from the midst of the stones of fire." "Thine heart was lifted up because of thy beauty, you have corrupted thy wisdom by reason of thy brightness: I will cast thee to the ground, I will lay thee before kings, that they may behold thee."*

When people are dealing in "*merchandise*", they buy low and sell high to make a profit for themselves. We use the wisdom that God put into our minds, and take our profit which is what business is all about: the gain of personal profits. God gave Satan those gifts for the protection of the mercy seat at the throne of God. Yet! Satan used his position for personal gain. That is exactly what is going on in the business part of the Church world today. A corporation is set up to benefit the people that own it, and along comes these little devils that corrupts the whole process for their personal gain.

Remember that Satan plays the role of the "*serpent and deceiver*" in the Garden of Eden. When Eve had Satan's child, Cain turned out to be just like his father. Cain was a murderer from the beginning and was hateful toward God's ways. He always hid from the rest of humanity. The offspring of Cain are called Kenites, who are the "*sons of Cain*", which are as set in their minds to follow Satan's ways as Cain was.

God opened the minds of His elect, and those who study and search for God's truth will not be deceived by the Kenites. These sons of Cain are also known as the *"tares"* in the parable of the sower, Jesus taught us about in Matthew 13, and Jesus tells us exactly where they came from in Matthew 13:36-38.

Matthew 13:36-38 *"Then Jesus sent the multitude away, and went into the house, and His disciples came unto Him, saying, "Declare unto us the parable of the tares of the field." "He answered and said unto His disciples." "He that soweth the good seed is the Son of man;* Jesus Christ *said" "The field is the world; and the good seed are the children of the kingdom; but the tares are the children of the wicked one;" which* is Satan the serpent.

Full understanding of these verses, are the foundation for all the other parables of Jesus Christ. The Kenite's are the negative side of God's plan. The Kenite's are the children of Cain from the Garden of Eden. They were the ones that took over the Levite priesthood when the House of Judah was in captivity in Babylon. They were also the scribes and Pharisees that tried to murder Jesus during His ministry.

Eve did not eat an apple in the Garden of Eden. It was a lie that, hides the people known as tares, who have mixed in with both the house of Israel and house of Judah. They cause trouble and deception even in these end times. Yet God used them to fulfill the act that would condemn their father Satan, and lay the final doom upon him, when the plan of God is finally fulfilled.

God the Father said he will put enmity between Satan and Eve, and between the Kenites and Jesus Christ' seed. Jesus Christ will bruise Satan's head, and the Kenites will bruise Jesus Christ's heal. Genesis 3:1

As the spike was driven into our Lord's heel on that very day Jesus would be raised on the cross and Satan's own kids were used to fulfill the sentence that God had placed on their father's (Satan's) head. They can lie and do what ever they want to cover their actions, but the fact still remains; Satan and his kids are doing what they do because God allows it. Their devices and acts fulfills the negative side of God's plan. The most important role for them to play was carrying out the sacrificial death, which was the blood of Jesus Christ, once and for all times.

Hebrews 10:7,8 "*Then said I, Lo, I come (in the volume of the book it is written of Me to do Thy will, O God.*" "*Above when He said, "Sacrifice and offering and burnt offerings and offering for sin Thou would not, neither had pleasure therein; which are offered by the law:*"

The will of God had to be fulfilled in every detail just as it was written in the Word of God, and that's why Christ pointed it out by saying, "*It is written*". As He spoke all those things took place. Every detail of God's Word will happen just as it was written, on schedule at God's appointed time. Even when they drove the spikes in Jesus' heels, and when our Lord endured His pain and died on the cross for our sins. All those details were all done to fulfill that part of the Old Testament, called "The Law."

Hebrews 10: 9,10 "*Then said He "Lo, I come to do Thy will, O God." He taketh away the first, that He may establish the second.*" "*By the which will we are sanctified through the offering of the body of Jesus Christ once for all.*"

The will of our Heavenly Father is, that all souls should come into the knowledge of Jesus Christ. God is fair and just, He will not force you to do what you don't want to do. There is hope even for a Kenite that chooses to believe and come into the knowledge of Christ, through repentance. God will use them in their blindness to continue to fulfill His will even in these end times. When Jesus was judged, lied about, took the stripes and thorns by these Kenites, it was to fulfill the will of God, as written in **Isaiah 53, Psalms 22** and many other passages of the Old Testament. Jesus prepared His disciples for what was to happen, yet they still turned away from the trial and all the suffering that Jesus went through.

Many Christians today will do the same thing when Satan arrives and presents himself as the Messiah. The Christian church as a whole will fall over themselves to be the first in line to do Satan's will because they were unprepared for the fulfillment of God's word to take place. Today the Kenites are placing a strangle hold on the Christian world, preventing His word from being taught in Schools and in public places, even removing the commands of God from public places.

II Corinthians 11:4 "*For if he that cometh preacheth another Jesus, whom we have not preached or if ye receive another gospel, which ye have not accepted, ye might well bear with him.*"

In **Genesis 2:17** Satan is called the "*tree of good and evil*", and our Lord is the "*Tree of Life*". People are called trees, just as our Heavenly Father calls Himself the "*Great Fir Tree*". Although the Kenites say they are from Abraham's seed, they are not. They moved in and mixed with the nation of Israel during the building of the Temple during King Solomon's day. One hundred and eighty thousand Kenites were skilled workmen in their crafts and the main suppliers of the materials that was used to build the Temple and the king's houses. When the temple was completed the people stayed and became part of the House of Judah, and never left.

When King Ahab of the northern House of Israel married the daughter of the king of the Kenites, she brought with her four hundred of their heathen priests. These wicked priests brought with them all their Baal traditions and sex symbols, and the Israelites mixed Baal worship into their way of worship. Within two hundred and fifty years the House of Israel was polluted with idolatry so much that God divorced Himself from them, and scattered all the people through out the world.

Yet when the House of Judah came out of captivity, I Chronicles 2:55 tells us that they had completely taken over the duties of the scribes of Judah. *"And the families of the scribes which dwelt at Jabez."* This was Jerusalem in it's fallen state; "*the Tirathites, the Shimeathites, and Suchathites*" had taken over. "*These are the Kenites that came of Hamath, the father of the house of Rechab.*" They are the offspring from Satan's son Cain from the Garden of Eden. Satan's kids took over the priests and scribes duties by the time of the birth of Christ, They are sill doing today.

The definition of the word "Kenite" is #7014 in Strong's Hebrew dictionary, "Qayin, *kah'-yin; the same as #7013 with a play on the affinity to # 7069) "Kajin, The name of the first child, also known as place in Palestine, and an Oriental tribe: Cain, Kenite."* definition comes, from, *Strong's Concordance Dictionary.*

Eve gave birth to Cain first, and continued in labor with her second son Abel. Two babies were born one right after the another, with two different fathers. Cain's father was Satan, and Abel's father was Adam. Adam and Eve both sinned when they entered into an orgy with Satan and from it came two babies. Cain murdered his brother Able, and God chased the whole family out of the Garden of Eden. Cain then went to the east and married into one of the other races from the sixth day creation, that's why it's written, *"an Oriental tribe."*

Ezra 8:15 tells us that the duties of the priests were controlled by the Kenite's. The Levite priests had fled, and they left their flock in the hands of these wolves. These Kenites skillfully brought in their false doctrine, and traditions of Satan, and by the time of our Lord's birth, they were on the watch for the Messiah of Judah who had been prophesied. At Christ's birth they killed all the children under the age of two, to make sure that they had killed the Promised Messiah. However their plot didn't work. Jesus lived to fulfill every part of God's written word that was prophesied about His coming; and He submitted

Himself willingly as He was taken to the cross and His blood become the sacrificial Lamb, and was given for the forgiveness of our sins, if we repent and believe in Him.

As we move into the end of these final days of this earth age, the Kenites have set up their "Central banking system", presenting their worthless paper money, backed by lies and deceptions. They have set up their "*One World Government*", with all its agencies to control the world. Through their "*World Council of Churches*", they have prepared the whole world to accept their father Satan when he arrives. Their "*Four Hidden Dynasties*" are controlled completely by these Kenites, they are also the hidden power behind the scenes so they can make or brake nations. Most Christian's remain unaware of their activities, however as they create their laws, and eliminate our laws under God, their system will crash world wide. Most preachers will follow them, because they are already members of their "*World Council of Churches,*" because they are very strong supporters of the Kenites. Many members are not aware of this truth, and they don't even know that the W.C.C. is a very important part of the United Nations known as the "*One World Government*".

There is a lot written about these Kenites through out the Bible, the Scriptures will prepare and teach us everything necessary to live in these latter days, so we won't fall into Satan's pit of deception. That's why this book was written to those who dare to read it.

PASSOVER
Chapter 3

Many Christians believe that the Easter festival is the happiest time of the year not Passover. The day before Easter they boil and color their Easter eggs. The Easter Sunday service was always filled with a lot of people. They would dress up in their Sunday best to show off their new dresses, hat's and gloves while and men were dressed in suits, ties and hats, everyone wore their Sunday best. It was as if they were in an Easter parade. Many only came to church once a year, because there was always a lively festivity following the early sunrise service, then in the evening they would go back to church for singing and celebration often time they served food and drinks. In the afternoon there was an Easter Egg hunt to entertain the children and they could keep all of the Easter eggs they found. Take note that the word Easter is recorded only once in the entire Scripture,

Acts 12:4 *"And when he had apprehended him, he put him in prison, and delivered him to four quaternion's of soldiers to keep him: intending after Easter to bring him forth to the people."*

Notice that King Herod's said the word Easter which was a quote. He was the wicked king who reigned over the Jews, and was always trying to perverted their Christian Churches. Herod was determined to kill Christ, and His followers, He had murdered James the brother of John with the sword, he also took Peter and put him in prison until after *"the days of unleavened bread"*. Jesus Christ never used that word in the Bible.

When we know that the "days of unleavened bread" is part of the Passover, it is obvious we are talking about Passover, not Easter. Although we know that the word Easter is only recorded once in the entire Bible, mankind still insists on calling Passover, Easter Sunday giving tribute to Istar the heathen goddess.

Why would any translators use the name Easter, when he should use the name Passover? When you look up the word Passover in the Strong's Greek dictionary, it's #3957. "Pascha, *pas-khah; The Passover, is (the meal, the day, the festival, and the special sacrifices connected with it: refers to Passover"*. They were in Egypt when the death angle passed over God's people.

The heathen goddess Astarte, is known as Easter. The word Easter came from the *Old Testament*. It was and still is a heathen term derived from the Saxon Goddess named Eastre and is also the name for the goddess Astarte. The Syrians called this goddess Venus, and the ancient Canaanite's called her Ashtoreth in the *Old Testament*, also recorded in II Kings 23:13, I Kings 11:5, I Kings 11:33. Passover and Easter are not the same day. One is evil the other is God's pure word.

Christian's have always celebrated the heathen goddess Easter, along with God's sacred day known as Passover, even though Our Heavenly Father gave us strict orders through His Ten Commandments; not to serve heathen god's like Easter. However today our modern churches still do it and think nothing of it.

Exodus 20:3,4 *"Thou shalt have no other gods before Me," "Thou shalt not make unto thee any graven image, or any likeness of any thing that is in heaven above, or that is in the earth beneath, or that is in the water under the earth."*

This instruction written to Christians is very clear, were told not to do such things. We should never worship false gods, nor images nor anything of any kind in heaven, or on the earth. Yet we have rosaries, candles, and images of Saints, people even bow to them and pray to them, they are all symbolic images of angels etc., which are traditions of men, and God is very angry about it. Don't under estimate God's Great Wrath that will come down upon this world for the evil that has been going on in His House of Prayer.

Exodus 20:5,7,8 "*Thou shalt not bow down thyself to them, nor serve them: for I the Lord thy God am a jealous God, visiting the iniquity of the fathers upon the children unto the third and forth generation of them that hate Me.*" "*Thou shalt not take the name of the Lord thy God in vain; for the Lord will not hold him guiltless that taketh His name in vain.*" "*Remember the sabbath day, to keep it holy.*"

God's commandments were given to us to set standards for His people. We all should know them and show proper respect toward Almighty God. However His people, choose to chase after heathen gods and heathen practices that were mixed and even substituted for the holy things of Our Lord God. He knows when we allow the activities of the heathen gods and goddess to be practiced in His Church, to make it even worse is the fact that they do it as part of His sacred and most Holy Day known as Passover. On the very day that Christ was sacrificed for the sins of mankind they were participating in their heathen traditions just like today. God knows every thing we do and every thought we have. Yet mankind continues to allow these ancient practices to be inter-woven into God's most sacred day. The story of Gideon tells us how it was historically, so we can compare those days with our end times. We can know and understand what will happen in the end times by studying the scriptures.

GIDEON'S ARMY OF GOD.

Gideon was a good Judge over Israel in the time of the Judges. Each year the Midianites would come into the promise land and plunder it, then went home with all their crops and what ever else they could get their hands on. Gideon gathered the men of Israel, he cut the numbers down to a few hundred and then went to war against the Midianites. He chased them completely out of the land, and the people turned to God. The Israelites followed the laws of God until Gideon died.

Judges 8:33 *"And it came to pass, as soon as Gideon was dead, that the children of Israel turned again, and went a whoring after Baalim, and made Baal-berith their god."*

This was nothing new for God's people because every time a judge in Israel died, the people departed from their faith, and drifted back into Baalim worship. The Judge of Israel made the people abide by the Laws and Commandments of God. When Gideon died they went back into making Baal-berith their god. They continued worshiping Baal-berrith, also known as grove worshiping. People may wonder what made this form of worship so inviting to the Israelites, when they were so willing to go back into Baalim worship.

The word, *"Baal-berith"* in the strong's Hebrew dictionary is #1170; "Ba'al Beriyth, *bah`-al-ath-beh-ayr"* from #1168 and #1285; *baal of the covenant, Baal Berith; a special deity of the Shachemites: Baal berith."* Under #1168 we are told that the Baal of the Phoenician deity is the same Baal as the Shechemite deity. However in #1285 we read, "Beriyth, *Ber-eeth'; comes from a sense of cutting; a compact (because it was made by passing between pieces of flesh: a covenant or league.*" This is from *Strong's Concord-ance Dictionary.* Compare this form of sex orgies, with modern day secret societies that practice wife swapping, there is no difference.

Where ever Baal worship exists groves are mentioned, as well as the word "*Asherah*". The word "*Asherah*" is from the root "*Ashar*", which is "*to be straight, erect or upright*". It is from this word that we get the terms, "to be upright", "to be happy and prosperous". Every place in Scripture where Asherah is used, it is in connection with Baal, groves or grove worship, and is used as a proper name. All of these names are tied together, and they all refer to the same sexual activities as those ancient heathen religions were practicing. It's no great wonder that God is so angry with the pastors who allow the word Easter to be used in His House of Prayer. They either don't know or just don't care.

This is where the idea of hunting for came from. Easter known as [Ishtar's] promoted their egg hunts for their children centuries ago. The only purpose for hunting Easter eggs, in Scripture; was having sex orgies in the groves in worshiping the goddess Ishtar, Venus, Eastre, or Astarte they were all the same person. God told us in Deuteronomy 16:21 "*Thou shalt not plant thee a grove of any trees near unto the altar of the Lord thy God, which thou shalt make thee.*" This is directed to all Christian, don't rename the Lords day with the heathen name, Easter. Don't imitate, or change the meaning of God's word, with the things that are symbolic of heathen gods, and then say it's of the Lord, especially on God's most sacred days. It's time to open our eyes and ask God for forgiveness before He returns.

When we take the word "groves" back into the Hebrew, here again we see the word "Asherah". They are all tied together. We are not talking about planting trees. This is in reference to making things with hands that deals with the phallic shapes made from the trees. These were symbols, shaped in the form of male or female organs, used to prepair those that went chasing in the groves.

Isaiah 17:8 "*And he shall not look to the altars, the work of his hands, neither shall respect that which his fingers have made, either the groves or the images.*"

Remember the second commandment of God; "*Thou shalt not make unto thee any graven image or any likeness of anything that is in heaven above or that is in the earth beneath . . .*" The Easter egg represents the Easter bunny, yet chicken eggs were used, and children were told, they came from the Easter bunny, which represented the orgies that the adults participated in their grove worshiping. That is supposed to make it all right in the world today, because "it's for the children" and that makes it acceptable even though these things over ride the Laws of Almighty God.

Gideon went throughout all of Israel, where ever there was a grove or trunk carved in such a fashion; he cut it down and destroyed it. When he died all the people including God's people immediately went out and reestablished their grove worshiping. The male part of Baal worship is called "Asherah which is distinguished from "Astoreth" the female goddess counterpart, yet these images were both worshipped together. This form of worship was used to worship the productive part of life, it was their way of worshiping their god. Almighty God hates that practice, and all of those that take part in this kind of heathen customs especially, hunting Easter eggs.

As a bride of Jesus Christ we should be a chased virgin. Jesus expects us to always remain true to Him in all things. When someone takes part in any of Satan's religious activities, they have gone whoring, and Jesus called it "with child" in Matthew 24:19.

Many Churches today have fallen into false religions like in the time of Noah which came from Ham's sons, the Canaanites. The Canaanites developed their forms of Baal and Ashtoreth, and the rest of the people followed them. Ham's grandson Nimrod was ruler over that ancient world government, and in time the people began to worship Nimrod, and his wife. Their worship spread over the entire earth, written in Genesis 11, and when that world kingdom split, fragments of those people and nations took part of their filthy heathen religious form with them.

Genesis 11:5,6 *"And the Lord came down to see the city and the tower, which the children of men builded." "And the Lord said, Behold, the people is one, and they have all one* *language; and this they begin to do: and now nothing will be restrained from them, which they have imagined to do."*

God's Word told us what beleivers should do to be saved; yet mankind continued doing evil even in these end days, they built their towers and devised their own way into salvation. Today we call it philosophy, and people think they can solve their own problems, by leaving God out of their lives. Even as far back as Genesis 3:15, God told man about the coming Messiah who would become the sacrifice for sins of mankind, yet mankind continues to reject God's plan and design their own religious beliefs. The term that *"came down,"* in the Hebrew text is "anthropo-patheia," ascribes to God the things that belong to people who rationalize, while they accepted the traditions of men as being from God.

Genesis 11:7-9 *"Go to, let us go down, and there confound their language, that they may not understand one another's speech." "So the Lord scattered them abroad from thence upon the face of all the earth: and they left off to build the city."*

The things they were doing were called Babel, it was not a location. The people began all kinds of religious practices saying, it was from God. They were also taking things of God and saying it was from man. "Anthropo-patheia". The word "Babel" in the Hebrew tongue means "confusion". God scattered the people across the face of the earth so they couldn't talk to each other. However their religious practice were established, and were carried through out the known world when they left. Nimrod was the male that was worshipped, and his wife Samurais became their goddess after her death, in his kingdom. Samurais became known as Shamash which took the name Ishtar universally, that's where we get the name Eastre. This heathen goddess was also known as Diana of Corinth in Paul's time.

All of the ancient idolatries connected with astrology and mythology were not new. Their ancient Canaanite Religion was twisted and corrupted. Every phallic form worshiped is a relic from the world system of Nimrod and Samurais, then when God scattered those people at the tower of Babel, they took all their filthy religious forms with them. Today they have multiplied into a movement just like it was, in Sodom and Gomorrah.

Just like in Gideon's day, after the death of Solomon, the nation of Israel was split in two Houses known as nations. They were the *House of Israel* to the north, and the *House of Judah* to the south. They continued their practices of various sacrifices in the Temple at Jerusalem, which was the capital city of Judah. The House of Israel formed two golden calves for worship, to stop their people from following the House of Judah. These people are known as the other ten tribes of Israel who were kept from going into Judah. Immediately after their nation was formed, they started Grove Worshiping, also called Baal Worshiping. All sorts of other heathen activities were going on while Israel continued as a nation for about two hundred years. They become so heathen, that even the heathen nations around them could not stand their filth. Their activities are still going on today throughout the world. While the righteous people turn their heads, and close their minds to their idolatry while their wickedness corruption and evil forces move into their homes and Church's, as the government controls the lives of their children.

God scattered the ten tribes of Israel, and this nations migrated into Europe, the Americas and Canada. The House of Judah continued for another century and they became worse than their brethren Israel, who were scattered. Through out the years those heathen forms of worship has never left the minds of God's people, and many today uphold their traditions in their Christian churches, by redefining the Word of God to fit their needs, they cover up these things with lies, because they don't want to accept God's truth. Many preachers today tell their people; "they don't need to study the Old Testament, because it's about the past", nor "the book of Revelations because they will be gone [Rapture] when it happens". If you're taught to believe in the Rapture your hearing one of Satan's lies, therefore there is no protection for you. When Satan arrives, he is in full charge and thousands of Christians will worship him in their churches, in ignorance. There is nothing new regarding sun worshiper's, they are still going to their early morning sunrise services, in their Christian Churches today. The pagan people went out to bow and worship their sun god Nimrod and the sun goddess Ishtar. Today the Christian's traditions go to their early morning sunrise service on the feast of Ishtar, called Easter Sunday, as they pretend to worship Jesus Christ. True Christians should never mix Ishtar, and Easter with Jesus Christ the son of the living God. Our Heavenly Father is very angry about mixing Satan's things with His churches, especially when we call Passover His most Holy day. Easter Sunday, is an abomina-tion to our Heavenly Father.

Jesus Christ told us how to worship him on Passover, which was that we should take the cup and the bread at the "*Communion Table*" in remembrances of Him. On the night before Jesus was crucified, He was with His disciples in the upper room. After the meal, Judas had departed, Jesus Christ took the bread, gave thanks, blessed it, and broke it and said; "*Take, eat; this is My body.*" He then took the cup and gave thanks then gave it to His disciples, saying; "*Drink ye all of it;*" then Jesus told us exactly what they had done.

The Passover in the end times, is when the people will be bowing to the antichrist Satan in ignorance. They will believe that Satan is the true Jesus Christ the son of God, because their churches will tell them so many lies. The biggest lie is the rapture theory. Remember the tribulation is when the Great Deceiver Satan comes to rule the world just before the true Messiah arrives at the seventh trumpet.

Matthew 26:28 "*For this is My blood of the new testament, which is shed for many for the remission of sins.*"

This was the reason God established a New Covenant between those people who accepted this New Covenant, that our Heavenly Father recorded in New Testament. When Jesus Christ paid the price on the cross, once and for all times made this all possible. If you accept that truth by faith, you are saved, if you do not, this covenant is not for you. If people accept the covenant that our Lord offered to them, and take His Communion His way and follows the instructions of His Word, they will know there is no other way. If people chose to follow mankind and all their traditions of men that God hates because of their ancient religions, remember even today it angers Him when people pervert or change His words, regarding to His sacred Covenant.

Matthew 26:29 "*But I say unto you, I will not drink henceforth of this fruit of the vine, until that day when I drink it new with you in My Father's kingdom.*"

From that night before His crucifixion, until the seventh trumpet sounds, we are to continue to take the "*Communion Table*", in remembrance of our Lord Jesus Christ's sacrifice day on the cross. You will not sit and take that Communion supper with the Lord in your flesh and blood body, because at the seventh trumpet all flesh is gone, and we are changed into our spiritual bodies as we enter into the Millennium Kingdom of our Lord Jesus Christ. In other words, if someone comes to you and says they are Christ, like Satan will do, and you are still in the flesh, that person is a deceiver or the Devil in person. Mark them well, and don't be deceived. We are all being tested to see if we will believe Satan's lies, or stay in the word of God, during the sixth trumpet just before the end of this earth age of mankind.

Don't call Passover by a heathen name. If you want to boil eggs, and chase bunnies; don't deface our Lord by making your own heathen ritual by calling it Easter Sunday, because that is exactly what is being done in these end times. If you have read this chapter, then you are not innocent when you stand before God on Judgment Day, because you know bunnies, eggs, bonnets, sunrise service, groves and all the rest are used in covering up the most sacred day of the Lord. His day is called Passover, which is when we are to take communion at the, *"Communion Table of the Lord."*

The day before Passover falls on the 14th day of Nisan, "*The Preparation Day*", which was the day of the crucifixion of our Lord Jesus Christ. This day in reality falls on our Tuesday from sunset to Wednesday sunset. This is the day that Christ was betrayed by Judas. During that Tuesday night, Jesus had dinner with His disciples, He taught them the meaning of "*The Communion Table"* and established the "*New Covenant" to* His followers who were told to keep doing it until the true Jesus Christ arrives at the seventh trumpet.

He was betrayed in the Garden, brought in and judged illegally by the Jewish court, and brought before Pilate to be tried and sentenced to death. On that Wednesday at noon Jesus was nailed to the cross, and from noon to three P.M. on that day in Jerusalem, the sun never gave light. Jesus was pierced by the spear before sundown, and taken from the cross and put into the tomb by 6 P.M. Wednesday evening.

Jesus was in the tomb from Wednesday evening at 6:pm; until Saturday evening at 6 P.M., which was, three days in the tomb. The tomb was secured by the Roman guards at the request of the Jewish court. The Resurrection of our Lord Jesus Christ happened sometime in the night after 6 PM Saturday night to Sunday morning, when the two women went to the tomb and found it empty. Good Friday was a man made day of celebration, no doubt for commercial reasons. However don't get the actual time line of our Lords death and resurrection mixed up with man made holidays that the Bible calls traditions of men, God Forbid.

Jesus walked and talked with his disciples so they knew him personally. He was seen by over 500 people at one time, and lived with people forty days before His ascension into heaven on the 40th day after His resurrection. He asked His believers not to leave Jerusalem but to remain there for the next ten days. On the 50th day after Passover was the day of Pentecost. That was when the Law was given to Moses on Mt. Sinai while 140 souls were gathered together. It was written in Acts 2:1-3

Acts 2:1,3 *"And when the day of Pentecost was fully come, they were all with one accord in one place." "And suddenly there came a sound from heaven as of a rushing mighty wind, and it filled all the house where they were sitting." "And there appeared unto them cloven tongues like as of fire, and it sat upon each of them."*

Those early Christians were obedient to the Lord, when he requested that they should not leave Jerusalem. At this very moment in time, the New Testament Church was established. It was established when, every person there was filled with the Holy Spirit of God.

Acts 2:4 *"And they were all filled with the Holy Ghost, and began to speak with other tongues, as the Spirit gave them utterance."* There is No mention of an unknown tongue.

Peter told us that in the last days, this same speaking of tongues would happen all over again. We should be looking forward to that day when the gospel goes out the mouths of God's elect, when everyone hears the gospel in his native tongue, no matter what language it was spoken in. All praise and glory goes to our Heavenly Father, and to His Son, Our Lord Jesus Christ.

CHRISTMAS
Chapter 4

There are many family traditions mixed within Christmas that help us remember that special time when our Lord came into this world age, born to the Virgin Mary. We have picked a date that most Churches believe to be the day that Jesus was born. However that misconception came from the Pharisees. We can't fully understand the birth and life of Jesus Christ, unless we search scripture for the truth of God's word for ourselves.

Before we start the study of Christmas, we must read John 7, which tells us about the time before feast of the Tabernacles when Jesus and His family were going to Jerusalem, for the third highest Holy day of the Law. The scribes and Pharisees were there and witnessed all the teachings and miracles that Jesus had taught since His ministry started after His Baptism and the death of John the Baptist.

John 7:1-3 *"After these things Jesus walked in Galilee: for He would not walk in Jewry, because the Jews sought to kill Him." "Now the Jew's feast of tabernacles was at hand." "His brethren therefore said unto Him, "Depart hence, and go into Judea, that Thy disciples also may see the works that Thou doest."*

From the time of the birth of Jesus, the Jews sought to kill Him. When He was born the three wise men saw the star in the east, and followed it with their gifts they planed to give to the Christ Child. Then some time later the three wise men went to King Herod to find out where Jesus was. After hearing the wise men speak, King Herod ordered, all of the two year old and younger boy's in Bethlehem to be killed, so that they would be sure to kill the young Messiah. The brethren of Jesus

Christ knew the works of Jesus, and they wanted Jesus to go to Jerusalem to speak and show His mighty works to all the people however they were not aware of the Jews plot to kill the baby. Jesus lived in Galilee, and the people in that area were friends of His family. Remember that the Kenite Jews were in charge of the Temple, and the sons of Satan wanted to kill Jesus.

John 7:4-6 "*For there is no man that doeth anything in secret, and he himself seeketh to be known openly. If Thou do these things, show thyself to the world.*" "*For Jesus said unto them,* "*My time is not yet come: but your time is always ready.*" "*Then Jesus said unto them, My time is not yet come: but your time is always ready.*"

Jesus knew every thing that was in the Old Testament, and He knew that His death would happen on time. Jesus would become the Passover Lamb once and for all times, and that day was not on the feast of Tabernacles. Jesus simply would not allow himself to be sacrificed before His time.

John 7:7,8 "*The world cannot hate you; but Me it hateth, because I testify of it, that the works thereof are evil.*" "*Go ye up unto this feast: I go not up yet unto this feast for my time is not yet full come.*"

These brethren then went up from Galilee to Jerusalem for the feast of Tabernacles, and after they departed, Jesus waited a while for them to get on their way, and He went up to Jerusalem by Himself. When the men of Galilee arrived at the Temple, the Jews were there looking for him. "*Then the Jews sought Him at the feast, and said,* "*Where is He?*" Then all the gossip and talk started. It is no different today than it was two thousand years ago. People like to lie, and tell stories and half of the people are anxious to hear and gossip about all the evil, so they can spread it around.

Remember the time of Babylon's captivity, some four hundred years before this time, when the Kenites took over the Levite priesthood. Their word was the final authority of the day, so the people were cautious of what they said in public, because they feared the Kenite Jews.

John 7:13-15 *"And Howbeit no man spake openly of Him for fear of the Jews." "Now about the midst of the feast Jesus went up into the temple and taught." "And the Jews marveled, saying, "How knoweth this Man letters, having never learned?"*

Today the Kenites control the Four Hidden Dynasties much like it was in Christ's day. A man of "letters", were people who were taught the law in their school system, and accepted a higher standard of learning. Jesus' had never sat under one of their Jewish Kenite teachers, however Jesus taught the law as they would have it taught. So when these Jews heard the words of Jesus they were amazed. They wanted to know who taught Jesus.

By this time the people listening to Jesus and were supporting what He was saying, and the Jews knew that this was not the time to lay hands on Him. The conversation between Jesus and the Jewish leaders continues up to John 13:31, when Jesus declared "*But I know Him: for I am from Him, and He hath sent Me.*" Jesus has just declared Himself to be the Messiah sent from God. The Jews knew who their father Satan was, because Satan is their god. This is also the way it will be when the sixth trumpet sounds. This was too much for these religious leaders so they sought to take Jesus, but no man was able to touch Jesus. The Jewish Kenite known as the chief priests, scribes and Pharisees sent for the officers of the Temple to take Jesus; but Jesus kept right on teaching.

John 7:40-42 *"Many of the people therefore, when they heard this saying, said, "Of a truth this is the Prophet." "Others said, "This is the Christ." But some said, "Shall Christ come out of Galilee?" "Hath not the scripture said, That Christ cometh* *of the seed of David, and out of the town of Bethlehem, where David was?"*

The truth is that when Jesus had spoken, notice very few people in the Temple had been taught about the Scriptures. The Kenites had laid out their teaching methods, to where the people simply could not put the scriptures together in an orderly fashion. This is what is going on today in many churches. Even when the police of the Temple came to take Jesus, they listened, and were astounded by what Jesus said and no one would touch Him.

John 7:46-48 "*The officers answered, "Never man spake like this Man." "Then answered them the Pharisees, "Are ye also deceived?" "Have any of the rulers of the Pharisees believed on Him?"*

Do you understand who is in control and what their teachings were in the Temple at that time? Is it any wonder that the Jews were out to kill Jesus, and even today it is forbidden to teach the Word of God in Jerusalem. These Hidden ones, known as Kenites, have complete control over what was taught back then and even today, and they accepted the teaching that went on in their churches back then just as they do today. They were much like the church boards of modern denominations of today. This is an example of how traditions got started, and was carried on generation after generation. Then the Kenite priests made the statement; "*But this people who knoweth not the law are cursed.*" These cursed are Satan's kids, and those in most modern churches today, because they changed and hid the truth of God's word from His sheep.

John 7:50,51 "*Nicodemus saith unto them, he that came to Jesus by night, being one of them," "Doth our law judge any man, before it hear him, and know what he doeth?"*

Nicodemus was the one that came to Jesus at night to inquire how he could be saved. He was a secret follower of

Christ, yet like Jesus' uncle Joseph they sat on the seat of the Sanhedrin, which was the court in Jerusalem. Nicodemus asked his piers if they were going to break their own Laws, and not allow the man to speak for himself. The laws were the same at that time as it is today, a man is innocent until proven guilty. It was a set back by their own leadership by asking such a question.

John 7:52,53 "*They answered and said unto him, "Art thou also of Galilee? Search and look: for out of Galilee ariseth no prophet." "And every man went unto his own house.*"

This is a sample of the school system today, and even in many churches in the U.S.A. Not one of the chief Priests or Pharisees stood before Jesus, knew about a prophet that came out of the Galilee area, the place where they knew Jesus grew up. That is exactly why most Christians are so confused today. People say they love the Lord, yet they simply cannot rightly divide the Word of God because no one taught them how to do it.

Many Great Prophets came out of Galilee, but they would just as soon forget many of them for their forefathers had murdered many of them. For example the book of Jonah, tells us he was in the fishes belly for three days and three nights. Hosea prophesied about the houses of Israel and Judah in the end times. Amos was the man that foretold, "the truth of the Word of God would dry up," and it simply would not be found in our generation were from Galilee. And of course the two most famous prophets, Elijah, and Elisha, the Prophets that God took, and they killed the four hundred prophets of Baal. No wonder that this cloud of ignorance covered over Jerusalem and people in the Temple at that time.

The reason that this study is brought up before Christmas is to show the lack of truth and understand that fell over Jerusalem before the crucifixion of our Lord Jesus Christ. Even at his birth, it took three men from a far to bring attention to the fact that the Messiah was born, yet they did not know where Messiah would be born. Today we sing, "Oh little town of Bethlehem", yet that is about the only part of the story that is true.

Luke 1:5 "*There was in the days of Herod, the king of Judaea, a certain priest named Zacharias, of the course of Abia: and His wife was of the daughters of Aaron, and her name was Elizabeth.*"

This time frame was establish, in 5:B.C., when King Herod took over the land of Judaea. Zacharias lived at the same time as Aaron, but he would not be able to serve at the course of Abia. Both Zacharias and his wife Elizabeth were full blooded Levites. Take note that this verse speaks of, "*the course of Abia*" which was the eighth feast and that places the time of this sacrifice between June 13th 19th annually. This course was assigned only to a Levite Priest, which was a day's travel from his home when Zacharias a Levite priest was on duty in the Temple.

Luke 1:6,7 "*And they were both righteous before God, walking in all the command-ments of ordinances of the Lord blameless,*" "*And they had no child, because that Elisabeth was barren, and they both were now well stricken in years.*"

This calls attention to the fact that both the priest and his wife met all the requirement's set forth by God in the law. Luke is about to give us a precise record of the lineage of our Lord, and it will be given in a simple way.

Luke 1:8,9 "*And it came to pass, that while he executed the priest's office, before God in the order of his course,*" "*According to the custom of the priest's office, his lot was to burn incense when he went into the Temple of the Lord.*"

This marks the exact time and place when this vision took place, because Zacharias was on duty in the Temple, serving the course of Abia. Notice that "his lot", or exact time he was to burn incense was at a precise time as directed by the priest's office, to follow the course and custom set down by God in the law. As Zacharias would burn the incense, the smoke would rise out of that holy place, and the people would stand out in the court yard watching for the smoke that was the offering for their sins. Then it would be time for prayers and repentance for sins.

Luke 1:10,11 *"And the whole multitude of the people were praying without at the time of incense." "And there appeared unto him an angel of the Lord standing on the right side of the altar of incense."*

A masses of people were in prayer outside at the right time, while the incense was being burnt at the altar inside; and an angel appeared to Zacharias. When he saw the angel fear came over him. The angel told Zacharias not to fear, but that he and his wife were going to have a son, and that his name should be called John. The name "John" means "Yah's gift". Zacharias didn't rejoice, because he knew that both he and Elizabeth were too old to bare children.

The reason that we are establishing what went on here at this exact time, which was during the feast of Abia, is that it gives us the exact date when Elizabeth's conception took place. Her son John the Baptist was conceived on June 23 of our calendar year.

Luke 1:23,24,25 *"And it came to pass, that, as soon as the days of his ministration were accomplished, he departed to his own house." "And after those days his wife Elisabeth conceived, and hid herself five months, saying," "Thus hath the Lord dealt with me in the days wherein He looked on me, to take away my reproach among men."*

Elizabeth had been pregnant for six month when Gabriel the angel appeared again, only this time the Virgin Mary was conceived by the Holy Spirit, in the city of Nazareth, in Galilee. This was the second appearance of Gabriel on December 24th at sundown, making it December 25 our time. This was the conception of Mary not the birth of Jesus Christ.

Luke 1:27,28 "*To a virgin espoused to a man whose name was Joseph, of the house of David; and the virgins name was Mary." "And the angel came in unto her, and said, "Hail, thou that art highly favored, The Lord is with thee: blessed art thou among women."*

This was right on schedule according to Isaiah 7:14, where God named this Child, the Son of God Immanuel." At first Mary was troubled because she was espoused to marry Joseph, but the marriage had not taken place yet.

Luke 1:30,31,32 "*And the angel said unto her, "Fear not, Mary: for thou hast found favour with God." "And, behold, thou shalt conceive in thy womb, and bring forth a Son, and shalt call His name JESUS." "He shall be great, and shall be called the Son of the Highest: and the Lord God shall give unto Him the throne of His father David:"*

This same night the Virgin Mary was conceived by the Holy Sprit of the living God. Her Son was Jesus Christ the savior of mankind. Who so ever that will accept His blood sacrifice and believe in repentance for their sins will be saved. Mary accepted every word the Holy Spirit told her. There were two miracle births in the same family, because the Virgin Mary and Elizabeth were related.

Luke 1:35 "*And the angel answered and said unto her." "The Holy Ghost shall come upon thee, and the power of the Highest shall overshadow thee: therefore also that holy Thing which shall be born of thee shall be called the Son of God."*

This was the fulfillment of the promise that goes all the way back to the time of Adam, in Genesis 3:15. It fulfills the prophecy of Isaiah 7:14 "*. . . Behold, a virgin shall conceive, and bear a son, and shall call his name Immanuel*". This will be the greatest gift that God has given to mankind, the Redeemer of our souls from the bonds of sins. This establishes what happened on the night of the December 24th, which is the day of the 25th, that we celebrate as the birth of Jesus Christ today.

Luke 1:36 "*And behold, thy cousin Elisabeth, she hath also conceived a son in her old age: and this is the sixth month with her, who was called barren.*"

This established the fact that the soul of the individual enters the embryo of a woman at conception. John the Baptist was six months in the womb, and Jesus had just been conceived. God has established the fact that the Son of God is now in the womb of Mary. If you want to dispute this, you can because Satan and all the heathens disputed it. This action proves that the conception of Jesus Christ was on December 25, and when you add nine months to that date, you have the feast of the Tabernacles, where we started this chapter, recorded back in John 7.

If the State and all the photospheres say that the soul forms at birth, then that should place a shadow over their entire profession. If you want to kill a baby, you just declare that it is not human, and it is like killing a rabbit. If the Christian world today celebrates rabbits on the day of Passover, I guess they can declare what ever they want. Yet the time will come when every person will be responsible for those little lives that they have destroyed. Historically it is known that abortion originated in Nazi Germany, and when the whole world went to war, they called it genocide. Today we call it abortion in the United States. If this has happened to you and you have asked the Lord for forgiveness then don't carry your burden to the grave. Your Heavenly Father forgives all our sins if we ask Him and your forgiven as if it had never happened.

This chapter was written to point out that the next time you give gifts on December 25, remember that you are nine months too early. Because that is the day of conception of our Lord, and let it be a reminder that it was recorded in Luke 1:35 "*Holy Ghost came upon thee, and the power of the Highest shall over shadow thee: therefore also that Holy Thing which shall be born of thee shall be called the Son of God.*"

UNKNOWN TONGUES
Chapter 5

Today most of the Church denominations have formed their central theme around the traditions of speaking in an *unknown* tongue. When any word in the Bible is in italics, it means that word was added by man. It's not the pure word of God. Before we can discuss what the tongues of the New Testament Church is, we must first identify the exact meaning of what the Apostles and prophets meant when they spoke about the "tongues" of the end times.

The Church of Jesus Christ was formed on the Day of Pentecost. The fiftieth day after, the first Passover Feast was the time that God freed the Israelites from their 400 year bondage in Egypt. When the death angel passed over the land and took the life of the first born of every man and animal that did not have the sacrificial blood over the door post of their homes.

That night the Israelites put the blood on the doorpost of their homes; they ate the lamb, and kept their clothes on so they could be ready to travel. The next day after the death angel passed over, the Israelites were packed, and heading for the promised land. God took the life of Pharaoh's first born son and that changed the mind of Pharaoh that night. Fifty days later, while on the road, the Israelites were at the base of Mount Sinai and Moses came down off the mountain with the book of the Law from God in His hand. That book is the Law that the Israelites would live by and be governed by when they entered the promise land. Many times they strayed from the instructions under the Law, but God gave them a way to approach the throne of God, by the blood sin sacrifice of animals.

When God set the times that the Israelites would follow from that day forward, and the first day of the year was at the Spring Vernal Equinox. Fourteen days after that moment in time is when the Passover took place, and that is also the feast day that was to be remembered forever. Even in our day, many churches claim the name of the Goddess Ishtar or Eastre, which means Easter, and they think God is pleased with them for mixing their heathen traditions with His most sacred and highly honored holy day of Passover.

The Israelites considered these two days as two of their three annual special holy days that they were to remember with the blood sacrifices of birds and animals. That third time of the year is the day of the feast of Trumpets, or Harvest at the harvest time of the year. This time will be studied in traditions of men in a later chapter.

Our Lord went to the Cross willingly, to be the pure sacrificial blood sacrifice for once and all times. His death on the cross took place at the same moment in time that the Passover sacrifice was to be offered. Hebrews 10:5-10 tells us that Jesus did this to fulfill the will of the Father and the Word of God, in every detail that was prophesied in the Old Testament. It was recorded in Psalms 22 and Isaiah 53 it all took place right on time, on the exact day and in the exact way that it was written.

The Crucifixion of Jesus Christ at the direction of the Kenite Jews and at the hands of the Roman soldiers were at the Passover, when the sacrificial animals was to be slain. That year, the sacrifice event did not happen, because the power of Almighty God tore the Vail of the holy of holies into pieces, and the day became night for three hours, in the middle of the day. Jesus was crucified on Wednesday, the day before Passover on Thursday of that week. Jesus was put into the tomb by sundown 6 P.M., this was the start of Passover in that particular year. He was in the tomb for three days and three nights, just as He said He would be, when He told the Pharisees that the only sign that He would give them was the sign of Jonah, being in the belly of the great fish for three days and three nights. Accept it or not, it happened. Those who don't believe this have chosen a heathen mind.

Jesus rose from the dead early Sunday morning, and was seen by many people after His resurrection. That is a recorded fact. The disciples of Jesus and many followers were gathered on the Mount Olivet, on the fourth day after His resurrection. They asked Jesus, when the Kingdom would be restored to Israel. Jesus answered in Acts 1:7, 8.

Acts 1:7,8 *"And He said unto them "It is not for you to know the times or the seasons, which the Father hath put in His own power." "But ye shall receive power, after that the Holy Ghost* [Spirit] *is come upon you: and ye shall be witnesses unto me both in Jerusalem, and in all Judaea, and in Samaria, and unto the uttermost part of the earth."*

When Jesus finished telling His followers that each of them would receive the power of the Holy Spirit, He started to rise into heaven while they were watching. He told them in Acts 1:11.

Acts 1:11. *"Ye men of Galilee, why stand ye gazing up into heaven? this same Jesus, which is taken up from you into heaven, shall so come in like manner as ye have seen Him go into heaven."*

There was a ten day period from the ascension of our Lord Jesus Christ into Heaven, to the feast day of Pentecost that would also take place in Jerusalem. Those ten days were days of meetings and planning, but the church could not be formed until after the arrival of the Holy Spirit. In that time, the disciples chose another person to fill the position of Judas, because at that moment in time, Judas was dead. There were three men, and only one of them could be chosen. The disciples and followers cast lots and they all fell on Matthias.

Acts 2:1,2 *"And when the day of Pentecost was fully come, they were all with one accord in one place." "And suddenly there came a sound from heaven as of a rushing mighty wind, and it filled the house where they were sitting."*

Think of it, these people that were to form the Church had waited patiently for ten days. They held fast to the promise of the Holy Spirit, who is their teacher and comforter that would lead each member of the body of Christ.

Acts 2:3,4 *"And there appeared unto them cloven tongues like as of fire, and it sat upon each of them." "And they were all filled with the Holy Ghost* [Spirit], *and began to speak with other tongues, as the Spirit gave them utterance."*

The word "*Tongues*" in the Strong's Greek Bible Dictionary is #1100. "*Glossa, gloce-sah'; a tongue, a language, specifically one naturally un-acquired: tongue.*" In other words the language that these followers of Christ were speaking, were languages that they had not learned by themselves. It was a "*cloven tongue*", meaning that it went out in many different directions, when one person spoke, each person heard what was said as it was spoken in their native language back home. There was no confusion to what was being said, for the Spirit of God was speaking through each of these souls. They all understood immediately, because they all heard what was said, in their own language.

Acts 2:5,6 *"And there were dwelling at Jerusalem Jews, devout men, out of every nation under heaven." "Now when this was noised abroad, the multitude came together, and were confounded, because that every man heard them speak in his own language."*

Remember it was Pentecost, and people came to Jerusalem from all over the world. You have ten different nations listed in verses nine through eleven. *"And they were all amazed and marveled, saying one to another, "Behold, are not all these which speak Galileans?"* in verse seven. The death and resurrection of Jesus was well known around Jerusalem at this time, for just prior to this Pentecost time, Jesus was crucified, and many, if not most of them took part in the false trial, the lies and torments that they put upon Jesus. Each of them knew very well who those Galileans were, because they were the followers of Jesus Christ the one that was accused of calling Himself God. To them that was a sin unto death.

THREE THINGS TO REMEMBER

First is the fact that every believer received the Holy Spirit all at the same time. Second is the language and words that were spoken were not jumbled, nor confusing. Everyone understood in your own language. Third, it was like fire as every word that God spoke went right into their heart and mind, with complete understanding and clarity. There was no interpreter, because God put the understanding in every one's mind that heard the cloven tongues. Man's ways will always have an interpreter, that's how you will know without a doubt, it's a false Christ.

Acts 2:9-11 *"Parthians, and Medes, and Elamites, and the dwellers in Mesopotamia, and in Judaea, and Cappadocia, in Pontus, and Ashia," "Phrygia, and Pamphylia, in Egypt, and in the parts of Libya about Cyrene, and strangers of Rome, Jews and proselytes," "Cretes and Arabians, we do hear them speak in our tongues the wonderful works of God."*

These men were from all parts of the known world at that time. Each of them were amazed, ". . . *Because we do hear them speak in our tongues the wonderful works of God."* There is only one True Holy Spirit, and when the Holy Spirit is part of something there is no confusion of what has been said. No one has to interpret what has been said because everyone will hear in their own language with understanding. When the true Spirit of God speaks through one of His Elect, it is the Holy Spirit speaking through them and there is no confusion. The leaders of the Jews listened and finally understood every word that was spoken, and they thought this was some sort of game. Others were mocking these men and women of God, saying "*These men are full of new wine*". They are drunk and sputtering.

Peter stood up before this massive number of people, along with the other eleven, including Matthias who was also a disciple. Peter told these Jews:

Acts 2:14-15 "*Ye men of Judaea, and all ye that dwell at Jerusalem, be this known unto you, and hearken to my words:*" "*For these are not drunken, as ye suppose, seeing it is but the third hour of the day.*"

It was 9:00 A.M. in the morning when the Pentecost feast day began and these hundred and forty men and women were not drunk. Peter spoke saying, "*But this is that which was spoken by the prophet Joel;*" Peter is quoting from the book of Joel, 2:28-32.

Joel 2:28-32 "*And it shall come to pass afterward, that I will pour out My spirit upon all flesh; and your sons and your daughters shall prophesy, your old men shall dream dreams, your young men shall see visions:*" "*And also upon the servants and upon the handmaids in those days will I pour out My spirit.*"

Peter was telling the Jews that had witnessed, all of those who were speaking in the cloven tongue. This was recorded as an "*ensample*" which means an example to us living today. This is giving a warning of how it will be in the final generation just before the return of the Lord. That time is at the seventh trumpet, after Satan has had his time in Jerusalem deceiving the whole world. One thing for sure, when you hear mankind speaking with cloven tongues it will be directly from the Holy Spirit of God, with no confusion, nor training. It will happen world wide all at the same time. Every one who hears will hear in their own tongue. Jesus warned us in;

Mark 13:9-10; "*But take heed to yourselves: for they shall deliver you up to councils; and in the synagogues ye shall be beaten: and ye shall be brought before rulers and kings for My sake, for a testimony against them.*" "*And the gospel must first be published among all nations.*"

The importance of this is that the *cloven tongue* is given by the Holy Spirit, to God's Elect and each of His witnesses must give a testimony, and every person no matter what language they speak, must be able to understand with clarity. There will be no training for the Elect, because the Holy Spirit can read the minds of the listener, and know exactly what should be said. In short it is the voice of God Almighty through His Holy Spirit, coming out of the mouth of His servants at that time.

Mark 13:11 "*But when they shall lead you, and deliver you up, take no thought beforehand what ye shall speak, neither do ye premeditate: but whatsoever shall be given You in that hour, that speak ye: you in that hour, that speak ye: for it is not ye that speak, but the Holy Ghost* [Spirit]."

This instruction by Jesus was given to His Elect of the final generation, in the time of the end. Satan will be on his throne in Jerusalem, pretending he is God, and most Christians will be worshipping him in ignorance. Friend, you don't set the course of what should be said, or mutter something like "Are you saved?". The words that the Holy Spirit will place in your mouth will be burning like fire in their ears, just as it was here on the day of Pentecost. It will be spoken by both men and women alike, and by young and old alike. Even the "gainsayers" will not know what to say, when they hear the words coming from the lips of the Elect on that day. Jesus told us in Luke.

Luke 21:31,32 "*So likewise ye, when ye see these things come to pass, know ye that the kingdom of God is nigh at hand.*" "*Verily I say unto you, This generation shall not pass away, till all be fulfilled.*"

When you hear the cloven tongues being spoken, people of many different languages all hearing what is said yet everyone will understand in their own language and only one person will be speaking. Either a man or woman will be speaking at a time, when you hear this happening you will know that the coming of the Lord is very close. If you are looking for rapture, you have already been sidetracked into looking for Satan, and probably have accepted the false Christ.

Peter continued speaking the words of the Prophet Joel:

Joel 2:30-32 *"And I will shew wonders in the heavens and in the earth, blood, and fire, and pillars of smoke." "The sun shall be turned into darkness, and the moon into blood, before the great and the terrible day of the Lord come." "And it shall come to pass, that whosoever shall call on the name of the Lord shall be delivered for in mount Zion and in Jerusalem shall be deliverance, as the Lord hath said, and in the remnant whom the Lord shall call."*

This has not happened yet but in those final days and hours of this earth age, those that call on the name of the Lord Jesus Christ, and remain true to Him to the end, shall be saved. Those that are sealed in their minds with the truth of the Word of God regarding these events and warnings from our Lord will not be deceived by Satan, nor will they chase after the traditions of men. However, Millions of Christians' will accept Satan because of the traditions they were taught in their churches. They will chose not pay any attention to any of God's warning. This is why this book was written to tell God's people about His warnings and how the Traditions of men will lead them into Satan's camp, and is so important to know.

Luke 21:33,34 *"Heaven and Earth shall pass away: but My words shall not pass away," "And take heed to yourselves, lest at any time your hearts be overcharged with surfeiting, and drunkenness, and cares of this life, and so that day come upon you unawares."*

Jesus is telling us to make sure were not involved in traditions of men, when we go to our churches. Such as chasing after Easter bunnies, putting on our bonnets, dancing around our Christmas trees or what ever the traditions of the day are. Be sure that you don't get carried away with the cares of this world so much that you loose sight of God's warnings. If people mutter something and it needs an interpreter, it's not of the Lord because the Holy Spirit does not need an interpreter. The flood of Satan is full of Mediums, soothsayers, and spirits of divination which are not of the Lord. Watch out for what you accept, and check it out with the living Word, your "*King James Bible*". Don't take any man's word, without getting your Bible out and studying it for yourself. If a word is from the Holy Spirit, it will burn in every ear with understanding, no matter how many languages are present. Everyone will hear it in their own language if it's from God. His truth and word will prevail above every else because He created all things. He alone is supreme and worthy of our full attention.

Luke 21:35,36 "*For as a snare shall it come on all them that dwell on the face of the whole earth*" "*Watch ye therefore, and pray always, that ye may be accounted worthy to escape all these things that shall come to pass, and to stand before the Son of man.*"

Most of your family members will not turn from their traditions of men, for they find comfort in the false foundation that those traditions give them. Your closest family members will be turned against you, when you don't accept the first Christ, who is Satan that comes. Father will turn against son, brother against brother, and mother against daughter. The fierceness of what is going to happen will be so great that Christians will even rejoice over the death of God's the two witnesses. How could that happen? They don't expect Satan to bring death nor killing and destroying every thing in his path. That's not how Satan will come. Read Daniel 8:23-25.

Satan is the king of fierce countenance in Ephesians 6:10-20 and he is the first king that will come. Satan's kingdom of the latter time will come to fulfill God's prophecy, and he will bring understanding to the people of His dark sentences. Those things that Satan will say will sound so good, that even Christians will believe that He is the Christ.

Daniel 8:24,25 "*And his power shall be mighty, but not by his own power: and he shall destroy wonderfully, and shall prosper, and practice, and shall destroy the mighty and the holy People.*" "*And through his policy also he shall cause craft to prosper in his hand; and he shall magnify himself in his heart, and by peace shall destroy many: he shall also stand up against the Prince of princes; but he shall be broken without hand.*"

Satan is the author of confusion. In Revelation 9:4,5 Jesus has told us through John that the Elect will understand what Satan, his fallen angels and Kenites will be doing. Those that don't want to study nor know God's truth, are allowed to remain ignorant, by their own choice. He allow them all to be sting by the "*scorpions that striketh a man.*". While the Elect are protected because they know God's truth. Satan will give them every thing to make them want to worship him as God. If your business is failing, he will back it and give you what ever it takes to get your soul. If you want fame He will give it to you because He controls the new papers, the press and the flow of information. Satan's policy will be to cause your craft of proper "in his hand". You will be successful in Satan's kingdom, when you have sold your soul to him, as you bow to him in worship.

The Elect of God will see and understand exactly what is going on and they will not accept any of Satan's programs. Five months is a very short time, once Satan has arrived it just doesn't matter what the business does, because all the things in this earth age of flesh man will be over and done with when Jesus Christ, the Prince of princes comes, and according to His Word, this earth age of the flesh will not exist any more.

We started this chapter looking into the traditions called tongues, because tongues are a sign of the end times. Most Christians today have already accepted the confusing babbling as the real thing. The Elect who are sealed in our minds with truth, will know better because Jesus has warned us to be aware of every one of these traditions, so that we are fully aware regarding the day of His return. Even today many Christians like to take strong drink, and "*surfeiting*" which is the nausea that comes after the drunken-ness that leaves people unable to think clearly. This is not a time to let their guard down. In order to be worthy and stand before the Lord requires our faithfulness to Him until the very end. The Elect of God will stand and will be found worthy of Jesus Kingdom in the Millennium age.

Our prayer is that the readers will consider this truth and compare it with the scripture. May God's truth dwell in your soul and set you free. We all stumble and fall short in life while searching for truth, and often times we fail to see truth even when the Spirit of God has laid it out before us. May His Holy Spirit open your understanding as you study to show your selves approved.

II Timothy 2:15,16. "*Study to shew thyself approved unto God, a workman that needeth not to be ashamed, rightly dividing the word of truth. But shun profane and vain babblings; for they will increase unto more ungodliness.*

SATAN'S OFFSPRING
Chapter 6

The Kenite's are the children of the evil and wicked soul that had an affair between Eve and Satan. By understanding this truth, the Bible will take on an entirely different meaning with a greater depth of truth. We will be studying in this chapter, because many churches have been taken over by these people that even the thought of the serpent's seed starts their blood boiling. So the only way to approach this subject is through the Scripture, and dealing with the words of Jesus, the Prophets, and the Apostles of the New Testament.

The word "Kenite" appears many times in the Scriptures. To most Christians it is just a reference to a nationality of people who have mingled with the Israelites throughout the ages. Sort of like how the immigrants have come to America, to blend in with the people here, become citizens, and called themselves Americans. Although these Kenites have mixed in with people all over the world today they have control over the House of Judah and also have key positions within other nations. Their allegiance is to their father Satan, and his agenda, it's the same in this earth age as it was in that first earth age that once was.

The word "Kenite" from the *Strong's Exhaustive Concordance* and dictionary is #7014; "Qayan, *kah'-yin; Kajin, The name of the first child, also a place in Pal., and of an Oriental tribe:—Cain, Kenite(s).*" This identifies the fact from the Scriptures that Kenite is a form of "*Cain*", and with "*ite*" added, which gives us the understanding that these are the children of Cain, or son's of Cain.

The obvious question is; if these Kenite people or offspring of Cain lived before the flood, how did they survive after the flood? Jesus, John, Moses, also other prophets talk about this in the Scriptures.

When God created Satan in that first earth age, God put into Satan the full pattern of beauty and wisdom. By this action we can know that God had a special purpose for Satan, and pride was the reason God turned against Satan.

Ezekiel 28:1,2,3 *"The word of the Lord came again unto me, saying" "Son of man* [Ezekiel], *say unto the prince of Tyrus* [Satan], *`Thus saith the Lord God; `Because thine* [Satan's] *heart is lifted up, and thou hast said, I am a God, I sit in the seat of God, and in the midst of the seas;' yet thou art a man, and not God, though thou set thine heart as the heart of God:" "Behold, thou* [Satan] *art wiser than Daniel; there is no secret that they can hide from thee:" "With thy wisdom and with thine understanding thou* [Satan] *hast gotten thee riches, and hast gotten gold and silver into thy treasures:"*

Satan was a cherub created to serve at the throne of God in heaven. Because of his duties, God put the full pattern of wisdom in his mind to fulfill that mission. To gain the confidence of the "stars" or souls that were also created, God made him in the full pattern of beauty, recorded in verse, 3.

Today gold or silver is not the backing of any government's monetary system, for it has moved into the standard of productivity. This gets into one of the, "Four Hidden Dynasties"; through Economics, they control the central banking system: Everything under that system is controlled by the hidden hands of it's board. Most people today think that the central banking systems are federally controlled, but in reality, the governments buy into it with worthless paper money to run their state of affairs. World Governments pay gold for worthless paper. This means that they can elevate any government of any nation through their interest rate and their manipulations. The leaders of all nations under this World Central Banking System are under the complete control of the Kenites, the Bible tells us about these offspring of Satan through Cain.

Ezekiel tells us that Satan was "*the anointed cherub that covereth;*" By cherub means that Satan was created as a supernatural being for the protection of the things of God. Satan was in the Garden of Eden as a protecting servant to God. By using the word "Perfect" here indicates he was part of God's creation.

Ezekiel 28:15 "Thou [Satan] *wast perfect in thy ways from the day that thou was created, till iniquity was found in thee.*"

So we see that Satan was a created being from that first earth age. God [YHVH] created Satan for a purpose, to protect and was the overseer regarding the things of God. *"Therefore, thus saith the Lord God; `Because thou hast set thine heart as the heart of God;"* because of Satan's pride, he had his fall. So before you blame Eve and her husband Adam for their fall, there is a time coming when every person on the face of the earth, will follow Satan once again as their god, all except for God's Elect,

Genesis 3:1 "*Now the serpent was more subtil than any beast of the field which the Lord God had made. And he said unto the woman, "Yea, hath God said, `Ye shall not eat of every tree of the garden'?"*

The word "serpent" in the Hebrew text is "Nachash" meaning "*a shining one*" The Apostle Paul warns us about Satan's actions in II Cor. 11:3.

II Corinthians 11:3 "*But I fear, lest by any means, as the serpent beguiled Eve through his subtility, so your minds should be corrupted from the simplicity that is in Christ.*"

Satan is the Great Deceiver; he will present himself as being the true Jesus Christ, he is not who he tries to make you think he is. Paul was using Satan's actions in the Garden of Eden to warn those of us living in these end times. He is telling us how Satan and his followers will present themselves.

I Corinthians 11:13-15 *"For such are false apostles, deceitful workers, transforming themselves into the apostles of Christ." "And no marvel; for Satan himself is transformed into an angel of light." "Therefore it is no great thing if his ministers also be transformed as the ministers of righteousness, whose end shall be according to their works."*

Strong's Greek dictionary for the word, "*transformed*" as used in the Greek text is #3345. "*Metaschematizo, met-askhay-mat-id-co; To transfigure or disguise, transform by accom-modation.*" Satan is going to do what ever it takes to accommodate you, as he tries to disguise himself as God, when in fact he is nothing more than a created soul like we are. The Kenites and all his ministers will use the same efforts to disguise Satan that he used to present himself as God. Today many calling themselves Christians pastors of various Church's, will disguise themselves in ignorance and will follow Satan.

This phrase means, ". . . *Whose end shall be according to their works.*" indicates that the things these false ministers did was done in ignorance. Their salvation will only come by proving themselves through the Millennium age after the second trumpet, when they are in their incorruptible bodies. This is what Revelation 20:11-15 is all about. For if they were of the Elect and had known that Satan was the devil and was not God they would not have followed him. However, these Kenites continue worshipping him, therefore there is no salvation given to them in Gen. 2:15-17.

Genesis 2:15-17 *"And the Lord God took the man, and put him into the Garden of Eden to dress it and to keep it.)" "And the Lord God commanded the man, saying," "Of every tree of the garden thou mayest freely eat:" "But of the "tree of the* *knowledge of good and evil, thou shalt not eat of it: for in the day that thou eatest thereof thou shalt surely die."*

Do you see how Satan changed the wording in Genesis 3:1, and made it mean something totally different. He disguised the words of the *King James Bible* by using other translations, to make a lie, and made God's statement confusing. That is how the Kainite's work today in their publications. The truth is hidden somewhere in the midst of misleading statements, and are bold lies. Even in the churches of our generation, most of them are like the seven churches of Revelations. Only two of those churches could identify those that were *"of the synagogue of Satan"*. They are Philadelphia and Smyrna.

Genesis 3:6,7 *"And when the woman saw that the tree was good for food, and that it was pleasant to the eyes, and a tree to be desired to make one wise, she took of the fruit thereof, and did eat, and gave also unto her husband with her, and he did eat." "And the eyes of them both were opened, and they knew that they were naked; and they sewed fig leaves together, and made themselves aprons."*

Eve conceived both Satan and Adam seeds. Not apples! Don't be deceived. They were in a fig orchard, and used fig leaves to make their aprons. Eve conceived, the seed of Satan first, who had transformed himself from a snake into a man. Later Eve conceived the seed of her husband Adam. From these two affairs, Eve conceived Cain first from Satan's seed, and then from Adam's seed, therefore Eve gave birth to maternal twins.

Genesis 4:1,2 *"And Adam knew Eve his wife; and she conceived, and bare Cain, and said, "I have gotten a man from the Lord." "And she again bare his brother Abel. And Abel was a keeper of sheep, but Cain was a tiller of the ground."*

Eve conceived not only from Adam, but from Satan, as we read in Genesis 3:6. Later she had twins. *"She again bare his brother*", meaning when you have one baby, and continue in labor to have the second child, you have twins. Not from the same father, but from the same mother. So Eve's sin in the Garden of Eden was, her two conceptions with both, Adam and Satan. Then in verse 8 were read; *"And Cain talked with Abel his brother: and it came to pass, when they were in the field, that Cain rose up against Abel his brother, and slew him."*

For this murderous act against his brother Abel, we read in verse 2 that God sent Cain to the east to take a wife outside the lineage of Adam [Seth], and that is why we read "*an Oriental tribe*" in Kainite's, under # 7014 of *Strong's Dictionary.*

Genesis 4:12, "*When thou tillest the ground, it shall not henceforth yield unto thee her strength; a fugitive and a vagabond shalt thou be in the earth.*"

How did those Kainite's survive the flood of Noah's day? After the people of the earth had time to multiply about seven hundred and fifty years, the population grew upon the earth. Not only from Adams seed, but also the Kainite's and the other races of the six day creation recorded in Genesis 1:26-28. Contrary to what many teach, the black race did not come from the sins of Ham. Because God created all races perfect, in accordance with His purpose for each race and he called it good!

Genesis 6:1,2 *"And it came to pass, when men began to multiply on the face of the earth, and daughters were born unto them," "That the sons of God saw the daughters of men that they were fair; and they took them wives of all which they chose."*

Don't get all spiritual with this, because we are talking about a common thing that happened before the flood, and it will happen again in our generation. When daughters were born to men, no matter what the race or generation, men take them for their wives. The sons of God, the "angels" came into this realm or dimension of our earth age as flesh man, and took these women for their wives to bear children. There are no apples from this apple seed, but children are born from the sperm of males. Over the course of many years, the entire population of the earth was genetically cursed with these misfits, called "giants", and all except for Adam and his immediate family were samed.

God was not pleased with what went on, so He told Noah to build a boat that would be sufficient to carry two of each kind, plus himself, his wife, their sons and wives.

Genesis 6:9 "*These are The Generations of Noah: Noah was a just man and perfect in his generations, and Noah walked with God.*"

The "*generations*" in the Hebrew text is "*tol'doth*" which deals with family history genetically. "Perfect", in the Hebrew text is "*tamin*", meaning, "*without blemish as to breed or pedigree.*" All of Noah's family was without blemish in reference to the contamination from the fallen angels that entered into this earth age, to destroy the fate of man in the flesh. However this is not aimed toward all races, because God had chosen Adam in Chapter two and through his generations would come the Messiah.

Genesis 6:17,18 "*And, behold, I, even I, do bring a flood of waters upon the earth, to destroy all flesh, wherein is the breath of life, from under heaven; and every thing that is in the earth shall perish.*" "*But with thee will I establish My covenant; and thou shalt come into the ark, thou and thy sons, and thy wife, they sons' wives with thee.*"

Your "*breath of life*" is your soul and spirit. All living flesh of mankind will be destroy-ed, including every thing that has life. The covenant between God and Adam is that his entire family would be saved from that destruction.

Genesis 6:19 *"And every living thing of all flesh, two of every sort shall thou bring into the ark, to keep them alive with thee; they shall be male and female."*

Every different kind of race of mankind was on the ark with Noah, two of each race both male and female was saved to reproduce and continue their race. Those races were all created good just as the Adam's race. Genetically the Kenite's had their two slots on the ark also, for they are a definite Oriental race, with Cain and their Oriental mother. So we see a continuation of all flesh kind from the first dispensation prior to the flood carried on after the flood.

KENITE'S AND THE TEMPLE OF GOD

God loved David and Solomon, Solomon like his father was dedicated to serving God. Because of the trouble in David's life, God did not allow David to build His house of God, the Temple. When God asked Solomon what he wanted, he asked for wisdom and knowledge, instead of riches and gold.

I Kings 3:5,6 *"In Gibeon the Lord appeared to Solomon in a dream by night: and God said, "Ask what I shall give thee." "And Solomon said, "Thou hast shewed unto Thy servant David my father great mercy, according as he walked before Thee in truth, and in righteousness, and in uprightness of heart with Thee; and Thou hast kept for him this great kindness, that Thou hast given him a son to sit on his throne, as it is this day."*

Solomon knew the character and dedication that his father David gave to God, and he was grateful that God blessed and kept his kingdom so that he, could reign over it.

I Kings 3:7-9 *"And now, O Lord my God, Thou hast made Thy servant king instead of David my father: and I am but a little child: I know not how to go out or come in." "And Thy servant is in the midst of Thy People which Thou hast chose, a great People, that cannot be numbered nor counted for multitude."*

"Give therefore Thy servant an understanding heart to judge Thy People, that I may discern between good and bad: for who is able to judge this Thy so great of People?"

God gave Solomon wisdom and knowledge and we can read about in the books of Ecclesiastes, and the book of Solomon. God also gave Solomon great riches, and along with those riches the right to build His Temple, the House of God. When it came time for the Temple to be built, Solomon had the wealth to buy the materials for the Temple, but King Hiram of the Kenite's who was in charge of the workers with full control of the materials. I Kings 5:1-12 tell us about the contract between Solomon, and King Hiram of Tyre, or the Kainite's. Remember symbolically, Satan is called the "King of Tyre", and Solomon is using these Kenite's to fulfill God command to build the Temple.

Hiram provided Solomon with cedar trees, all the gold and material that were required for God's temple and other houses of Solomon including 180,000 Kainite's to work on all the projects of Solomon. In the contract, Solomon gave Hiram the food for the men, and twenty measures of pure oil. God gave Solomon the wisdom to do the job, and the building of the Temple began.

I Kings 5:12 *"And the Lord gave Solomon wisdom as He promised him: and there was peace between Hiram and Solomon; and they two made a league together."*

This sounds like what is going on today. The first thing Solomon did was to raise the levy or taxes upon God's people to give to Hiram to finish the job. After Solomon's death, the kingdom split in two houses, or nations, called the House of Israel, and the House of Judah. The King line of the Kenite's married into the king line of both houses or nations of Israel and Judah. We know from a vision God gave to Jeremiah in Jeremiah 24, that there are good figs and bad figs. The problem today is that most people don't know who these figs are. God said he would protect the good figs of Judah that would be carried away captive into Babylon. But the bad figs that are evil would remain captive in Judah, and then scattered into Egypt, and many other nations around the world.

It is from the offspring of the fig Tree known as the Kenite's who went into Babylon for 70 years of captivity and they took over the Levite Priesthood. Their children and offspring were the scribes and Pharisees that confronted Jesus and caused His death. As we discussed in an earlier chapter, they controlled the priests and scribes who were going back to Jerusalem.

I Chronicles 2:55 "*And* the family of the scribes which dwelt at Jabez *[Jerusalem]; the Tirathites, the Shimeathites, and Suchathites. These are the Kenite's that came of Hamath, the father of the house of Rechab.*"

These Kenites were talented people they have the seed genetic line of Satan in them. In most cases they cannot exist as a nation by themselves, because as we were told in Genesis 4 they could not raise their own food. That is why they are like their father Satan, for he was specialized in Commerce, money and trade, buying low and selling high that is their business. The Kenites will remain the hidden ones, that are directing the course of things to come. Are they of God? No, but God uses them in their blindness to fulfill His Word, and His Will. The first prophecy in the Scriptures is all based on that hidden mission.

Genesis 3:15 "*And I* [God] *will put enmity between thee* [Satan] *and the woman* [Eve], *and between thy seed* [the Kenites] *and her Seed* [Jesus Christ]*; It* [Jesus] *shall bruise thy* [Satan's] *head, and thou* [the Kenites] *shalt bruise His* [Jesus Christ's] *heel*"

This is what Passover is all about, the crucifixion of Jesus Christ at the instigation of the Kenites, which completes the sentence by Satan, and completes salvation for all those that believe on Jesus name, and come under the blood of Christ in repentance. That sentence on Satan though will not come until after God has used him to fulfill the negative part of His plan.

KENITES OF THE END GENERATION.

The term Jew, as we use it in the Bible, has two meanings. The Jew is either an offspring of Judah by blood, or he is a resident of the land of Judah, that southern kingdom when the Israelite's split into two separate nations. Jesus referred to the Kenite's, as "the synagogue of Satan", and there were only two types of the seven churches of the end times that knew who they were and how to identify them. Through the warnings of Jesus Christ to His Elect, that living in this end time generation. He told us to learn the parable of the fig tree. That parable identifies the Kenite's as the seed, and offspring of Satan through their Mother Eve. Through Cain came The Kenite's who are called the seed of the serpent. Jesus identified these Kenites when he was telling us who they are and how they work.

Earlier we discussed these Kenite's of the synagogue of Satan over many centuries they have blended in with Brother Judah, and disguised their real identity. Today they have a definite purpose, which is deception and preparing for the coming of their father Satan, at the sixth trump.

Revelation 2:8,9 *"And the angel of the church in Smyrna write; `These things saith the First and the Last, Which was dead, and is alive;" "I know thy works, and tribulation, and poverty (but thou art rich), and I know the blasphemy of them which say they are Jews, and are not, but are the synagogue of Satan."*

Though the Church of Smyrna of the end generation was a very poor church, yet Jesus called them rich. They were rich because they could identify who the Kenite's were if they were in their midst. Today they may call themselves Christian or

Jew, but in reality they are Kenite's, children of Satan. We see from Revelation 3:8,9 that the church of Philadelphia also could identify the fake follower that were among them, that were from the synagogue of Satan. When Jesus saw them face to face, He told them exactly who they are, and what they were trying to do within His churches.

John 8:44, "*Ye* [Kenite Jewish scribes and Pharisees] *are of your father the devil, and the lusts of your father ye will do. He* [Cain] *was a murderer from the beginning, and abode not in the truth, because there is no truth in him. When he speaketh a lie, he speaketh of his own: for he is a liar, and the father of it.*"

When a high ranking newsman was asked why he used false documents to frame the president, he said he would use what ever was necessary to bring about his fall. That is Satan's goal, for the truth is not in him nor in his kids. When they lie, that's their nature. If they commit murder to cover up their intent to destroy, that's standard for them. Like we read in II Corinthians 11:13,14 Those false teachers and prophets who present themselves as preachers, and disguise themselves as angels of light as they spread their lies to their followers. It's no wonder that they do so much evil, because Satan himself will present himself as God and that's what the "*abomination of desola-tion*" is all about, and that's what Jesus spoke about.

Our generation is being prepared to accept Satan as the angel of light. Christians are given a false hope of these Kenite's, as they are preparing themselves for Satan's coming, he is not the true Lord. People are looking for safety, prosperity, and comfort. Christians today are looking for the great escape, and the Kenite's are giving them what ever will make their dream world come true. Amos talked about that time of the "*Great Tribulations*" in Amos 8:11, and we can see that preparation taking place today. Scripture is being removed from the school's, and government buildings, and people are told to watch what you say about these hidden ones. The public is being told not be prejudice or offensive toward anyone, yet at the same time they are blaspheming our Lord, and making fun of Christians in the press. If you think that it is bad now, in a short time it will become impossible to find a copy of the Holy Bible. That's why we must know the hidden truth of God's Holy word in our minds. If you finish reading this book you will know most of God's warnings to His people.

Amos 8:11,12 "*Behold, the days come, saith the Lord God, that I will send a famine in the land, not a famine of bread, nor a thirst for water, but of hearing the words of the Lord:" "And they shall wander from sea to sea, and from the north even to the east, they shall run to and fro to seek the Word of the Lord, and shall not find it.*"

This is exactly why Jesus warned us to learn the parable of the fig tree, for there will be no fruit of Salvation, when the word of God is dried up. That is why we are told to learn the seven seals of Revelation 6, for those seals are the same events that Jesus warned us about in Matthew 24, Mark 13, and Luke 21. The Elect will learn those seals before the final trumpet sounds, for there will be no written warning after the sixth trumpet sounds because that's when Satan arrives. These warning are nothing new, for all of the prophets of the Old Testament wrote God's warnings to our generation.

The great tribulation is going to happen and most every body living today will be part of the "*Great Deception*" and blasphemy that will take place. God has warned us to get ready, learn the seal, but only the Elect will be ready and those who are the bride of Jesus Christ.

Revelation 9:4,5 "*And it was commanded them that they should not hurt the grass of the earth, neither any green thing, neither any tree; men* [the Elect of God], *but only those which have not the seal of God* [the trumpets are in the order of their importance] *in their foreheads* [minds]." "*And to them it was given that they should not kill them, but that they should be* *tormented as the torment of a scorpion when he striketh a man."*

Our job in these end times is to store the truth of the Word in our minds so we will not be deceived. God will allow all those who are not sealed to become part of Satan's kingdom, once the sixth trumpet is sounded. This is why most Christians will be rejoicing when Satan calls himself God, as he kills the Two Witnesses of God. Things will be so distorted that good will be called evil, right will be called wrong. Satan will be doing things that the Christian people, will accept because they believe he is the true Jesus Christ. God's two witnesses that were sent by God will be known as the destructive ones, and when they are murdered by Satan, the entire world will rejoice for three and a half days over their deaths.

Revelation 11:9-11 *"And they of the people and kindreds and tongues and nations shall see their dead bodies three days and an half, and shall not suffer their dead bodies to be put in graves." "And they that dwell upon the earth shall rejoice over them, and make merry, and shall send gifts one to another; because those two prophets tormented them that dwelt on the earth." "And after three days and an half the spirit of life from God entered into them, and they stood upon their feet; and great fear fell upon them which saw them."*

Most of the Christian world will be part of those who are rejoicing over the death of the two witnesses because they brought fire down from heaven upon this earth by their supernatural powers. After the death of the two witnesses of God, Satan has just declared himself to be Jesus Christ. Recorded in Daniel 8:23-25; Satan will bring peace and prosperity, he fills your pot with food and gives you what ever it takes to buy your soul for himself. Today the definitions and meanings of words are perverting the meaning of God's pure word. Kenites are trying to making evil look good, and has turned good into evil by perverting God's holy word. The words of the Prophets, and Apostles that Jesus taught them, has been mistranslated. This is what the Kenite's are doing because they control the schools, governments and the churches. They distort every thing God has written.

The Kenites, sons of Satan through Cain now control the four hidden dynasties, so when a disaster happens, they will tell you who caused it, and why you should hate them. If you talk against their agendas, they will say that your promoting hate and you are branded as a member of a hate group. They can blow up buildings, start wars and blame other people as they destroy the reputation of people, with lies in the press and they appear to be righteous for doing it, because it is fulfilling their hidden agenda.

They have gone into their little cells within their hidden societies, and through their hidden agenda they fulfill their goals of preparation for the coming of their father Satan. If you are one of the Elect, and have prepared yourself by knowing the Word of God during "*The Great Deception*" that is coming, it will be like watching a movie that you have seen many times. You know the ending and you know what is coming next. It becomes a matter of watching as the events take place until the very end when the seventh trumpet sounds. You will know when the true Jesus Christ will return to this earth with His army of Saints, and when He set this world back on the right track.

Judgment is coming upon the earth and it will be at God's appointed time. God told us what to look for and the approximate order of events. Jesus told us the order of importance through the seals, but it is up to each of us to make preparations and wait until the Millennium begins. Now is the time to study to make yourself a proved unto God, by our works before the thousand year period of time is over. It's your choice to learn the parable of the fig tree or become one of those in the synagogue of Satan and allow some false prophet to lure you to sleep with false hopes. The choice is yours.

The arms of the Lord is waiting for us to repent and accept His truth as you study his word for yourself. All we have to do is ask him to forgive us for believing these traditions of men for so many years. Remember He alone has died for each of us and we all have to face him when this world ends.

SANCTITY OF LIFE
Chapter 7

This is one of the *Traditions of men* that we are studying in this chapter, there are two trains of thought, the first deal's with abortion, and the second part reveals what the Bible says about cloning human cells to make a copy of people. The problem with abortion in our modern day, is that it hinges on the "*Quality of life*"; and the "*Sanctity of Life.*" On the surface, those promoting free choice, allowing the woman to have an abortion, seems to be the mother's choice rather than God's choice. However, the intent of their plan is to promote abortion for an entirely different reason.

This movement promoted the free choice of a mother to abort their child is not new, it was common in Germany following the First World War. The purpose of the German society was to promote a better life style and give each individual a *"quality life"*. This battle was between Quality of life, verses the Sanctity of Life. President Ronald Reagan wrote a book on this subject called "*Abortion and the conscience of a nation*". The "hidden ones" are known as the Kenites in our land who made sure that his book was rejected from the start, therefore not many of these books reached the book stores or library shelves. His book was a view of Nazi Germany and it told how a Christian nation could become just like it was under Hitler's rule.

The German people were recovering from the First World War, and were wanting a better life style. The people wanted quality in their life, so psychologist and psychiatrist joined with the legal profession and "*gave the people what they wanted*". This process was to take the stressed minds of the people that were shattered from the war and give them a better "quality of life". Their life styles became free and easy as their activities increased and they eliminated their "unwanted babies". This was not a Nazi plot, because the Nazi's were not in power, nor was Hitler in the spotlight. Under disguise the psychiatric community joined with the legal profession and laws were passed to allow "abortion" to take place on a massive scale, legally. This was a blessing for the people who wanted their free life style, with no threat of obligations. Later Sex was taught to little children in our school system. Then later free condoms were given to children by our United States Government.

Attached to that came a process of eliminating people that had mental defects. The handicapped members of society were a drain on those who had to care for them. Those given the task of determining the future for the mentally ill person were the same ones who were promoting the quality lifestyle through the abortion process. When any of these doctors fail in their work regarding the mentally ill, it is always the patient's fault. In time, the legal profession assisted those doctors and it became law to eliminate the mentally ill and unborn babies of today.

This opened a new field in the medical profession. The fetus of the mentally ill was tagged as being useless. The soul of those subjects were legally nullified by the courts and their body parts, whether living or dead became nothing more than laboratory specimens. At this point, it is important to point out that the majority of these doctors, lawyers and judges were Kenite Jews. They were playing a game with life, and later their game came back to haunt them, when Hitler and the Nazi's came into power.

Once they declared an unborn baby as being mentally ill, it is marked as useless because it is a drain upon society. The next group of people they focused on were the elderly who can not care for themselves. They thought that they had lived their lives and it was time to get rid of them. They were also considered a drain on the society, they thought that the money to care for them should be spent elsewhere. Once a nation has grown into thinking that there is no "Sanctity to life", the only thing left that matters is their "quality of life".

The next time you hear the expression, "Quality of Life and Free will" it refers to "freedom of Speech" in a speech or political statement, remember that these are the works that led Germany into their evil activities under their demonic leadership. It was the most barbaric nation this world has ever known. Watch out who you cast your vote for. Remember this is what President Ronald Reagan wrote about in his book, *"Abortion and the conscience of a nation".*

The title of that book was "*Nazi Doctor*". Their laws brought about their free and easy life styles in Germany. Their laws are the same laws that have been introduced in our nation, as President Reagan stated, they opened the flood gates for the murder of millions of unborn children in the U.S.A. Although they say, these laws give the mother free choice. The only way that the laws of abortion today could be accepted, is if you believe that mankind is an animal without a soul.

Once the "killing of the unborn" became law, it set the standards that tear down all of God's biblical standards. Sodomy became another form of life style. This also defends the raping of innocent children. Once a rape takes place, the legal remedy for the cure, is abortion not the death penalty as written in God's word. Remember the point of this chapter is "Quality of life, verses Sanctity of Life". The victim's quality of life is performed by a doctor who decapitates that little baby in the womb, piece by piece that little child is pulled from the safety of his mother's womb. The quality of life is not better after that child has departed. Often times the mother lives with emotional scares for the rest of her life, even though it was the doctor who killed that living soul.

The word, Sanctity" in the dictionary reads; "*Saintliness or holiness, in face of being sacred or inviolable, anything held sacred."* Not much in our nation is sacred anymore. Even our churches as well and those with disease are wanting for new body parts to live longer, today. We hold the Kenite Jewish and their Federal Reserve System more sacred than the life of the unborn child. Hitler promised to give the German's their quality of life, at the time people brought Hitler into power. Today our churches and people have turned away from God's truth and began to allow the sex educations into public schools to teach their children all about sex in grade school. The Kenites created the atmosphere for their wickedness as they came into power just as Hitler did.

There has been three Babylon World Governments come into power, and we are entering into the fourth time when the New Babylon will coming into power again for the last time.

Genesis 10:8,9,10 *"And Cush begat Nimrod: he began to be a mighty one in the earth." "He was a mighty hunter before the Lord: wherefore it is said, "Even as Nimrod the mighty hunter before the Lord." "And the beginning of his kingdom was Babel, and Erich, and Accad, and Calneh, in the land of Shinar."*

The words, *"His kingdom"* is *"Nimrod's kingdom"* The word, "Babel in the Hebrew tongue is *"Bab-ili"* from the root word #1101: *"Confusion, Babylon, a government of confusion"*, *"From Strong's Concordance."* Nimrod's kingdom was the first attempt by man to create this kind of confusion. The earth had only one language and one speech for all the races and peoples upon the earth. Everyone came together to build this tower, for their protection.

Genesis 11:4 *"And they said, "Go to, let us build us a city and a tower, whose top may reach unto heaven; and let us make us a name, lest we be scattered abroad upon the face of the whole earth."*

The Hebrew text, *"let us make us a name"* means, "let us provide our own salvation." All of the souls that lived through the flood of Noah's day were alive and part of Nimrod's kingdom. They did not believe in God. They chose to follow the ways of Nimrod. They trusted Nimrod, just as the German people trusted Hitler, when he gave them the quality of life that they were holding on to. They wanted their peace and prosperity, but they didn't consider the cost they had to pay for it. They knew the devastation that took place on the earth, more importantly, they knew it was God who brought it about.

The people in Nimrod's day didn't believe in the covenants nor the instructions God gave them after the flood, and they banded together for protection from the wild animals and relied on their tower to give them salvation. They thought the tower would give them access to heaven. The term *"a name"* in the Hebrew text shows us their independence from God, and their reliance on Nimrod. So Nimrod's Babylonian System was built upon false hope, peace and salvation. People took their eyes off of God's ways, and formed their own ways by trusting in their own traditions of men, just as they are doing today.

Our Heavenly Father is always in control. Although Nimrod had his tower to bypass God's ways just as Nebuchadnezzar had his image's built by the hand of man back then and forced every one in Babylon to bow to their image's. The end time Babylon of Satan's Kingdom will be no different. Revelation 17:5 tells us about, Mystery, Babylon the Great, Mother of Harlots and Abominations of the Earth. "The Babylon" of our time is not a city, but a condition that is about to occur and will cover the whole earth. The word, *Babylon* means, "Confusion" that controls all the people in the entire world. Satan's system will control all the religions of the world, and it's confusion will cause millions of souls to follow Satan as their God. Mankind will accept Satan, because their minds have been prepared in ignorance, to follow their system with out question. This is just as it was in Nimrod's day, and in the other two Babylon's. God told Abraham to pack up and leave the land of Ur, and to go to another place that He had prepared for him.

In our day people believe they will fly away in their false rapture while others don't even believe there is a God. Many believe that salvation comes from knowledge and science. Today this type of confusion is being sealed in the minds of many Christian Churches, because they refuse to study God's Word. They don't believe the Bible is true. They are being deceived by relying on false doctrine rather then reading God's written Word for themselves.

We are living in the end generation filled with confusion, known as the New Babylon, when most Christians will trust in their doctrines and traditions of men. They are conditioned into accepting the ways of this *New World Order,* rather than being sealed with the truth before the sounding of the sixth trumpet. When Satan arrives, only the Elect of God and those sealed with the Word of God in their minds ahead of time, will not be deceived by Satan when he comes to rule on this earth. This warning is real, it's the truth that is recorded in the living Word of God in Revelation 9:4,5. It will be like it was when millions of Christians in Germany were drawn under the control of Adolf Hitler's power during world war II. Today Christians are being brain washed and conditioned to accept the new *One World System* which will bring Satan into power. Today we are reliving the days of Nimrod, and most people have no idea what we are talking about.

In Genesis 11:7,8 God put a stop to that ancient kingdom of Nimrod's by confusing their language, by scattering them across the face of the earth. In our generation God will also put an end to this earth age before the seventh year prescribed time of Satan's rule. When the seventh trumpet sounds, life as we know it is all over. We are approaching a time that this world has never seen before. Taking the lives of the unborn and cloning the stem cells to make creatures of the same likeness, leading mankind to accept a different way for his own salvation. Most people are unaware of the seriousness of these things that are going on today.

We are now living under the *New Word Order* today, called the United Nations. Their laws are continuing to be passed that will set us up to receive their One World Religious System that will be far worse than Hitler ever thought of. The political system that now exists will come to an end shortly, because God's word tells us in Revelation.

Revelation 13:3,4. *"And I saw one of the heads as it were wounded to death; and his deadly wound was healed: and all the world wondered after the beast." "And they worshipped the dragon which gave power unto the beast: and they worshipped the beast, saying, "Who is like unto the beast? who is able to make war with him?"*

The only reason that this political head or governmental system fell and the religious system came into power, is that the people of the world learned to trust and rely on it by what they were taught and experienced in their lives. That's why the people of the world chased after Nimrod in his day, and also in the days of Nebuchadnezzar. Promises, promises; lies, lies; and visual conditioning prepared the people to accept what was going on in their day. Fifty years ago, Sodomy and rape were as bad as murder, yet after laws were passed, new definitions in the churches were made, as their pastors looked the other way, while evil became an acceptable way of life.

Going back to John 3, where it tells us that, each soul must be born from above to have eternal salvation. If you have killed a child before it was born, you have kept it from entering into this earth age. If you have already gone through this process in ignorance, then it is time for repentance, for there is salvation through the blood of our Lord Jesus Christ, and that is why our prayers must be *"in Jesus name"*. Satan will set up the policy for the New World Order that is coming upon us very soon, and it will be exactly what the world is looking for. The policies of Satan's Kingdom will be applied to businesses and churches world wide. Laws will control what people can say and things that are forbidden.

Daniel 8:24,25 *"And his power shall be mighty, but not by his own power: and he shall destroy wonderfully, and shall prosper, and practice, and destroy the mighty and the holy People." "And through his policy also he shall cause craft to prosper in his hand; and he shall magnify himself in his heart, and by peace shall destroy many: he shall also stand up against the Prince of princes; but he shall be broken without hand."*

God warned us to know what was recorded in both the Old and New Testament. God's Elect will understand and will be prepared for the end times as things are taking place. Our only protection is knowing the Word of God that is sealed in our minds. God's "mighty Power" is activating everything that is coming to pass before our eyes. When Satan uses those supernatural powers, to deceive God's holy people, the Elect will have their eyes opened by the Spirit of God to see through Satan's deception. Today the, "Quality lifestyle" will become the playground for the elimination of both Jews and Christians who stand in it's way. This time is coming very soon, only God's Elect and the Bride of Jesus Christ will know these truths.

If those who read and fully understand this entire book "*Men's Traditions Revised*" and accept it as the truth. They are either a Bride of Christ Jesus or one God's Elect. However if you find this book a burden to you this is a good time to stop reading at this point in time. If you have fallen into deception and despair you can repent and ask the Lord to cleanse you from, Men's Traditions and ask God for forgiveness. He died for you and loves you just as you are. All you have to do is ask him to cleanse your life and make you into a new person. Its up to you to chose to whom you will follow. This is why this book has been written to those who didn't know God's truth. Remember the truth sets us free in Jesus Christ, King of Kings.

Many will be destroyed spiritually because they didn't know these things nor do they want to know about the warnings written in God in His Word. We are living in the end times, and many of the trumpets have already sounded. Sodomy is running wild and murder is common today. These souls are being sent back to the Father who gave them life and also those babies who were aborted. It is time to put your spiritual armor on and be ready to make a stand. This *"king of fierce countenance and understanding dark sentences" is* Satan who will stand up, and the whole world will follow him immediately except God's Elect and the Bride of Christ. The final battle here on earth is a spiritual battle for the souls of mankind, and if you are one of the Elect, or a bride of Christ, then this message is recorded for you. Those who are not sealed with the truth will not except this book nor any part of it.

Remember Daniel wanted to know more about what God had revealed to him, and he couldn't sleep for two weeks. Then God told Daniel, "*the words are sealed until the end*".

Daniel 12:8,9 *"And I heard, but I understood not: then said I, O My Lord, what shall be the end of these things?" "And He said, `Go thy way, Daniel: for the words are close up and sealed till the time of the end."*

Next time a person tells you, he is for *"quality of life"*; stop and think for a moment; ask yourself, "At what cost?" Most of the church world today will find this chapter offensive, but as one of the Elect, you are placed in this generation by God to make your stand. We are living in this flesh Age of Grace and it is coming to an end very shortly, after five months of Satan's testing all of mankind. Then we all will be changed into the "*Millennium age*" of Christ's Kingdom here on earth. This senseless loss of life of the unborn is a prime example of the times we are living in, and it was all prophesied. Maybe that is why Daniel was not allowed to writing about it taking place. The concerns written here are only for the end generation, and did not apply in Daniel's day. He was used by God as a messenger for Christian believers' living today.

It saddens my soul that pastors don't teach their followers these things that are recorded in the Bible. Scripture tells us that they will be held accountable for leading their congregations into Traditions' of Men.

SOUL SLEEP
Chapter 8

Whenever mankind perverts God's plan, it causes Almighty God to poor out His wrath upon them. God has created every living soul back in the first earth age, and one third of His children were deceived into following Satan at that time. Because our Lord is a loving and merciful God He ended that first earth age and completely destroyed it. The body of every living soul was created like the angels with spirit bodies. As mankind searches for their beginning, they have discovered artifacts of many kinds of creatures from that first earth age, yet there are no remains of human beings found. Because our souls were spirit bodies, not in a fleshly body at that time, therefore we were all in our Spiritual bodies, and we will be changed back into our Spiritual bodies once again at the end of this flesh earth age.

God created every living soul in that first earth known as the world age that once was, and the process of testing each of those souls was because of the fall that many of His children made at that time. That is why God created this second earth age of mankind in fleshly bodies and He gave us all a free will. In the 19th chapter, titled *Salvation*, Jesus told Nicodemus in John 3:3

John 3:3 *"Jesus answered and said unto him, "Verily, verily, I say unto thee, Except a man be born again, he cannot see the kingdom of God."*

This was not only confusing to Nicodemus in his day, but it's also confusing for many Christians today. In the Greek Text, *"born again"*, reads *"born from above"*. This passage is talking about the birthing process, *"being born of water . . ."* from the womb of a child's mother. Every soul born must enter into this earth age innocent of the first age that once was, and will have their own choice to follow the ways of God, or Satan.

All life forms are important to God, and each was created to reproduce and multiply after its own kind. At this point in time, the use of cloning, or copying genes into identical animals has been limited to the minds of the movie makers. This is not according to God's plan, it's not even in plant life or animal life, much less human life. The Apostle Paul presented thoughts regarding this in I Corinthians 15:34-44.

I Corinthians 15:34 "Awake to righteousness, and sin not; for some have not the knowledge of God: *speak this to your shame."*

This verse tells us to get a little common sense about yourself and think before you act. There are many that do not have the knowledge of God concerning the resurrection of Christ. They don't know things concerning life after death, nor what happens to a soul after the physical body dies. This knowledge of God is contained within His Word. If you don't know, its a shame because you will stumble into all sorts of false doctrine, by teachers that lead you into their spiritually dead avenues, at the end of the road.

I Corinthians 15:35 *"But some man will say, "How are the dead raised up? and with what body do they come?"*

Paul gives us the answers regarding, what happens after death and when a person is buried in the ground, so that we can fully understand with out confusion. If we believe in the resurrection, we have hope. Where does it take place, and with what body does the dead rise? This is talking about the changing of the physical body into a soul spiritual body. In other words, when our flesh body dies it will instantly be changed into our spiritual bodies which has departed from the flesh body the instant we died. That old flesh body will return to dust in which it was made of.

I Corinthians 15:36 *"Thou fool, that which thou sewest is not quickened, except it die:"*

It is important to understand the word *"quickened"*, Earlier Paul said in verse 22; *"in Adam all die, so in Christ shall all be made alive."* This Greek word for *"quickened"* is the same Greek word for *"coming alive"*. It means that all, sinners and saints are made alive through Christ. It doesn't mean that the soul is raised to eternal life, because the soul is not the subject here, but the question is what happens to the physical body?

To *"revitalize"* #2227 in "*Strong's"* the soul is to become conscience and ready for judgment. This doesn't mean that all souls are saved, but that all souls are given life to continue as they were after they were created in this flesh earth age. If that soul was lost, it will still be lost, but there is a final death which is, the death of our soul bodies, called also spiritual bodies that lives after this flesh body has died. All soul bodies will go into heaven. After the Seventh trumpet sounds the Millennium age comes and then the "*Great White Throne Judgment"*, and those who are still against Christ will see hell fire and the destruction. The *"second death"* is known as, the death of all those lost souls. It means that the soul has put off the flesh body, and put on their spiritual body, yet their soul is still condemned to death if that soul is not in right standing with God.

Hebrews 4:12 *"For the word of God is quick, and powerful, and sharper than any two-edged sword, piercing even to the dividing asunder of soul and spirit, and of the joints and marrow, and is a discerner of the thoughts and intents of the heart."*

By placing the Word of God in our minds, it becomes our standard of thinking, and directs the intent of our minds that fills our hearts. Jesus Christ is the Living Word, and He can give us discernment, wisdom, and understanding in all things, He also knows the intent of our thoughts. His Holy Spirit, heals, leads and directs us through our spirit when we pray and ask Him to fill us and teach us, our intellect becomes part of His thought process as we study His word, where by we begin to know and understand His living word.

To understand the resurrection we must understand what Paul is going to explain to us about our flesh body, not the soul, and spirit body but, the thought process, of our flesh body.

I Corinthians 15:37 *"And that which thou sowest, thou sowest not that body that shall be, but bare grain, it may chance of wheat, or of some other grain:"*

Paul is comparing our flesh body with other living things, such as a grain of wheat. When the seed is separated from it's parent plant it is as naked as a new born baby. This is the body of the wheat, and this is not the grain that you see coming up as new plants next year. This seed of wheat that you set aside for the next year's crop is what must die before it can rise up again into a new form. That body of wheat is gone, and that is what happens to our flesh. It must die before the new beautiful spiritual body can come forth.

The flesh body must die and be buried in the ground. Christ's body was raised again, because He paid the price for our sins, once and for all times. However, when Christ's body came out of the tomb, it had to be transformed before flesh man could see Him.

The body of the wheat or of flesh that dies and is planted in the ground is not the same body that springs forth into new life. It is the Spiritual body that ascends to be with the Father, not the flesh. Again, the subject is the physical body.

When you plant a seed; flowers, corn, or wheat, there is an embryo deep inside of the body of that plant. As the body of the parent plant decays, it feeds this little embryo that is deep within that seed or kernel of corn. Then when the water, temperature, and soil are just right, the embryo springs forth into new life, and a plant is formed. That is exactly as it is with our flesh body; the old flesh body must die before our new spiritual soul body can come forth. The time that it takes for the new spiritual life to come from the death of the old flesh body is instant.

The instant the flesh body dies, the soul and spirit body is present with the Lord who created it. The flesh decays back into the elements of the earth that it is made of, and your soul always returns to our Heavenly Father. Paul could not have made it any clearer than using the grain of wheat in comparison to our flesh bodies and soul bodies. Just as all of natures functions, so it is with mankind.

I Corinthians 15:38 *"But God giveth it a body as it hath pleased Him, and to every seed his own body."*

Our bodies were given to each of us because it pleased God. We are talking about physical bodies here, not the soul bodies. Our physical body were created for our soul and spirit bodies to live in while were living here on earth. Although the flesh body may lose a leg or body part, our spiritual body living within us is still whole and complete. All of nature has been given seeds within them, through their embryos so their seed can continue to live after their flesh body dies. The seeds of mankind brings forth their offspring.

Why did God create the different races on the sixth day and Adam on the eighth day? To give Him pleasure with the different human seeds. God created different races of people for His pleasure, and He called them Good. We all should be thrilled with whatever race we are, especially proud to be just as God made us. Remember He not only created us just as we are, but He died for the human race, and looks upon us as His unique creations that we all are. Remember God never created a nobody.

I Corinthians 15:39 *"All flesh is not the same flesh: but there is one kind of flesh of men, another flesh of beasts, another of fishes, and another of birds."*

This is still talking about the flesh bodies not the soul or spiritual bodies. God created all animal life in various types of creatures and not any of them are created alike. Dogs, cats, bird's, and fish and animals of all kinds have different kinds of physical bodies. They don't look alike, nor act alike, yet they all have their own unique beauty. When the female dog has pups its not possible for her to have a baby fish or a cat, she will only give birth to puppies. God's creations are all perfect just as God has planed. Mankind was created after their own kind just as the animals' were created after their own kind. Their are different species of both mankind and animal life. Animals were created first, and then mankind was created.

Genesis 1:24 *"And God said, "Let the earth bring forth the living creature after his kind, cattle, and creeping things, and the beast of the earth after his kind: and it was so."*

Genesis 1:25 *"And God made the beast of the earth after his kind, and cattle after their kind, and every thing that creepeth upon the earth after his kind: and God saw it was good."*

God's plan didn't order the snakes to breed kitties, nor sheep to breed with cows. He doesn't want man to cross with an animal, but each flesh which man is, to bring forth it's own kind. God has a plan and we are all part of that plan. That kernel of corn, the fish and all of mankind are all part of God's plan. Every soul that God has created must enter into the embryo of a woman or female in order to give birth. Every soul must go through this flesh age only once, and then give up it's flesh body. It is from the death of this flesh body that the soul can return to the Father to be judged for their actions while living in our flesh body. While in the flesh, we're innocent of that first earth age, every living soul has the right to freely choose to follow either God or Satan.

The conflict started back in the first earth age at the rebellion of Satan, when one third of all souls, known as the children of God, rebelled and followed Satan. Now in this flesh age God has provided a way that all souls can be brought back to commune with Him, and is given a fresh start in our flesh bodies to choose Christ's way or follow Satan. God created every soul for His pleasure, and each flesh body has a soul body during this part of God's plan. When your flesh body dies, then it is time for the soul to return back to the Father, from where it came. He placed your soul body into the embryo of your mother at conception.

There are many different thoughts on this subject in the Christian community, but remember that Satan likes to twist the truth, and make God's reality into a lie. Its very important what you believe, because its what determines your faith; and what saves or condemns your soul. When our flesh body dies, your soul body returns to our Heavenly Father where we will give account for all those things that we have said and done while living in your flesh bodies. When believers return to the Father they will rejoice, while non believers will be sent to the other side of the gulf.

People who teach *"soul sleep"* believe that their soul body sleeps in the grave until the resurrection and the final judgment. This teaching is one of Satan's deceptive plans to destroy souls because its a lie. The word sleep in Luke 8:52; and 1Cor. 15:6 does not mean literal sleep, its just a way to describe death because a dead body appears to be asleep. We are told to mark those who teach "*false doctrines*". The Churches today that teach and believe in *"soul sleep," are* the Seventh *Day Adventist Church, Jehovah's Witnesses,* and others. They teach that there is no hope for the dead souls in the ground after death,. That's not what the scriptures tell us. They are teaching "soul sleep" that condemns mankind to hell! Where as God's word sets them free.

God's word tells us that Hell will not occur until after the 1000 Millennium Age and after judgment day at the *"Great White Throne"* of all Mighty God. That is when those souls who followed Satan will be judged. God would not send anyone to hell until after judgment day, because our Heavenly Father is a fair and merciful God. He gives every-one a chance in the Millennium age to learn all truth and follow him for a 1000 years. We should thank God every day for His great love and mercy, knowing that He alone is the final judge, not mankind. God is very angry with pastors who teach false doctrines because they deceive his flocks. Its time to repent and stop teaching such things in His House of Prayer. Our goal is to reveal the truth of God's word not to pass judgment upon anyone. For no greater love has any man than to lay his life down for his brother. This book is full of all kinds of truths to remind those we love to change their ways and rededicate their lives to our Heavenly Father.

I Corinthians 15:40 *"There are also celestial bodies, and bodies terrestrial: but the glory of the celestial is one, and the glory of the terrestrial is another."*

We are still taking about bodies, and not souls. *"Celestial bodies"* are heavenly bodies, while *"terrestrial bodies"* are earthly bodies. Paul is telling us that within us is what we call "self", you have two bodies. One is the earthly body that will die and return to the earth. Our heavenly body is known as our soul body that returns to the heavenly realm that it came from. Each of these two bodies has their own glory, dignity and honor.

I Corinthians 15:41 *"There is one glory of the sun, and another glory of the moon, and another glory of the stars: for one star differeth from another star in glory."*

God's words are very clear. This is the reason that God calls His children *"stars"*. God asked Job to give Him an answer to this question in Job 38:7.

Job 38:7, "*When the morning stars sang together, and all the sons of God shouted for joy?*"

Each star is different and so are each of the children that God created. Every one of them has a different body. Yet, every last one of them was created for God's pleasure.

Revelation 4:11 *"Thou art worthy, O Lord, to receive glory and honour and power: for Thou hast created all things, and for Thy pleasure they are and were created"*

I Corinthians 15:42 *"So also is the resurrection of the dead. It is sown in corruption; it is raised in incorruption:"*

The *"resurrection of the dead"* is what happens to the dead body, for this body is doomed to corruption and decay from the day we were born, until we die. There is an ageing process, and no matter how we try to extend our life, it will not be for more than a few years. When our flesh body is dead, our soul body that was living within our flesh body is raised into our incorruptible body, immediately. This happens to everyone who lived in their flesh bodies.

All of our flesh bodies, have a living soul body within our flesh bodies, we all will look the same through out the vast expanse of time, just as the day that they were created. Souls or spiritual bodies never gets sick, and they all have complete knowledge and memory of the past. The differences between these two bodies are that one is used in the fleshly realm of this earth age, while the other is a spiritual body living in a spiritual realm.

Our flesh bodies are corruptible, and filled with pollutions of all kinds. Mankind has caused all kinds of pollutions in the air, in the waters, and across our land to satisfy their own needs. Flesh is corruptible, however when the corruptible body is buried at death into the earth, and our Soul body goes directly into God's heavenly realm and we become incorruptible.

I Corinthians 15:43 *"It is sown in dishonor; it is raised in glory: it is sown in weakness; it is raised in power:"*

In the flesh body we fall short every day, but when our soul body is raised, it's changed at death, and we have God's power within us. In that new body we will never be weak, get sick nor age. When our soul is released at death, it is like being turned loose into a freedom that these fleshly minds can not understand. We are never to commit suicide or shorten the lives that God has given us, because we have a duty and mission on earth in our flesh bodies. However on that day when it is all over, we will be given power and glory that God has placed within our new incorruptible bodies.

Those people living from Adam's seed have all die in the flesh, but those living in Christ are raised incorruptible. Even sinners are replenished and brought back into their incorruptible state, some will be held for judgment and trial, while others will receive eternal rewards. Your flesh body is not what is judged its your soul body that lives within our flesh body that will returned to the Lord for judgments or it's rewards.

I Corinthians 15:44 *"It is sown a natural body; it is raised a spiritual body. There is a natural body, and there is a spiritual body."*

There is a natural body called our flesh body, and a spiritual or body with a soul body. The two are different, when the natural body or flesh body dies the spiritual body is *"raised"*. In the Greek text "egiro, *awakened, become active from its death"*. You have two bodies, one is your flesh body and the other is your spiritual body. Our spiritual body is released and awakened into a new life, when the flesh body dies. Your spirit and soul is in one body. Our spirit body is "the intellect that lives within our soul body". Just as our spirit body that once lived within our flesh body. It is through these two parts, that our Heavenly Father leads us by His Spirit and teaches us all things. When we pray, we grow in His Spirit and we walk in

His Spirit. Only by His Spirit can we understand the deeper things of God's word because it's His Holy Spirit who teaches our spirit.

Your spirit never leaves your soul body, even at the death of your flesh body. Satan does not have any power over your spiritual body, just your flesh body. Man and Satan can tear this flesh body into pieces and cause people to do all sorts of evil things, but no one on earth can harm your soul body, no man on earth, Satan himself, nor his angels. God is the only one that can destroy the soul and that will not be until the end of the Millennium age after the final judgment. However, through the great deception of Satan, he can cause you to sin against God, through his various deceptions' and many will fall away from Almighty God. But that is why we have been given repentance, in the name of Jesus so that believers can have forgiveness and a right standing before the Father again if we ask Him to forgive us in Jesus Name.

It can't be made any clearer than what Paul has written in the next verse. We all have two bodies, the flesh body that we can see, and the spiritual body within no one can see. When the flesh body dies, then the spiritual body is awakened and come alive. It starts to live a life without baggage of the flesh body confining it to the limits of the flesh.

Ecclesiastes 12:7 *"Then* [at death] *shall the dust* [flesh body] *return to the earth as it was: and the spirit* [spiritual body *shall return* [instantly] *to God* [our Father] *Who gave it."*

Ecclesiastes 9:5 *"For the living know that they shall die: but the dead know not any thing, neither have they any more a reward; for the memory of them is forgotten."*

This is written by Solomon to the flesh man that walks under the sun, and when the life of the flesh is over with, it has no more knowledge nor thoughts because it has died. It's useless, but the soul body that was within it has gone to be with our Heavenly Father.

I Corinthians 15:48 *"As is the earthy, such are they also that are earthy: and as is the heavenly, such are they also that are heavenly."*

When a person builds his life around the things of the flesh, and lives only for the pleasures of life, then his fleshly nature controls him. However, when we are living in the Spirit, our inner man forces our flesh body to be under the control of His spirit body. It is a matter of which part of you controls your life, the one that is in tune with God, or your selfish nature. We all have a choice to make.

I Corinthians 15:49 *"And as we have borne the image of the earthy, we shall also bear the image of the heavenly."*

Every living soul that God created will pass through this life in a flesh body. There are many souls that refuse to be born of woman through the birthing process, and they are called the *"Nethilim"*, or "fallen angels". In Genesis 6:6, they are called the *"sons of God "*, and they are the same angels Jude wrote about in Jude 6.

Jude 1:6 *"And the angels which kept not their first estate, but left their own habitation, He hath reserved in everlasting chains under darkness unto the judgment of the great day."*

These fallen angels came to earth and married the daughters of flesh man, then transformed themselves into a human form. Paul is telling us that everyone is going to be raised into that spiritual body on judgment day. Judgment day for the unjust is at the end of the Millennium age. All living souls will be raised up into heaven in their spiritual bodies. Their flesh body has nothing to do with the condition of their soul bodies. This verse is talking about soul bodies that were transformed into a human body.

I Corinthians 15:50 *"Now this I say, brethren, that flesh and blood cannot inherit the kingdom of God; neither doth corruption inherit incorruption."*

Paul is saying that this is the truth, flesh and blood cannot be part of the Kingdom of God. Your flesh body is going to allow you to sin and that is it's human nature. When you are under the nature of your flesh body, it will not allow your inner man to control you. There is no way that flesh and blood can become part of the Kingdom of God. As long as you are living in your flesh body, you simply cannot keep from breaking parts of the laws of God. Your mind is incapable of retaining all of the laws, and applying it all to your life. This is why we have repentance, and it is also why flesh and blood will not be here when Jesus Christ's Kingdom is established here on this earth for the Millennium Kingdom, many people don't know this truth.

You may be spiritually dead, but you will also take on your new incorruptible body, that you will live in through out the Millennium age which is in Jesus Christ's Kingdom. Everyone is going to enter into a spiritual dimension whereby all souls will be judged. Every flesh body is changed from their flesh body into your new spiritual body, known as our incorruptible body, which has nothing to do with the condition of your soul. If you were lost before, you will still be lost, and if you have received Jesus Christ and are under His shed blood, you will be in that same spiritual condition with Him. This is going to happen at the sounding of the seventh and last trumpet when all physical bodies will be done away with, and all souls will be changed into their spiritual bodies. Mankind can not make a spirit nor a living soul body! Only God Almighty has mastered that creation.

CLONING
Chapter 9

The term Cloning, is taking an embryo and trying to make something identical out of it by using cells, tissue, DNA and various body parts. They mix human with animal DNA, to create some sort of distortion, they claimed to prolong human life by this research. They are trying to make an exact copy of humans with the D.N.A. implants in women, and has called it "cloning human beings". Their cloning is a body without a soul, only God can create a soul. When cloning is done by man, he can only alter the physical process of flesh man, and he cannot tamper with the soul or spirit body we call the incorruptible body that lives within the flesh body. That is not God's way, it's all unnatural. They are creating a body without a soul.

God created every female in a flesh body. There is an exact image of her soul body within it, and He also placed an embryo where by she could conceive. Because each of these bodies that go to make up the human being has weaknesses, God gave us a set of rules to follow to maintain a good healthy body, and laws to govern the moral condition of our soul.

When they began to clone other human beings, they are tampering with God's creation and that makes God very angry. God doesn't like it when anyone tampers with the souls of His children. God warned us in Isaiah.

Isaiah 45:9-11 "*Woe unto him that striveth with his Maker! Let the potsherd strive with the potsherds of the earth. Shall the clay say to him that fashioneth it,` What makest thou?' or thy work, "He hath no hands?" "Woe unto him that saith unto his father, `What begettest thou?' or to the woman, `What hast thou brought forth?" "Thus saith the Lord the Holy One of Israel, and his Maker, "Ask Me of things to come concerning*

My sons, and concerning the work of My hands command ye Me."

Do you really think that God is going to sit back and allow mankind to tamper with His normal reproduction process? Our Heavenly Father has told us here exactly what He thinks of people who tries to change his processes. God put a living soul in each flesh body at conception, and that soul and spirit will stay together until the human body dies. How do you think they can put a soul into a body that they have created? Mankind can not make a living soul's. Only God can create a living soul. God's plan is perfect because at death, the soul and spirit goes back to the Father to be judged or rewarded. Every time mankind has tried to tamper or mix the two realms, an advent has happened, and that is what will be determined here.

God told us in Jeremiah 4:22 what He thinks of His people when they do such things. He calls them "*sottish*" in the Hebrew text, meaning "stupid". When they tried to do similar things in that first earth age, Jeremiah 4:23-25 says that God destroyed all their cities, and all the life that existed upon this earth in that first earth age that once was. This activity is a sign that we are approaching the end of this earth age of flesh man.

In Genesis 3:15 we read the results about Satan deceiving Eve in the Garden of Eden, and from that sexual seduction of Eve, came Satan's children, the Kenites. It was by the Kenites hand that our Lord Jesus Christ was crucified on the cross. Satan was not a human being, but a supernatural being from another angelic realm. Through the sin of Adam and Eve, came another unnatural DNA life-form, part human, part angelic, outside of the plan of God's plan. The result of this action was when God sent Adam and Eve out of the Garden of Eden.

Genesis 6 tells us of another influx of the angelic realm, called the fallen angels that saw the daughters of men, and they took them for their wives. These fallen angels were known as "*Nephilim*", and were the fallen ones that had children, called "*giants*" by the daughter's of men. By this time, only Noah and his family were the only ones that were not part of that polluted mixture. The men of that first earth age that once was, left their habitation and they entered into this first earth age to disrupt the plan that God had for His children.

Jude 6,7 *"And the angels which kept not their first estate, but left their own habitation, He hath reserved in everlasting chains under darkness unto the judgment of the great day." "Even as Sodom and Gomorrah, and the cities about them, in like manner giving themselves over to fornication, and going after strange flesh, are set forth for an example suffering the vengeance of eternal fire."*

God knows the actions of Satan, the actions of the fallen angels, and those that practice and have given themselves over to Sodomy, and homosexual life style. If you think that what Satan does and the sexual activities of his angels with the daughters of men, and that the actions of Sodomites is just another life style, your wrong, because God is preparing a place for those who do such abominations after Judgment. That place is called "the lake of fire", "*These are examples of the suffering the vengeance of eternal fire*". Because they were tampering and changing the normal birthing process of mankind such as cloning which falls into this next verse of Jude.

Jude 1:8 *"Likewise also these filthy dreamers defile the flesh, despise dominion, and speak evil of dignities."*

God knows the intent of every one's mind who tries to defile their flesh bodies, and the birthing process that was designed to bring living souls into this earth age. We are here because of the sins of that first earth age, whereby each soul was to be given the opportunity to come back to the Father. The flood of Noah's day is written in Genesis.

Genesis 6:9 "*These are the generations of Noah: Noah was a just man and perfect in his generations, and Noah walked with God." Noah's family was "perfect" in the Hebrew text, "tamim without blemish as to breed or pedigree* ".

The rest of mankind was not perfect because they had mixed and bred with the fallen angels that produce their offspring, known as Gerber's who are giants, recorded in 1Kings 4:13-19. God had to do something or the promised Messiah would not have a blood line of human flesh to come through, therefore He destroyed that dispensation, and all of those who violated His creation of life. He will do the same thing in these end times just before His return.

Then after the flood, mankind came together with one mind under Nimrod. The people had one language and they looked to a man for their protection, instead of our Heavenly Father. When God saw mankind starting to build their own tower for salvation and protection. He confused their minds with different languages, the building process stopped, and the people were scattered. Babylon is known as confusion and historically this was the first attempt to create a One World System. Mankind built their great city and world system, and God destroyed it.

Jesus gave us the warning of the fig tree as one of the signs of the end times. After telling us about each of the events recorded in the seven seals and written in Matthew 24,32-34.

Matthew 24:32-34 "*Now learn a parable of the fig tree; When his branch is yet tender, and putteth forth leaves, ye know that summer is nigh:" "O likewise ye, when ye shall see all these things, know that it is near, even at the doors. "Verily I say unto you, this generation shall not pass, till all these things be fulfilled.*"

This parable alerts us to the works of the Kenites, the only way to have a fig tree is to clone it, take a branch from one tree and it becomes the second tree of it's kind. This is the same way to get sweet potatoes. Mankind has continually tried to play God in areas that are contrary to our God's perfect plan.

Daniel lived in Babylon many centuries after Nimrod's Babylon ended. Daniel had a dream of a great tree, in the book of Daniel.

Daniel 4:11,12; *"The tree grew, and was strong, and the height thereof reached unto heaven, and the sight thereof to the end of all the earth." "The Leaves thereof were fair, and the fruit thereof much, and in it was meat for all: the beasts of the field had shadow under it, and the fowls of the heaven dwelt in the boughs thereof, and all flesh was fed of it."*

Today we're living in the Babylon of Daniel's dream. The One World System of our end times will see all flesh coming together for their protection under the branches of that "great tree". The events that we are seeing coming to pass before our eyes are going to draw all of the nations of the world into the Babylon of the end time. Everything that is happening is part of the plan of God, to bring about the will of God as prophesied in His Holy Word. There was a meeting of the great nations of this earth in July 8, 2005 and the shadow of protection and feeding the people of the world that come under the shadow of this great tree is called "*The United Nations*" of our day.

In the end time, all the beasts of the field, the birds of the air including all of mankind who think that they are dwelling safely by man's own design, God will bring His judgment down upon them just as He did once before. The purpose of cloning is to extend man's life, so that his soul will not come under the judgment of God. If mankind thinks that he can clone himself, and move his life form one body to another that he has created, or renew his body parts to replace the old, this is going against God's plan for the life span of mankind. It is tampering with God's plan for this earth age of flesh man, and we are now well into the final generation of this earth age. This political system of plotting and planning is about to end; and mankind will move under this great tree that Daniel saw.

Daniel 4:13-15 *"I saw in the vision of my head upon my bed, and behold, a watcher and an holy one came down from heaven;" "He cried aloud, and said thus, `Hew down the tree, and cut off his branches, shake off his leaves, and scatter his fruit: let the beasts get away from under it, and the fowls from his branches:" "Nevertheless leave the stump of his roots in the earth, even with a band of iron and brass, in the tender grass of the field; and let it be wet with the dew of heaven, and let his portion be with the beasts in the grass of the earth:"*

God will cut that great tree of the *"Religious World System"*, known as the, *"World Council of Churches"* that Satan will control when he arrives at the sixth trumpet. Cutting down this great tree will come at the sounding of the seventh trumpet, by our Lord Jesus Christ; and only a stump will remain. That stump will continue right on through until the Millennium age of our Lord Jesus Christ, when Satan will be cast into the pit, and his army of fallen angels will be disposed of, from off the earth through out the Millennium age. Then at the close of the thousand years, Satan will be released for a season, and the final testing comes about for a very short season. Then the finial Judgment takes place.

We are told in **Revelation 15:3** that those that will be victorious in this earth age will be singing the song of Moses as they march into the Millennium age to receive their rewards. Those that sing this song know the difference between the Rock of our Lord, and the rock of Satan. Each of the Elect knows the difference between spots and way of God, and the ways of the devil.

The events like cloning, abortion, sodomy, and all the other filth that are happening today will be no surprise to God's Elect, that are fixed, sealed and focused on the Word of the living God, and not on the traditions of men. God is coming back, and He will make all things right. He did it in the first earth age, then in the time of Noah's flood, and when He scattered the people of Nimrod's Babylon and destroyed his tower, and in the Babylon of Daniel's day. God has His master plan, and no man will pervert, distort, or change Gods creation or His children and get away with it. Today we serve a very angry God.

Those people who think that they can play God with the genetic forms of God's creation, and get away with it. They should know that God has every one of them marked well, and unless they turn from their wicked ways and come into repentance and turn back to the Father in Jesus name, there is no eternal hope for them. We are living in the time of Grace today, but this time is coming to a close. No matter what plans mankind makes for themselves, one thing is for sure; only the plan of God will come to pass exactly as it is written in His Living Word.

APOSTASY
Chapter 10

God revealed warnings to His people through Ezekiel, regarding how it will be in the

House of Israel in the end times. These warnings came to pass when all of the House of Judah, were in captivity in Babylon. The house of Israel are the ten tribes that separated themselves from Judah and were taken captive by the Assyrians about 300 years before this happened. The people of the Northern Kingdom were taken to a place in Iraq of our day, and in a very short period of time they divided into tribal units and migrated north through the Caucasus Mountains. They formed many nations of the world, and are known as Celts, Gauls, Cimmerons, Brits, Sakka. They are still called "Caucasians", known as white race.

Ezekiel 3:4 *"And He said unto me, "Son of man, go, get thee unto the house of Israel and speak with My words unto them."*

Hosea 1:10 *"Yet the number of the Children of Israel shall be as the sand of the sea, which cannot be measured nor numbered; and It shall come to pass, that in the place where it was said unto them, "Ye are not My People," There it shall be said unto them, "Ye are the sons of the Living God."*

The *"sons of the Living God"* are called Christians today. Jesus Christ overcame death and arose to set on the right hand of the Father. Jesus Christ is the Living God, and God will use these sons of God to give the gospel of Christ to all nations of the world. God is telling Ezekiel to write this warning to those Christian nations of the house of Israel. Most Christians today think that God has lost this ancient house of Israel, when in fact they are the "sons of the Living God ", known as the Caucasians that have lost their own identity regarding their past.

Ezekiel 3:5,6 *"For thou art not sent to a people of a strange speech and of an hard language, but to the house of Israel," "Not to many people of a strange speech and of an hard language, whose words thou canst not understand. Surely, had I sent thee to them, they would have hearkened unto thee."*

At the time of this writing, both houses spoke Hebrew, their terms and expressions of God's Holy Word were known to all of them. The people in all of Israel were well aware of the laws of God, and the written Word of Moses and the rest of the prophets. This writing is directed to those people living in the end times that have put their trust in the Lord Jesus Christ and accepted the teachings of our Lord. If Ezekiel had sent these prophecies to heathen Gentile nations, they would not understand the meaning. However, like the example of Jonah's preaching to Nineveh, when they heard the word of God, they were converted.

Ezekiel 3:7,8 *"But the house of Israel will not hearken unto thee; for they will not hearken unto Me: for all the house of Israel are impudent and hard hearted." "Behold, I have made thy face strong against their faces, and thy forehead strong against their foreheads."*

After King Solomon died, the House of Israel separated themselves from God's house, they built two golden calves and then they placed these golden calves at both ends of Israel. In time King Ahab of Israel married the Kenite Jezebel and she brought four hundred of her satanic priests to lead the people of Israel. She tried to kill all the priests and prophets of God, and turn their minds away from God. This is going on even today in our land amongst the Christian nations of the World. People here in the U.S.A. and most of the Christian Church world today are so hard hearted that they refuse to accept God's written Word. They would rather go chasing after the fairy tales of the world, such as evolution, the rapture doctrine, abortion, and today sodomy is accepted in many Christian Churches. They say they don't want to judge nor offend any of them.

Ezekiel 3:9,10 *"As an adamant harder than flint have I made thy forehead: fear them not, neither be dismayed at their looks, though be a rebellious house." "Moreover He said unto me, "Son of man, all My words that I shall speak unto thee receive in thine heart, and hear with thine ears."*

In these final days of this earth age, Christian's minds are so fixed and hardened into their fairy-tales and traditions of men that it will be impossible to change their minds into accepting the truth of His Word. Many preachers today are bound by the controls of their deacon's where by their traditions are approved through their church system. It is like putting a chain or bondage around the neck of a gifted teacher of the Word of God. This system of confusion and pressure keep the truth from being taught, it is part of the Babylon system of these end times. These traditions are what is keeping the flock from being fed the truth of God's word. The greatest sin in the world today is to teach a lie to please the world, when you know the truth and withhold that truth from the flock. God is telling Ezekiel to "let it all sink into your mind with understanding and let your ears hear".

Ezekiel 3:11,12 *"And go, get thee to them of the captivity, unto the children of thy People, and speak unto them, and tell them, "Thus saith the Lord God; "Whether they will hear, or whether they will forbear." "Then the spirit took me up, and I hear behind me a voice of a great rushing, saying, "Blessed be the glory of the Lord from His place."*

When you go forth to preach the Word of God, don't listen to any of those self appointed critics, just preach the pure word of God. When you teach from the Word of God, You always say, *"Thus saith the Lord God "*. Once the truth of God's Holy

Word is given by you to another with understanding, then their blood will not be on your hands or head. In these end times we are sent out to teach the truth, recorded in the Bible, although we reveal the pure Word most people will reject it. However, it is not your responsibility to make anyone accept the truth, the Holy Spirit of God is the teacher. Most people will reject the truth and continue to follow traditions of men in these end times.

God prepared Ezekiel first regarding what was going to happen, and then in the next three verses in Ezekiel 3:12,13,14 is when His spirit is being taken up.

Ezekiel. 3:12,13,14 *"Then the spirit took me up, and I heard behind me a voice of a great rushing, saying, "Blessed be the glory of the Lord from His place." "I heard also the noise of the wings of the living creatures that touched one another, and a noise of a great rushing." "So the spirit lifted me up, and took me away, and I went in bitterness, in the heat of my spirit; but the hand of the Lord was strong upon me."*

Ezekiel talked about this highly polished vehicle with the protective creatures in the first chapter. Here Ezekiel is taken in the spirit into the future and as it leaves, the noise gets louder. God's time with Ezekiel is about over, but Ezekiel is given a clearer picture of the message that he is putting forth. Ezekiel saw the presence of the Living God, and he was given a view of the future technology. Ezekiel was given two separate views of this vehicle that lasted seven days. God made Ezekiel a watchman for our end genera-tion, as he viewed those things that are going on today.

Ezekiel 3:17,18 *"Son of man, I have made thee a watchman unto the house of Israel: therefore hear the world at My mouth, and give them warning from Me." "When I say unto the wicked, `thou shalt surely die; and thou givest them not warning, nor speakest to warn the wicked from his wicked way, to save his* *life; the same wicked man shall die in his iniquity; but his blood will I require at thine hand."*

Ezekiel was given a view into these end time, and he saw all of the false teachings and traditions of men that are going on today. He saw the mass murdering of the unborn, and the spread of sodomy. He became a watchman on the wall of our day, and now God is going to warn him of his duties as a watchman. This letter from Ezekiel is his warning to all of us living in the house of Israel today. All Christian nations of today regarding our obligation toward those who are spiritually blind. It is our duty to plant the seeds of truth from the Word of God in their minds, and allow the Holy Spirit to bring it to light in their minds. Once you have planted the seed of truth in Israel, to our neighbors, family and friends, then they will be without excuse.

As we study the Word, God gives each of us wisdom and knowledge from His Word, and we have the responsibility to share that knowledge. The Word will either save Israel from their sins, or they will reject it and die a physical death in their iniquity. However, when we know the truth and refuse to share it with others, then the blood of their iniquity and sins, will be on your hands. And this is the fear of the Lord for the Christian's who knows truth and fail to tell others. As Christians we are compelled by God, to plant the seeds of truth and allow the Holy Spirit to work in the minds of others.

Ezekiel 3:19,20 *"Yet if thou warn the wicked, and he turn not from his wickedness, nor from his wicked way, he shall die in his iniquity; but thou hast delivered thy soul" "Again, When a righteous man doth turn from his righteousness, and commit iniquity, and I lay a stumbling block before him, he shall die: because thou hast not given him warning, he shall die in his sin, and his righteousness which he hath done shall not be remembered; but his blood will I require at thine hand."*

Once you have warned a wicked man of his wicked way, your soul is delivered from any blame for whatever that person decides to do. He or she has the right to choose the path that he will follow, and you have warned him that his path of iniquity is the way of destruction. However, if a righteous man gets all wrapped up in the ways and tradit-ions of this world, that will become a stumbling block to other Christians and causes them to sin; then what ever righteous acts that person has done will not be remembered in heaven. In fact, when judgment day comes, the sins of the pastors and righteous men, who led their congregations astray because they neglected to tell them the truth of God's word.

We are living in a time just prior to the coming of Satan in the role of the Antichrist. The traditions of today are leading many righteous men, preachers and teachers of the Word of God are told to instruct their flocks to follow the first Christ that comes to take them away. They are told that as a Christian they will not have to prepare for *"The Great Tribulation"* because they will not be here on earth, and that God will remove them before Satan and his army of fallen angels arrives on earth in Revelation 12:7-9. This warning is from God to Ezekiel, but it's directed to Christians that are living in our day, who claims the name of Jesus Christ as their Savior.

After all of Ezekiel's warnings, God told Ezekiel to stand to his feet, and He reminded him that there is a time and place for everything in God's plan. God prepared Ezekiel for His mission, just as He has prepared those of us who came into the understanding of His Word. God told Ezekiel to go to his house and lock himself away, therefore this message was not for our day. There were many years remaining to the 70 years of captivity in Babylon, this message was to be passed on from one generation to the next and on into this final generation. It is for "the rebellious house of Israel" of our day.

Ezekiel 3:27 *"But when I speak with thee, I will open thy mouth, and thou shalt say unto them, `Thus saith the Lord God;*

He that heareth, let him hear, and he that forbeareth, let him forbear: for they are a rebellious house."

As each of the Elect watch the events that are going on around us, and the wickedness that is spreading over the land; it's time to open our mouths and speak out when things are not right. We are to voice our opinion when the world moves against what we know to be true from the Word of God. Although there will be many who will rebel's against God's word, that's the time we are to stand our ground with the truth so it can be heard. God has His chosen people at this time, and each of those chosen ones knows the truth from God's holy Word. He will reward those that are diligent in their mission, and each of them will become joint heirs with Christ in His Millennium Kingdom.

This sets the stage for a lesson that God will use as a sign of those witnessing in these end times. Remember that Jerusalem will always be a very special place for our Heavenly Father. This lesson was given in the day of Ezekiel, but it is given as a warning to each of us living in these final days in this earth age.

Ezekiel 4:1 "Thou *also, son of man, take thee a tile, and lay it before thee, and pourtray upon it the city, even Jerusalem:"*

God is telling Ezekiel to take a flat piece of slate of Babylonian brick which is a symbolic object given to portray the city of Jerusalem as becoming Babylon. This lesson is for the end times and it will relate to the final siege when the Antichrist takes over. This is a picture that was projected far into the future, on into the time that we now live in. A model of Jerusalem is drawn on a tile and given for an object lesson for the house of Israel, which is the Christian nation of today.

Ezekiel 4:2 *"And lay siege against it, and build a fort against it, and cast a mount against it; set the camp also against it, and set battering rams against it round about."*

Notice that *"against it"* is used five times, and in biblical numeric', five stands for "Grace". It is time that we wake up and stand against the "Judas goats", and make a stand against everything that is unholy. When you go into a church house and see that the Word is not being taught there, mark that place well in your mind.

Ezekiel 4:3 *"Moreover take thou unto thee an iron pan, and set it for a wall of Iron between thee and the city: and set thy face against it, and it shall be besieged, and thou shalt lay siege against it. this shall be a sign to the house of Israel."*

At this time, *"the iron pan"* was a flat iron skillet used in baking bread. Jesus Christ is the Word known as the bread of life. He offered Grace to those who follow His Word and walk on the path that He has prepared for us. The placement of the pan between Ezekiel and this tile with the city of Jerusalem drawn on it is a demonstration given to show what is going to happen. When those false teachings and traditions come against us, we are to set this bread pan, or Christ as our wall of protection. This is on an individual basis and is a special message to the Christian nations, the House of Israel and individuals of our day. It is one of the signs that God is giving, it tells us that the time of the end is near. Each of the items of warnings has their own meaning,

This sign of the end times are showing us what's happening in Jerusalem today, by the events that are taking place there today. Jesus talked about these abominations that would take place in Jerusalem, as He has written in Daniel 9:27 in Matthew 24:15. He warned us and gave us special instruction regarding, what we are to do when we see these *"abomination of desolation"* coming to pass. This abomination is given also in II Thessalonians 2:3, 4.

II Thessalonians 2:3,4 *"Let no man deceive you by any means: for that day shall not come, except there come a falling away first. and the man of sin be revealed, the son of perdition,"*

"Who opposeth and exalteth himself above all that is called God, or that is worshipped; so that he as God sitteth in the Temple of God, shewing himself that he is God."

The common teaching today in many churches is that Christians will not be here on earth when Satan is sitting in Jerusalem, presenting himself as God. They think that they will be ruptured from this earth, to a place of protection from Satan, and they will miss the entire time of testing of the Christians. This belief Satan's biggest lie. Satan is the man of sin that is coming to earth at the sixth trumpet. He is the son of perdition, and he is the one that will exalt himself above every thing on earth. He is the one who claims to be Jesus Christ. Satan will sit in his temple in Jerusalem during that five months of "*The Great Tribulation*", and after he kills the two witnesses, the whole world including the Christians will worship and exalt him as their god because their pastors have taught them to believe it. The Elect of God will be sealed in their minds with the truth, and will know that this false Christ known as Satan. He will not be tempting to any of God's elect, because each of the elect know that the end is only a matter of days until the seventh and final trumpet is sounded.

The subject in this chapter is in Jerusalem, and all of the dedicated servants of Christ are told to be against those false teachings concerning Jerusalem**.** That is why we are against Jerusalem when certain events take place there today. It is the reason that Ezekiel was to take an *"iron bread pan,"* and put the truth of God's Word between him and this painted tile of Jerusalem. Ezekiel 38 & 39 allows us to see that the Christian needs only one wall, regardless of where we are. Our wall is God, our Heavenly Father. That wall is our common sense that we use once we understand His entire Word. God's Word gives us instructions on how to protect ourselves, and then He will do the rest.

Iron is always given as a symbol of strength, and an Iron mountain stands for nations with strength and protection. These special instructions to all Christian's tells us exactly what the "*iron bread pan*" means, that Jesus Christ and His Word is the absolute truth. Our protection is given in Ephesians 6.10-20. That Iron bread pan is your breast plate, and that breast plate is part of the gospel armor. That armor is part of our protection that we must have on and in place in our minds in order to understand the signs and events of these end times.

Ephesians 6:14-17 *"Stand therefore, having your loins girt about with truth, and having on the breastplate of righteousness;" "And your feet shod with the preparation of the gospel of peace;" "Above all, taking on the shield of faith, wherewith ye shall be able to quench all the fiery darts of the wicked." "And take the helmet of salvation and the sword of the spirit, which is the word of God:"*

This gospel armor is our protection against Satan's deception's and His false prophets that will come into Jerusalem. God's warning is directed only to Christian nations of the House of Israel, and not to the House of Judah or the Jews. God will give the Jews special instructions later because Ezekiel is the chief watchman for the *"House of Israel."* The prophecies of Ezekiel gives us the complete details, explaining fully within the Scriptures all about the watchmen of this generation.

Ezekiel 4:4 "*Lie thou also upon thy left side, and lay the iniquity of the house of Israel upon it: according to the number of the days that thou shalt lie upon it thou shalt bare their iniquity."*

This is one of the signs God gave to Ezekiel. God is telling Ezekiel to lie on his left side for a period of time, and for the total number of days, Ezekiel will bear their sin. This is prophecy to be remembered always that when you lie on one side there is one arm pinned.

Ezekiel 4:5 "*For I have laid upon thee the years of their iniquity, according to the number of the days, three hundred* *and ninety days: so shalt thou bear the iniquity of the house of Israel."*

The book of Ezekiel is the sign, whereby people will be able to understand.

Ezekiel 4:6 *"And when thou hast accomplished them, lie again on thy right side, and thou shalt bear the iniquity of the house of Judah forty days: I have appointed thee each day for a year."*

When Ezekiel laid on his right side, his right arm is covered, which is symbolic of the time, when the word is applied to the house of Judah, the Jews today.

In biblical numbers forty means probation. We also know from the parable of the fig tree that Judah would return to the city of Jerusalem, and when the house of Judah returns in the end times, they will also be accompanied by bad figs known as the Kenites. These bad figs have caused a great deal of trouble to the house of Judah since the Babylonian captivity of Ezekiel's day.

It was forty years of probation tested the Israelites when they came out of Egypt, until they entered the Promised Land. There will also be the period of probation for the House of Israel's Christian nations at the close of this flesh age. Then all souls will enter into the promised land in the Millennium age.

To find the start of this time of three hundred and ninety years when the House of Israel known as the British and American people, became the powers of the world, you have to go back beyond the two hundred years since we became a nation. From that time of the House of Israel, all the Christian nations have experienced a form of life that no other nations have. Yet we are sinking into the lowest form of degradation.

While **Ezekiel 4:9** represents the paralyzing degradation that the Houses of Israel will fall into. It will be like in the days of Sodom and Gomorrah. We have seen the rapid decline in all Christian nations, as crime, drugs, false doctrines and foreign religious forms are taking a grip on most of our churches that call them selves Christian today.

As the degradation of the world continues to increase, God's wall of protection is around His Elect as they stands firm with their protective gospel armor on. The events and deceptions of the satanic "*One World System*" will not tempt the Elect. God's Elect will see through, these man's traditions and false doctrines, as well as the lies of their false prophets because, the truth of Almighty God is known to His elect.

Ezekiel 4:7 *"Therefore thou shalt set thy face toward the siege of Jerusalem, and thine arm shall be uncovered, and thou shalt prophecy against it."*

When this siege of Jerusalem takes place, we are not to run from it, or hide from it, or try to escape to some far off place. When this time comes, God is telling us how to know when these signs of the times become active. When you know, "*thine arm shall be uncovered.* When it's uncovered that will be the time to speak out and tell others. We will all be prophesying against it. If you had laid on your arm for a year, you would become paralyzed. God is saying that we were once paralyzed holding back our knowledge, He will remove it from us and the Lord God will speak through us. You will know for that is the time that God's Elect will be delivered up before the synagogue of Satan as recorded in Mark 13:9-11.

Ezekiel 4:8 *"And, behold, I will lay bands upon thee, and thou shalt not turn thee from one side to another, till thou hast ended the days of thy siege."*

God is telling Ezekiel that His Word will come to pass exactly as it is written, and He will put blinders on the Christians so that they simply won't be able to identify the events nor interfere with them until the time of witnessing and speaking against these events has come. God has His set times, since the foundation of this earth age, the times and events came to pass, exactly as "it is written" in His Word. Those set times were right on time when Israel came out of Egypt, when Jesus the Christ child was born. Even today they are right on time.

Today many people are writing books on Bible prophecy and as fast as they make their false statements, they have to put out another book to correct their first set of lies. These are false prophets just like those that existed in Jeremiah and Jesus' day. There are many today that are peddling their lies and deceptions to obtain money for their cause. Vanity and pride over shadow their words, to obtain authority and popularity that gives them power over their subjects on TV. They sell books, prayer clothes and trinkets and etc. to promote their business, when in fact, they are deceivers. They try to fit their fairy-tales and false doctrines into the Word of God, and it just does not fit. When we hear one of them be sure to check them out with the Word of God and then if what they say doesn't fit, mark them well, and stay away from them.

Ezekiel 4:9 *"Take thou also unto thee wheat, and barley, and beans, and lentiles, and millet, and fitches, and put them in one vessel, and make thee bread thereof, according to the number of the days that thou shalt lie upon thy side, three hundred and ninety days shalt thou eat there of."*

This is an object lesson that God is teaching to Ezekiel. Remember from the prior chapters that God came to earth in those highly polished bronze vehicles with cherubim's to give a message personally to Ezekiel. This is part of those words that God spoke.

Each of these things, the wheat, barley, beans and so on, represents items that will make up the bread that will sustain those living in the last days. It is obvious that when you make bread you do not include all these things in the mixture and have the baked bread fit to eat. The Christian's bread is the staff of life, and that bread is symbolic of hearing the Word of God that Jesus told us in the book of John.

John 6:35; *"Jesus said unto them, "I am the bread of life: he that cometh to me shall never hunger; and he that believeth on Me shall never thirst."*

This is told by Christ over and over in the Gospels; Jesus is the only bread that we need. This is why the Iron Bread pan is used as our wall of protection in this chapter. It represents Christ. This one is different bread that is to be made and will reflect exactly what most of the so called Christians will try to sustain themselves on in the latter days. Notice that along with the ingredients for real bread, the wheat and the barley, we have things that are not intended for bread and also things that should not be eaten. When people add words or change the meaning of the living Word of God it turns His truth into a lie. That is what Satan did when he tempted Jesus, and that is also what he will do when he is here on earth presenting himself as the true Christ.

This is a spiritual lesson that God is making into another object lesson to believers that are living in these latter days so we can understand. In Ezekiel 3:1, God had Ezekiel eat the whole book [roll], for that is the whole loaf. The time is coming where the true Word will be removed from us by the false Christ Antichrist, and in it's place will come a false book and teachings to sustain their church. We must understand the reason for mixing all the foreign things that went into making up the spiritual bread, which is symbolic of God's spiritual truth of the last times. Are you going to rely on the pure Word of God, which is our living bread or the mixture of half truths, and foreign dogma of the heathen religions that is filtering into the entire church world today? Our souls are at steak here, we must choose one way or the other.

Ezekiel 4:10 *"And thy meat which thou shalt eat shall be by weight, twenty shekels a day: form time to time shalt thou eat it."*

God is saying that the meat or truth of God's Word that you receive will be weighed out for you. This means that the only spiritual teachings given from the Word of God has been changed by the Kenites who want to deceive you. This is the same way that Satan tried to deceive Jesus with lies and half truths. The time is coming when we will receive only what these Kenite traditionalists want us to know, and that could cause millions to loose their souls.

Amos 8:11,12 *"Behold the days come, saith the Lord God, that I will send a famine in the land, not a famine of bread, nor a thirst for water, but of hearing the words of the Lord:" "And they shall wander from sea to sea, and from the north even to the east, they shall run to and fro to seek the word of the Lord, and shall not find it."*

This is the lesson that Ezekiel is presenting to us. Our generation will see this time come to pass. Their will be a famine for the truths recorded in the Word of God. The truths of the events of the latter days will be sealed in the minds of the Elect before Satan arrives, and those not sealed will be deceived. The true Gospel will not be allowed once the Antichrist is here.

Amos 8:13,14 *"In that day shall the fair virgins and young men faint for thirst." "They that swear by the sin of Samaria, and say, `Thy god, O Dan, liveth;' and, `The manner of Beer-sheba liveth;' even they shall fall, and never rise up again."*

The *"sin of Samaria"* and the *"manner of Beer-sheba"* is where the Israelites set up their calf worship. They turned from the True God, to follow their man made heathen ways. Once Satan has arrived it's too late, for God will turn all those who are not sealed with the truth in their minds, over to Satan and his fallen angels.

Revelation 9:5 *"And to them it was given that they should not kill them, but that they should be tormented five months: and their torment was as the torment of a scorpion, when he striketh a man."*

When the scorpion strikes a man, he is left defenseless, unable to protect himself. If you are not sealed with the truth by the time the sixth trumpet sounds, God will allow you to go chasing after the devil and you will become his harlot. You made the choice by not reading and understanding the Bible when you were free to read it.

Ezekiel 4:11 *"Thou shalt drink also water by measure, the sixth part of an hin: form time to time shalt thou drink."*

"The sixth part of an hin" is a sixth part of a gallon, and there is a part of this liquid that you will not like, and that is because of Satan's pollution into the world. This water is not from the fountain of the Living Word, but from all the lies and distortions that are presented by that harlot church of Revelation 17.

Ezekiel 4:12 *"And thou shalt eat it as barley cakes, and thou shalt bake it with dung that cometh out of man, in their sight."*

God is showing His objection, and disapproval in this lesson, because of these polluted cakes, or bread mixed with the dung of man, baked and eaten in the sight of everyone. God is tell us that He is against Satan and his teachings and this lesson will bring your attention to his message, of how corrupt and polluted people have allowed themselves to become, in this end generation.

Remember both Ezekiel and Jerusalem are to be a sign to our generation; are you beginning to see the signs that God would have you see? Amos tells us that in the end times there will be a famine, for the lack of God's truth word. Your reading God's truth in these end time so pay attention to the following verses

Amos 8:11 *"Behold, the days come, saith the Lord God, that I will send a famine in the land, not a famine of bread, nor a thirst for water, but of hearing the words of the Lord:"*

Let's get these things in proper order. This is an object lesson to show us a spiritual truth and though these things of pollution which are of a physical nature, relate all this to how God's word will become polluted, and will be filled with all sorts of heathen traditions of men. Then in this twelfth verse, God is adding man's dung into the making of the bread. If that doesn't turn your stomach, I don't know what will. However, this mess that is called bread, is how God looks at the teaching that is taking place today, and is part of the so-called Christian church world and it will get worse. This polluted bread is analogies of the deception that will take place when Satan comes to earth and he will be accepted as their new messiah the Antichrist.

God is getting very graphic in this lesson in order to wake us up regarding the changes taking place today. The entire Christian world is being prepared to accept Satan as their true Christ when he comes. This spiritual cake is filled with all of these impurities, the term, *"man's dung"*, shocks us and we wonder! When you find out what it all means it fits the lesson perfectly. The term, *"True bread"* is Jesus Christ, which is to say the "Word of God". The Word of God is going to be polluted with the dung of Satan, and his lies, distortions, and corruption in these end times. This is how God feels about what is being taught in *"God's House of Prayer"* in these end times. Its revolting!

This is the abomination that was spoken of regarding "*The Great Apostasy*" that will come upon the whole earth with a perverted religion that will capture all except the elect of God.

Ezekiel 4:13 *"And the Lord said, "Even thus shall the children of Israel eat their defiled bread among the Gentiles, whither I will drive them."*

This disgusting mixture of bread and dung is the "*bread of life*" of the Antichrist. Christian's and Gentile's alike will all eat of this spiritual bread and everyone except the Elect of God who knows the truth. When you go into a church where false teaching and doctrines that goes against the Word of God, mark that place well. Separate yourself from their false teaching because if you don't it will become part of your thinking as it festers and distorts your mind.

Ezekiel 4:14 *"Then said I, "Ah Lord God! behold, my soul hath not been polluted: for from my youth up even till now have I not eaten of that which dieth of itself, or is torn in pieces; neither came there abominable flesh into my mouth."*

Ezekiel is telling God that he simply could not eat this bread and this is in reference to God's health laws. He is telling God, "Don't make me eat bread made of that evil stuff." After God told Ezekiel what to do and how to make this polluted kind of bread, it is obvious how much of an abomination this bread will be to our flesh bodies and that will be just as destructive to our soul spiritually speaking.

Ezekiel 4:15 *"Then He said unto me, "Lo, I have given thee cow's dung for Man's dung, and thou shalt prepare thy bread therewith."*

God heard Ezekiel's plea and allowed him to substitute cow's dung for man's dung, but the example still has to be given by him. When you ask God to use you and make you a vessel for him, then you are expected to follow the instructions that He gives you. Ezekiel is the example to the house of Israel, the Christian's, of what will take place through out the forty days before his coming. In this scripture God changes the formula of the bread and adds cow dung, instead of man's dung.

Ezekiel 4:16 *"Moreover He said unto me, "Son of man, behold, I will break the staff of bread in Jerusalem: and they shall eat bread by weight, and with care; and they shall drink water by measure, and with astonishment;"*

In the historical sense there was a time of great shortages in Jerusalem, however this is another spiritual lesson for the end time. This astonishment that the world and Jerusalem will have, as they take their spiritual bread of Satan's filth, is what will cause them to bow down to him. There will be a small number of people that will be saved from partaking in the abominations of Satan deceptions and wonders. These people are God's Elect, and they will escape because they took of the true bread of life, the Word of God. The signs and events of the end times was sealed in their minds.

The "True Bread" is Jesus Christ, the Word of God, and by studying that Word we will have the knowledge and the council to see the truth, and the deceptions and lies of Satan will not be tempting to those who know these truth written within this book.

Ezekiel 4:17 *"That they may want bread and water, and be astonied one with another, and consumed away for their iniquity."*

Stop and apply this to those living around us today. Today not very many people care what is in the Word, nor the details of warnings in the Old Testament. Many pastors even tell their flocks that the book of Revelation, revealed by Jesus Christ Himself is not for them to understand. How ridiculous, for a man of God to stand and tell his flock that Revelation is not to be learned, or any part of the Bible, when God told us to learn it. Know it and make it part of your life, which is the seal of God in your life. We are told to be sealed in our mind.

Today the Christian world as a whole are lazy, and they don't want to take the time to understand or become part of anything that would come between them, their family and friends. The Kenites have caused it and taught them to be lazy. Studying and learning God's Word takes time and courage to stand for what is true and righteous.

There are seven churches that are mentioned in Revelation 2 & 3. Out of these seven churches only two were acceptable by God, they were the church of "*Smyrna*" and "*Philadelphia*". These two churches knew who the Kenites were back then, and what they stood for and where they came from. This also applies to us living today. They knew that the Kenites were the sons of Satan through Eve, and that the teachings of their synagogues were defiled. Because they knew who the Kenites were, these two churches wouldn't allow them to take over their church houses, but marked them and their false doctrines well.

Revelation 2:9 *"I know thy works, and tribulation, and poverty (but thou art rich), and I know the blasphemy of them which say they are Jews, and are not, but are the synagogue of Satan."*

In closing this chapter, there is only one question to you as a Christian, How can you ever defend yourself from these Kenites if you have no idea who the Kenites are, where they came from, what their traditions are, or what their purpose in life is? Jesus told you to learn the parable of the fig tree, because it tells us the identity of the Kenites and what they stand for. They took over Jerusalem when they came out of Babylon in Daniels day, and they controlled the temple in Jesus day. They are setting the stage for what is taught in the church houses of today, and that is why it is so important for every

Christian to know exactly who they are and what they are teaching in their churches.

The Kenites want you to be blind regarding their tactics, drugs, perverted sex, and all their wicked ways. They want you to become slaves to Satan when he arrives. Their two systems are called, "The *One World Government", and* the Bible call's it the *"New Babylon."* Satan will become their god, for five months, rest assured he and his fallen angels will completely rule this earth and he will set on his throne and claim to be God. He robs you of your dignity and fills you with his vial so he can control your soul. Satan's handy works has saturated TV programs and news media. Almighty God will give, Satan's followers over to reprobate minds because they chose to follow Satan.

If you are following the ways of the world, you will accept Sodomites into your churches, if you buy and sell like many churches do today, you're going to follow Satan in ignorance and the Lord God will deal with those people. Jesus Christ said, *"get out of her,"* because she is, "*The Great Whore"* known as the Modern Churches of today. Scripture tells us this is from God's Holy words. This is not taught in the modern Churches of these end times. God's wrath against modern Churches is made very clear.

Before it's too late you should study *"The Companion Bible"* that has the *"King James Bible"* within it, *and the "Strong's Exhaustive Concordance of the Bible,"* with numbers, that corresponds to the words of any K.J. Bible. God has recorded His truth for us to know and understand in these end times. Remember that the *Holy Spirit* is our teacher and the Lord will reveal all of these things to us if we ask Him, to open our blind eyes and if we seek the living word who as Jesus Christ our personal savior. He will show us all things through His written word.

LEGALISM
Chapter 11

The Apostle Paul addressed the topic of legalism in his letter to the church at Galatia. This letter was written prior to the letter he wrote to the church of Romans, and so there are many things common in both of these letters, or books. One thing that Paul stressed to the Galatians' was that we are to take the ceremony out of our teachings that was concerning Christ. The problem with teaching law in the form that many churches teach today; is that there are no absolutes. The Law always brings conditions and variations, for example, one brother may read it to mean one thing, and the other brother read's it differently, one will set someone free while the other one may ask for a conviction. However, when we are in Christ, we have an absolute. Whenever a law is taken to court, or before the deacon board, their decision is not an absolute, but a "precedent". That precedent or decision made by a court or church board sets the example of what can or will be accepted from that day forward. In other words, the "precedent" set by a church council is nothing but an opinion from the minds of men, a compromise to satisfy all those on that church board.

The true law points to "The Way", and that Way is through Jesus Christ. The word "Torah" in the Hebrew tongue is "*The Law.*" It's meaning was "*to point to something.*" That Way or Law will point directly to Jesus Christ, and in Christ there is an absolute. By repenting in the name of Jesus, there are no conditions or terms to meet, except that you have to believe that you are completely forgiven. This is the root of all of Paul's teachings. When Paul went into a town to establish a church of Christ, he presented that Way, the Gospel of Christ. The fundamental truth that stands out in all of the churches that Paul established was that there is no difference between Jew and Gentile before God. The problem in the church at Galatia was that the Jews in this church out numbered the Gentiles. In time, the Jews put their beliefs under the law and upon the Gentiles. These Jews were teaching under the old law, such as circumcision, that became a bondage for the Gentiles.

These conditions of the Law were accepted by this church board in Galatia, thus this Jewish tradition was being accepted by the Gentiles there as a condition of their salvation. Paul told these Gentiles then, when you accept this tradition, you did not receive it as a revelation of Jesus Christ, nor from me, but as men's traditions, from the Jews [Kenite or Brother Judah].

Before Paul's conversion, Paul thought he was doing the work of God when he was doing the will and work of the Kenite religious leaders in the temple. The Kenites took control over the direction and teaching of the House of Judah when they were captive in Babylon, also when they came out of captivity and returned back to Babylon, there wasn't one Levite among the 280 priests, amongst 43,000 returning to build the walls, temple and streets of Jerusalem. These Kenites had set the course for what was to be taught in their worship; and Paul was educated to think according to the law. However many parts of the law, were just as in many church houses of today, whereby the men and women that set the course for that church board, want to please everyone.

Paul was trained under the Law of that day by the finest educator of the time. Gamaliel was the scholar that all the other scholars looked up to, during the time of Jesus Christ. Paul used this training to let others know the authority that he was speaking from.

Acts 22:3, "*I am verily a man which am a Jew, born in Tarsus, a city in Cilicia, yet brought up in this city at the feet of Gamaliel, and taught according to the perfect manner of the law of the fathers, and was zealous toward God, as ye all are this day.*"

Then Once Paul met Christ, he was a completely changed man; and Paul let us know that it was Jesus Christ that trained him to understand the full meaning of the complete law of God, as written in the Old Testament; not as the Jewish Kenite priests were teaching.

REASONS CHRIST WENT TO THE CROSS.

Galatians 1:4 *"Who gave Himself for our sins, that He might deliver us from this present evil world, according to the will of God and our Father:" "To whom be glory for ever and ever. Amen."*

Jesus went to the cross to become the only human sacrifice that was perfect. His suffering was for the sins of those that would by faith believe in His name, and accept His sacrifice for their sins. By accepting this sacrifice every single soul can be delivered from the evils of this present world age of flesh man. This shows a kinship we each have with the Father, by God's Will and through the Word of God that provides us with a path to follow is made clear to us. Jesus made it very clear when he declared in the book of John.

John 14:6; *"Jesus saith unto him, "I am the way, the truth, and the life: no man cometh unto the Father, but by Me."*

Jesus Christ gave himself for our sins for a reason, and that reason is to deliver every soul that will believe in him and repent of their sins from the wickedness of this world age. There is much more to salvation in Christ than standing and uttering the sinner's prayer. Once you have said the prayer of confession, it is your duty to God to study His Word, and follow the instructions written in it. To overcome the evils of this world age, we must first overcome the one that rules over it. Satan, the devil, the serpent from the Garden of Eden played different roles to confuses people, as he tries to keep us from following our commitment to our Heavenly Father.

When you accept Jesus Christ as your savior you become a "Christian". You also receive the power that comes to you with your position as one of the sons of God. Our Heavenly Father sends His Holy Spirit to dwell within us and He also gives us His heavenly power. We are living in the end times and most of the people living today will see Satan in person, face to face. After he is kicked out of heaven onto the earth He appears as a handsome, luring man. Satan will present himself as being the true Jesus Christ," But he is "*The Great Deceiver*" we know as the "*Antichrist*". He will say things that cause people most Christians to believe is the true Jesus Christ as he performs his supernatural acts.

Hebrews tells us why Jesus came to earth to be born of a woman; He came in the flesh to be crucified so that He could destroy death, which is to say the Devil.

Hebrews 2:14 "*Forasmuch then as the children are partakers of flesh and blood, He also Himself likewise took part in the same; that through death He might destroy him that had the power of death, that is the devil;*"

When Jesus came out of the grave at His resurrection, both Satan and death were defeated. When Satan's angels left their place of habitation and came to earth, they also were called "the dead", just as Satan is called death, because they entered this earth age in other ways rather than the birthing process through the womb.

Titus a Greek went with Paul to Jerusalem to teach, and when he got there, these Kenite religious Jews followed Titus into the toilet to spy on him. When they saw that he was not circumcised, they forced him to follow their laws set forth in their church house.

Galatians 2:4 "*And that because of false brethren unawares brought in, who came in privily to spy out our liberty which we have in Christ Jesus, that they might bring us into bondage.*"

These "*false brethren*" spoken of here are those Kenites that were the spies, because the religious leaders at the temple were sending out their spies to plant their laws and traditions, to confuse the Christian community. These religious spies were planted for the sole purpose of bringing the Christians in Jerusalem back under their laws and traditional bondage. Paul explains it to the Christians back then and to us today in Galatians.

Galatians 2:5 "*To whom we gave place by subjection, no not for an hour; that the truth of the gospel might continue with you.*"

The so called super preachers will have their special little ways and words to belittle you when you do not follow their man-made paths through their legal process of the law. However, they saw that there was no compromise between Legalism and the Gospel of Christ. The moment that our Lord Jesus Christ shed His blood and died on the cross; all ceremonial statutes, and blood sacrifice, didn't exist any longer. It doesn't matter if you are for circumcision or not; Jew or Gentile laws governing blood ordinances don't exist any longer since Christ died on the cross for all of mankind.

There was a problem between Peter and Paul for a while, because when Peter went to Antioch, Peter left all the legalism that was present in Jerusalem. When the church leaders in Jerusalem sent men to visit Peter in Antioch, Peter pulled away from these Gentiles that he was teaching, and went back to the traditions of Jerusalem. The Christians at Jerusalem got caught up with the men of the temple, and to please them, followed the ceremonial customs of washing, not for cleansing, but for religious matters. When Paul heard that Peter was back into following the traditions with James and the other Jews, he was upset.

This was also the reason that Jesus Christ was not accepted by the Jewish Leaders when He was on earth during

His ministry. These Priests and Pharisees called Jesus a wine bibber and an eater with the publicans. This is the reason that many Christians today believe that the health laws were done away with, right along with the ceremonial laws and blood ordinances. Yet the health laws govern the health of your physical body; and when you put poisons into your blood stream, and that poison flows into the cells of your body, they do not function like God created them to function and produce. In time, the protective mechanism of the body breaks down and you become sick and open to many diseases.

Today many blame God for their sickness, and just like Jobs friends told Job that it must have been because something that he did wrong to cause God to bring this upon him. Today people bring ill health upon themselves when they turn away from God's health laws. God has warned us through His Word that we must rightly divide the Word, and apply it to where it fits in your lives.

Galatians 2:14 "*But when I saw that they walked not uprightly according to the truth of the gospel, I said unto Peter before them all, "If thou, being a Jew, livest after the manner of Gentiles, and not as do the Jews, why compellest thou the Gentiles to live as do the Jews?*"

Paul confronted Peter right in front of the entire congregation to make a point of the error in Peter's teaching before the Gentiles. Paul is telling him to just use a little common sense in his teaching. The bottom line to the problem is that no person can be saved by the law through the way they live. The reason that we all fall short of the law, is that it is impossible to be without sin under the law. This is why Christ came to earth, to give us life and grace by washing away our sins, and we can have forgiveness because were under the blood of Jesus Christ's. There is only one way that people can have perfection and that is through repentance under Christ's blood. If you think that you can be good and perfect under the law and you break just one part of the law in your whole life, then you are condemned from that point on, for eternity. There is no salvation or eternal life in the law.

Galatians 2:15,16 "*We who are Jews by nature, and not sinners of the Gentiles," "Knowing that a man is not justified by the works of the law, but by the faith of Jesus Christ, even we have believed in Jesus Christ, that we might be justified by the faith of Christ, and not by the works of the law: for by the works of the law shall no flesh be justified.*"

As Christians we should try to live and maintain the law within us, but there comes a time when we stray from the letter of the law. When you break even the least of the law, you have broken the entire law, according to God. It is impossible to keep the Law, and to say you have kept the entire Law is a lie. The Law is God's standard, and no one can be justified by the Law, which is to say; "*made perfect by the law*". "*Justified*" in Strong's Greek dictionary is #1344; "Dikaioo, *dik-ah-yo-o; to render (e.i. show or regard as) just or innocent: free, justified righteous.*" The Law is given only to condemn but in Christ we obtain our salvation. Our perfection must come through our faith in Christ, for our perfection is Christ's perfection, when we are under the blood of Christ.

That is our only hope of Salvation and Eternal life, and it comes from our Heavenly Father, but we can only claim in through the name of Jesus. Jesus paid the price, and when we approach Our Heavenly Father it must be in "Jesus Name". "There is no other name under heaven whereby we can be saved."

Galatians 3:1,3 "*O foolish Galatians, who hath bewitched you, that ye should not obey the truth, before whose eyes Jesus Christ hath been evidently set forth, crucified among you?" "This only would I learn of you, Received ye the Spirit by the works of the law, or by the hearing of faith?" "Are ye so foolish? having begun in the Spirit are ye now made perfect by the flesh?*"

Paul did not try to soft peddle the Word of God, he said what was on his mind. Paul asked these Galatians', Christians: Who has bewitched you into the acceptance of ceremonial religion? He is telling them that they understood the death of Christ when he taught it, so why have they allowed these Kenite Jews to come into their midst and do this to them. Paul taught them how to receive the Spirit of God, and by using God's Spirit build your faith in Jesus Christ; and now he is asking them; Did you receive the Spirit of God by the works; the traditions and ceremonies of the law: or by hearing about Christ's death on the cross, and through your faith and repentance in Jesus name. Paul then asked, are you so foolish that after you have started your good works in Christ that you would throw it all out, and place yourself back under legalism? All forms of legalism were nailed to the cross with Christ.

Stop and think for a moment; when our flesh body dies it decays and returns to the elements that it is made of. The inner man is called our soul and spirit bodies, that instantly returns to our Heavenly Father. All flesh does the same, as we read in Ecclesiastes 12:5-7. God has revealed through His Word, that our doctrines of faith is in Jesus Christ; and when anyone tries to teach any other doctrine through legalism, it is a doctrine of the Kenites, Satan is their father. We do not need to respect any day over another to be in the will of God, because Christ became our Passover. We respect Jesus Christ every day of the year and every moment of every day. Any time we fall short, we do not have to wait until we go into a little room, or for a certain day to repent, Our Heavenly Father hears our prayers of repentance any moment of the day or night. Don't allow anyone to make that promise from our Lord void through legalism because it's a Gift of God that He has given to you.

Galatians 3:4,5 "*Have ye suffered so many things in vain? if it be yet in vain." "He therefore That minsiterth to you the Spirit, and worketh miracles among you, doeth He it by the works of the law, or by the hearing of faith?*"

So Paul is asking these Galatians, *"are you going to throw the entire works of Jesus Christ away"* ?. When you put yourself back under the law, you are going to throw away the entire effect of the gospel, and I just can't believe that you would be so foolish. God loves each of us and He wants us to use His Word as our authority. This is why it is essential that when a person accepts the Lord, they should immediately try to get into the Word. The knowledge of the Word of God is the authority that gives us the power that He has promised to each Christian. We must learn how to rightly divide the Word of God. Learn to use the tools of the Bible so that the figures of speech, the idioms, and the correct meaning can be understood.

Jesus used idioms in expressing his instructions in what will occur in these final days of this earth age of flesh man, when Satan is cast out upon the earth.

Luke 10:19 *"Behold, I give unto you power to tread on serpents and scorpions, over all the power of the enemy: and nothing shall by any means hurt you."*

Jesus is telling us in this verse that Satan is the serpent, and his offspring through Cain are the scorpions. These scorpions are the fallen angels that will also be thrown out of heaven by Michael and his army, during "*The Great Tribulation*". This has nothing to do with the snake in the woods, or the scorpions that live at the waters edge, but it is given to help us understand a deeper spiritual meaning.

Paul was telling the Galatians to stop and think; when there was a miracle performed by Jesus or one of the apostles, do you think that those miracles were done by the Law? No! Those miracles happened under the works by the faith of the one administering the miracle. Paul is asking them, did the law work the miracles, or the Holy Spirit of God, acting by the hearing of faith? No miracle has ever been performed under the Law. When a miracle occurs it is the touch of God, through the Holy Spirit of God that works the miracles.

Galatians 3:11,12 *"But that no man is justified by the law in the sight of God, it is evident for, The just shall live by faith." "And the law is not of faith: but, the Man that doeth them shall live in them."*

Not one human being except Christ is perfect, and the only way that the just can live is by faith in Jesus Christ. This verse by Paul is from Habakkak 2:4.

Habakkuk 2:4 *"Behold, his soul which is lifted up is not upright in him: but the Just shall live by his faith."*

Our justification only comes when we have repented all of our sins in Jesus Christ's name, and then our Heavenly Father will forgive us. His justification takes effect in our lives when we have done wrong He make it right in the eyes of God if we confess our sins. The only way we can become perfect is through Jesus Christ's righteousness.

The purpose of the law is to be our school-master to show each of us that we simply cannot live by the law. The law was designed to direct us toward the cross of Jesus Christ, because He is the only one who can give us complete perfection in Him.

Galatians 3:13 *"Christ hath redeemed us from the curse of the law, being made a curse for us: for it is written, "Cursed is every one that hangeth on the tree:"*

Jesus Christ took the stripes so that we could be healed both physically and spiritually. He did it all because He loved each of His children. God created us and He knows all of our weaknesses and strengths that He has placed within each of us. He provided a way for us even when we fall short, it is by faith and through repentance in Jesus name. We have the Grace that Our Heavenly Father has offered to those who will accept it.

Jesus came into this world to fulfill the will of our Heavenly Father, and redeem lost souls back to the Father. The choice of receiving the gift of Salvation is up to each individually. The Lord's clock is set, right up to the pouring out of the vials of the cup of wrath upon the earth, every single event will be at God's selected moment in time. The details are all recorded in the "*The Companion Bible*", with the "*King James Bible*" version, foot notes and 197 Appendixes. If you really want to know more, it's up to us to study to show ourselves approved unto God and rightly divide the Word of God. See our References in the back of this book.

OLD AND NEW COVENANT
Chapter 12

The Old and New Covenant's were the laws of the land, during two different periods of times. The Old Covenant was when they used animal sacrifices for the forgiveness of sin. The New Covenant was when Jesus Christ became the sacrifices for our sins, recorded in the new Testament, where as, The Old Covenant occurred in the Old Testament. These first animal sacrifices, all began after the Children of Israel were released from bondage in Egypt and they crossed through the Red Sea and wandered south to the base of Mount Sinai. This was where God gave Moses a set of instructions to govern the children of Israel to live by. Through out their time in the wilderness and after they moved into the promised land God gave them a way to have forgiveness of sins, through animal sacrifices.

The books of Leviticus and Numbers were written at the time when they were numbering all of males, for service in the army. Their numbering continued throughout thirty eight years of wandering in the wilderness until they entered into the promised land of Canaan. Males over the age of twenty within each of the tribes of Israel were in the military service. God would redeem each of the firstborn of the other tribes, at the age of one month or older.

However, this didn't apply to the males from the tribe of Levi. This was done to allow the tribe of Levi to be given completely over to serving God in the Tabernacle, of the Lord. They were called Levite High Priests. They were told to protect God's word, and record them exactly as God wrote it.

In "***I Corinthians 10:1-12***" Paul told us that the events that took place in the time of wandering, were examples to us, regarding how it will be just before the second coming of Our Lord Jesus Christ. When our forefathers came to the Red Sea they had to stop because they couldn't cross the sea, so they prayed and God opened the sea so they could walk across on dry ground. When they ran out of food, God gave them manna from heaven. When there was no water, they prayed and God made water came out of a rock.

These things were examples written to people living today. Jesus Christ is the *"Rock",* the foundation that our salvation is built upon; and He is the *"Bread of life"*; He is the "*Living water"* that flows from the Word of God refreshes our souls. Without the instructions that God gave to Moses, we would be wandering aimlessly without any direction through life.

I Corinthians 10:11 *"Now all these things happened unto them for ensamples* [Examples]: *and they are written for our admonition* [warning], *upon whom the ends of the world* [age] *are come." "Wherefore let him that thinketh he standeth take heed lest he fall."*

These things happened way back in the wilderness thirty five hundred years ago. These examples have been preserved for us today. The people began to burden Moses and Aaron because they lost faith in God and they constantly murmured and complained because they wanted to return to their old ways of worshiping their Egyptian idols. They sent out their own spies to spy the land and when they returned they believed their lies. They took their eyes off of the promises that the Lord had given to them. They trusted in their own abilities and their desires to serve ideals'. Therefore, God allowed their own words to condemn them, where by many of them died in the wilderness.

This part of **Numbers 19:1,2**, are things we are told to remember. The first two verses of chapter 19 begins with something that is in the news even today regarding the *"red heifer"*. There is a warning to us in this particular topic. The Jews have returned to Palestine in the holy lands, and established their nation. Today's news reports coming out of Jerusalem say that the Israeli rabbinical council is involved with reestablishing the "*old Sanhedrin*," and they are calling all of people involved in the Temple Mount to prepare detailed architectural plans for the reconstruction of their Jewish Holy Temple.

Today they are forming their old councils and their ancient religious practices, there religious leaders are turning to the Scriptures and their traditions to see how things use to be. The "red heifer" was to be sacrificed, which was an important part of those ancient times, yet when our Lord Jesus Christ went to the cross, He fulfilled all of the requirements under the law for the sacrifice of sin. However Jews never don't believe that when Jesus Christ died on the cross, that He was the true Messiah. So they are going back into worshiping their "*red heifer*" like it was in their ancient traditions.

Hebrews 10:7,8,9 "*Then said I, Lo, I come (in the volume of the book it is written of Me) to do Thy will, O God" "Above when He said, "Sacrifice and offering and burnt offerings and offering for sin Thou wouldest not, neither had pleasure therein: "which are offered by the law." "Then said He, "Lo, I come to do Thy will, O God." He taketh away the first,* which is all forms of animal sacrifices*, so that He can establish the second, which is* our salvation by grace through the blood of Christ".

Numbers 19:1 *"And the Lord spake unto Moses and unto Aaron, saying,"*

When Numbers 19 took place, there was a lot of rebellion by Korah, and his followers that was going on. God separated the followers of Moses from the followers of Korah and the ground opened and swallowed up all those people who rebelled. Before the rebellion ended over fourteen thousand people of the Children of Israel were killed. Imagine that happening to a town the size of Atlanta. At the close of this chapter, the children of Israel had turned around and went back to Kadesh, from where they came from. They refused to enter into the promised land which was about the time of that chapter 19 took place. Much of the wanderings had already taken place, and they were about to inter into the promised land. Remember most of the people were over 20 years old when they left Egypt and many had died and were buried in the wilderness. Death is always symbolic of sin, and the "wages of sin is death".

Numbers 19:2 *"This is the ordinance of the law which the Lord hath commanded, saying. `Speak unto the children of Israel, that they bring thee a red heifer without spot, wherein is no blemish, and upon which never came yoke:"*

This she goat offering of the *"red heifer"* is a statute of instruction, known as *"a law statute"*, given here. Numbers 15:27 lists the only other "female sacrifice" that God required by the Israelites. That sacrifice was a *"she goat"* for the sin of ignorance. *"And if any soul sin through ignorance, then he shall bring a she goat of the first year for a sin offering."* The *"red heifer"* given here is symbolic of the Lord Jesus Christ. The color "red" shows the intensity for life, while the yoke had never been on her, shows us that she was a young she goat, and had never worked before. Sin in this verse is represented by death, and the antidote for sin back them was the sin offering.

During their wanderings, this third punishment is one of the three events recorded. The other two events are found in Numbers 15:32-36, the punishment of the Sabbath breaker. In Numbers 16:1 & 17:13, was dealing with Korah after he tried to undermine the authority of Moses, that cause the death of him, and the 250 that followed him, including his three neighbors and their families. This ordinance is emphasizing a lesson regarding the red heifer.

This *"red heifer"* was a "antitype" of Christ: So God required that an animal without spot or blemish must be offered as a sacrifice at that time. In Hebrews 8, Paul talked about the *"old tabernacle"* which was the "The *Old Covenant"* that was given, but would not stand very long. God promised that there would not only be a "*New Tabernacle*", but also a "*New Covenant*" that would be given to mankind. That "*New Tabernacle*" is made up of His people who were believers, which is "*The New Covenant" that* would be given at a time when one neighbor would not have to ask his neighbor, "Do you know the Lord?", because in the Millennium age, everyone will know the Lord and His Word.

Hebrews 9:1 "*Then verily the first covenant had also ordinances of divine service, and a worldly sanctuary.*"

The first sanctuary was the tent that the Levites and Kohathites were assigned to move and set up where ever they went. Those *"ordinances of divine service"* were all the sacrifices and offerings we are reading about that were required by Aaron and his sons for the sins committed by them and the people.

Hebrews 9:2 "*For there was a tabernacle made; the first, wherein was the candle-stick, and the table, and the shewbread; which is called the sanctuary.*"

These things were kept within the holy of holies, and used in their service to the Lord.

Hebrews 9:3,4 "*And after the second veil, the tabernacle which is called the Holiest of all;*" "*Which had the golden censer, and the ark of the covenant overlaid round about with gold wherein was the golden pot that had manna, and Aaron's rod that budded, and the tables of the covenant;*"

This place that Paul is referring to was *"the Holiest of all"* known as the "*Holy of Holies*", it was the place where God dwelled with man in Old Testament time. The Ark of the Covenant was where man went to talk to God, and His Mercy seat was where God judged His people. The "*Holy of Holies"* was where God dwelt among men at that time. God's Kingdom is where God lives. At this point in time, God had a veil placed between His place, and the place where the people were meeting in the sanctuary. The High Priest used the *"Golden censer"* to offer the incense offering in praise to God.

Hebrews 9:5 *"And over it the cherubim's of glory shadowing the mercy seat;' of which we cannot now speak particularly."*

These cherubim's of glory were protecting the mercy seat, of which we just can't speak of today in detail. This mercy seat might be thought of as the lid or top to the Ark of the Covenant. Back in the first earth age, Ezekiel tells us in Ezekiel 28 that God made Satan in the full pattern of wisdom, and placed Satan the Cherubim to guard His mercy seat.

Ezekiel 28:12 *"Son of man, take up a lamentation upon the king of Tyrus, and say unto him, 'Thus saith the Lord God; Thou sealest up the sum, full of wisdom, and perfect in Beauty."*

Satan was a cherubim created with wisdom and beauty for the purpose of protecting the mercy seat of Almighty God. But Satan's pride overtook him and he rebelled against God. His pride was his downfall, when he choose not to seat on the mercy seat of God, because he wanted to become God, himself.

Ezekiel 28:14,15 *"Thou* [Satan] *art the anointed cherub that covereth; and I have set thee so: thou was upon the holy mountain of God; thou hast walked up and down in the midst of the stones of fire." "Thou was perfect in thy ways from the day thou was created, till iniquity was found in thee."*

Satan was created, not eternal as YHVH our Heavenly Father, but a soul just as we are, except God made him with the full pattern of wisdom and beauty. This was the cause of his downfall, because he strutted up and down in the presence of God, when he was the anointed cherubim. Pride was lifted up in his heart, "*and corrupted his thinking or wisdom by reason of his brightness*". Paul told us in Hebrew.

Hebrews 9:6 "*Now when these things were thus ordained, the priests went always into the first tabernacle, accomplishing the service of God.*"

Aaron and his sons went into the holy place of the Sanctuary. The book of Numbers tells us what His assigned duties were. This is talking about the first veil that goes into the main Sanctuary.

Hebrew 9:7 "*But into the second [Holy of Holies] once each year to sacrifice first for his own sins, and then for the sins of the people.*"

When the High Priest entered into the "*Holy of Holies*" he entered with the blood of goats and calves that were to be their sacrifice. This blood was temporary because it was a type of that which would come later, known as the blood of our Lord Jesus Christ who became the perfect and unblemished sacrifice.

Hebrew 9:8,9 "*The Holy Ghost this signifying, that the way into the Holiest of all was not yet made manifest, while as the first tabernacle was yet standing:*" "*Which was a figure for the time then present, in which were offered both gifts and sacrifices, that could not make him that did the service perfect, as pertaining to the conscience;*"

When we come under the blood of Christ through repentance in Jesus name, we enter into the "*Holy of Holies*", that was the place where they came into our Heavenly Father presents. Today the Holy Spirit has made this plain to each of us. The way that we can approach the holiest of all places wasn't made known until after the death and resurrection of our Lord Jesus Christ. When that first tabernacle was still in place, the only way to approach the Father was under the Old covenant, through the gifts and sacrifices of animals made by the High Priest. However, when Jesus Christ came to earth. His body became the inner tabernacle. Only through Jesus Christ and the workings of the Holy Spirit, through our faith and repentance, is only through the blood of Jesus Christ who can eliminate guilt from our conscience. Because Jesus Christ lives within the hearts of all His believers.

Hebrews 9:10 "*Which stood only in meats and drinks, and divers washings, and carnal ordinances, imposed on them until the time of reformation.*"

Back then their rites and ceremonies, consisted of meat and drink offerings, and washings. These practices were done to cover their sins until the time of Christ's crucifixion and resurrection.

Hebrews 9:11,12 "*But Christ being come an High Priest of good things to come, by a greater and more perfect tabernacle, not made with hands, that is to say, not of this building;*" "*Neither by the blood of goats and calves, but by His own blood He entered in once into the holy place, having obtained eternal redemption for us.*"

It was through the blood of Jesus Christ at the cross that changed the way of the Old Covenant into the ways of the New Covenant. Jesus Christ became our High Priest. There is no others. The veil leading into the Holy of Holies was rent in two, so each of us can approach the throne of God personally, when we place ourselves under the Blood of Jesus Christ. Our New Tabernacle is now in heaven at the right hand of the Father; and we can enter His tabernacle today through prayer at any time or any place. His door is always open to His believers. You don't have to wait until Christ returns. We can enjoy living in your mansions which means, having a peace of mind through prayer, right here on earth when we pray to our Heavenly Father in Jesus Christ's name. That alone should make us jump with joy!

Hebrews 9:13 "*For if the blood of bulls and of goats, and the ashes of an heifer sprinkling the unclean, sanctified to the purifying of the flesh:*"

This was the ordinance statutes of the red heifer that was spoken of in Numbers 19:2. Sprinkling the blood of the red heifer could make someone clean back in those days; this cleansing only lasted for one year. Thank the Lord God we don't have to do that today!

Hebrews 9:14 "*How much more shall the blood of Christ, Who through the eternal Spirit offered Himself with out spot to God, purge your conscience from dead works to serve the living God.*

Today Jesus Christ is the God of the living. As we study the red heifer in Numbers, always remember that the heifer's blood is always symbolic of the blood of Jesus Christ. The Blood of Jesus Christ is offered only to people living today and in times of the New Testament. Christ has given us much more than those who lived in the Old Testament. We can call upon Him at any time and ask for help, as we give Him our praise or ask for understanding. Rest assured His love is always with us when we're studying.

Hebrews 9:15 "*And for this cause He is the Mediator of the new testament that by means of death, for the redemption of the transgressions that were under the first testament, they which are called might receive the promise of eternal inheritance.*"

Our Lord Jesus Christ became the final sacrifice on the cross when His precious blood without spot or blemish poured out of His body, upon the earth. Today He is our Mediator, our Savior and redeemer who has given us our eternal inheritance when we die, which is our reward.

1 Peter 1:19-21 "*But with the precious blood of Christ as of a Lamb without blemish and without sport:*" "*Who verily* *was foreordained before the foundation of the world, but was manifest in these last times for you," "Who by Him do believe in God, That raised Him up from the dead, and gave Him glory; that your faith and hope might be in God* ".

Today we have an antidote that cleanses us from all sin through the precious blood of Jesus Christ known as "The Lamb of God". The whole purpose of our studies is to understand why we are here on earth, and where we fit into God's perfect plan. We are told to plant the seed of God's truth in these end times, God's warnings are revealed to His followers who will know His truth, just before the Great and mighty day of the Jesus Christ's return.

John 14: 1-3 "*Let not your heart be troubled; ye believe in God, believe also in Me." "In My Father's house are many mansions: if it were not so, I would have told you. I go to prepare a place for you." "And if I go and prepare a place for you, I will come again and receive you unto Myself; that where I am, there ye may be also.*"

The first time Jesus Christ came He lived without spot nor blemish, and was the perfect sacrifice, but the next time Jesus comes, it will be to receive His believers unto Himself. That is a promise He gave to us all. The way in Moses' day was through sacrifices at the alter in side of the Holy of Holies. That "*Old Covenant*" was done away with. When Jesus died on the cross and went into heaven, where by God established a *"New Covenant"*, today mankind can go through His Son Jesus Christ in prayer. People can not go to YHVH the Creator, except through His son Jesus Christ.

John 14:12 "*Verily, verily, I say unto you, He that believeth on Me, the works that I do shall he do also; and greater works than these shall he do; because I go unto My Father.*"

When Jesus died and rose from the dead, He went directly to set on the right hand of our Heavenly Father who is our advocate; He is there with the Father, Jesus told you personally that you can ask anything in His Name and Jesus will give it to you if it be His will. His third promise from John14 was that when He goes to the Father, he would send a Comforter that would come into our hearts. He is our teacher who gives us wisdom and under standing. Our comfort and direction comes through the Holy Spirit, when our minds are opened to His Word. Not only does He keep His promises, but understanding events that are going on in this world are being revealed to us, where by we can know the complete plan of God. God's Spirit give's us peace of mind which is our "*Mansion*", when we come to know God's plan and how we fit into His plan we have the peace of mind that surpasses all understanding in Jesus Christ.

John 14:13 "*And whatsoever ye shall ask in My name, that will I do, that the Father may be glorified in the Son.*"

This verse is a continuation of the prior verse, whereby Jesus promised us that we will do even greater works after He has gone to set on the right hand of the Father in Heaven. It's up to us whether we have the peace of mind that only our Savior can give us, through His Holy Spirit. We don't have to wait on the High priest today to enter into the Holy of Holies, because we can live in that mansion today, which means we will have a peace of mind in the Father and the Lord Jesus Christ after prayer. He also gave us grace, when the veil was rent two when Jesus Christ's died on the cross for our sins. The way was opened for us to have direct access to the throne of God in heaven through our prayers.

Stop and think of what a wonderful Heavenly Father we have, and our Savior the Lord Jesus Christ. He is there for us the moment that we ask Him for help, those things that are done in our Lord Jesus' name, are done so that Our Heavenly Father will be glorified through Jesus Christ. Keep this in mind as we continue in the book of Numbers. The Old Testament methods of salvation won't work any more, for the blood of dead animals is not the way to worship any more. The only way today is through prayer to our Lord and savior Jesus Christ.

Let's continue in Number 19, remembering that what we are about to study is the way it was before Jesus Christ lived and died. We can thank God every day that we don't have to do any of these things today.

Numbers 19:3 *"And ye shall give her [the red heifer] unto Eleazar the priest, that he may bring her forth without the camp, and one shall slay her before his face:"*

The word "her" spoken of here is a female "red heifer" that was to be used as their animal sacrifice. Normally in the "sin offering" it was the High Priest that would take care of the animal sacrifice. However because of the limits set on the High Priest in Leviticus 21, the high priest was not allowed to approach a dead body of man, animal, or his own immediate family. Eleazar was the priest and the son of Aaron who was chosen to give this sacrifice out side of the camp, rather than the High Priest. Remember that sin offerings, as pointed out in verse seventeen of this chapter, would have been offered in the area of the sanctuary following the customs and instructions for the sin offering.

This female "red heifer" was not allowed to be sacrificed in the camp site, and just as this is an ensample for us. Remember our Lord Jesus Christ was also taken out side the city limits of Jerusalem to the hill of Calvary and was slain.

Numbers 19:4 *"And Eleazar the priest shall take of her blood with his finger, and sprinkle of her blood direct before the tabernacle of the congregation seven times:"*

Keep in mind that this sacrifice was out side of the camp, but the blood would be taken on Eleazar's finger then be sprinkled seven times toward the tabernacle.

Numbers 19:5 *"And the priest shall take cedar wood, and hyssop, and scarlet, and cast it into the midst of the burning of the heifer."*

The burning of the sacrifices would not included all these parts of the animal if the sacrifice was back at the alter of burnt offerings in side of the tabernacle. Remember that this female, the "red heifer sacrifice" was once used for "the purification of death, or sin". However our antidote for sin and death today, and our entry into the Holy of Holies at the throne of God, is through the blood of Christ. When Jesus blood was shed on the cross, the veil was rent in two, which gave us direct access to our Heavenly Father.

Numbers 19:6 *"And the priest shall take cedar wood, and hyssop, and scarlet, and cast it into the midst of the burning of the heifer."*

When you added the cedar wood, the Hyssop and the scarlet in the living water, it would make "the water of separation". This is what was used to purify one from the uncleanness of death. The "Cedar wood" is symbolic of the incorruptible continuance of life. The "Hyssop" had many purifying qualities about it, and the "scarlet" was the strongest strength of life, and the scarlet represented the blood of our Lord Jesus Christ.

Numbers 19:7 *"Then the priest shall wash his clothes, and he shall bathe his flesh in water, and afterward he shall come into the camp, and the priest shall be unclean until the even."*

So after Eleazar the priest came in contact with this sin offering sacrifice, he had to bathe, and wash his clothes completely before he was allowed to enter back into the camp.

On the tenth day of the seventh month of each year, the High Priest would enter into the Holy of Holies, and make the offering for atonement for the sins of himself and the people.

It was a national holiday. A bullock was offered for the sins of the High Priest first, and then two goats were also selected, one to be sacrificed, and the other to be turned loose into the wilderness. One goat was taken by lot for God, and the other to represent the scapegoat "Azazel" in the Hebrew. "Azazel" is another name for Satan, so you have one goat for the Lord, and one goat for Satan. This is discussed again in Leviticus 16:9-22.

Numbers 19:8 *"And he that burneth her shall wash his clothes in water, and bathe his flesh in water and shall be unclean until the ever."*

So the priest, Eleazar, that burnt the red heifer, or any one that came in contact with the ashes or any part of this sacrifice was to bathe and wash his clothes, and that evening he shall be considered clean again. This act is symbolic of death, but now we will see an example of this next verse.

Numbers 19:9 *"And the man that is clean shall gather up the ashes of the red heifer, and lay them up without the camp in a clean place, and it shall be kept for the congregation of the children of Israel for a water of separation; it is a purification for sin."*

Keep in mind that the red "heifer" was a substitute for Jesus Christ. It was Joseph of Arimathea who was the one who declared himself to have the right to claim the body of Jesus Christ. Because Joseph of Arimathea was the rich uncle of Jesus that went to Pilate, and as next of kin, he demanded that he had the right to prepare the body of Jesus for burial. By Roman law only the next of kin could claim a dead man's body. Joseph was a voting member of the Sanhedrin, and a follower of Christ but was also known as the very rich uncle of our Lord Jesus Christ. Recorded in Matthew 27:57-60, Luke 23:50-53 and in John 19. Notice that this scripture was recorded three times, remember that the Bible always proves it's self because it's the living word of God.

The "water of separation" was a "purification for sin" from the death sacrifice of the female heifer was basically a sin offering. It was the purification for sin, and not just for death. "Sin" and "death" are tied together, because, "*the wages of sin is death*".

Numbers 19:10 *"And he that gathered the ashes of the heifer shall wash his clothes, and be unclean until the even: and it shall be unto the children of Israel, and unto the stranger that sojourned among them, for a statute for ever."*

The burning of the female red heifer, was called a "*law statute*" in verse two of this chapter, applied not only to the children of Israel, but also to those who were living amongst them at the time, the sacrifice was made.

Numbers 19:11: "*He that toucheth the dead body of any man shall be unclean seven days.*"

This is how the "*water of sacrifices or separation*" was to be used when anyone came in contact with the dead. Anyone that touches a dead body of man or animal shall be unclean for seven days. Remember that this law is eternal, even into the Millennium age, after the return of Christ at the seventh trumpet. Ezekiel reminds us of this law even after flesh and blood corruptible bodies are done away with, so this is dealing with the spiritually dead.

Ezekiel 44:25 *"And they shall come at no dead person to defile themselves; but for father, or for mother, or for son, or for daughter, for brother or for sister that hath had no husband, they may defile themselves."*

This verse is unique because it is applied to the Zadok, those who did not bow a knee to Satan in their flesh bodies at the sixth trumpet. They were not Satan's bride. The just or Zadok knew the truth; they were the Elect that did not bow a knee to Satan. Their family members ran to Satan asking him to save their loved ones. Of course it was all done in ignorance, however their choice still left their soul and spiritual bodies dead at the seventh trumpet, when the true Jesus Christ returns. This verse is in the Millennium period of time, when God allows the "Elect" called the Zadok, the right to go to their loved ones who did not except God's truth in the time of Grace here on earth. Today mankind can accept by faith through repentance in Jesus wonderful name, but not in the Millennium age when all flesh has been changed into their Spiritual bodies, when the Elect can urge those relatives to pay attention, and follow their works according to the ways of the eternal God.

Ezekiel 44:26 *"And after he is cleaned, they shall reckon unto him seven days."*

After the Zadok came into contact with their unclean relatives, they could not enter back into the tabernacle of God where Jesus is for seven days. The Zadok became unclean by touching and coming in contact with the spiritually dead relative. This is in the Millennium age.

Ezekiel 44:27 *"And in the day that he goeth into the sanctuary, unto the inner court, to minister in the sanctuary, he shall offer his sin offering, saith the Lord God."*

Remember that the blood of lambs and goats was done away with at Christ's death on the cross, then our sin offering became acceptable toward the new way that our Lord provided through repentance. The New Way is our acceptance through repentance in Jesus Name. When we pray in Jesus Name, we are telling God that Jesus is the only begotten Son of YHVH our Heavenly Father. Jesus was perfect with unblemished blood who became the sacrifice for our sins.

We know that the Millennium age is Jesus Christ's Kingdom is here on earth and all of mankind living in flesh bodies are instantly changed into their, incorruptible bodies like the angles. Many will still have mortal soul bodies that are still liable to die.

This Millennium period of time is a thousand years of testing, when all souls will know the truths from God's Word. They will know exactly what to expect, at the close of the thousand year Millennium age, which is when the "*Great White Throne Judgment*" *takes place.*

Revelation 20:11,12 "*And I saw a great white throne, and him that sat on it, from whose face the earth and the heaven fled away; and there was found no place for them.*" "*And I saw the dead, small and great, stand before God; and the books were opened: and another book was opened, which is the book of life; and the dead were judged out of those things which were written in the books, according to their works.*"

At the close of the Millennium age, the dead and those souls in their incorruptible bodies that lived through the Millennium who were not part of the first resurrection of the coming of Christ at the seventh trumpet will stand before God. Each of their acts from the Millennium age will be recorded in their "books". Only those who accepted Jesus Christ as their personal savior before they died in their flesh bodies, have their names written in the "book of life".

Revelation 20:13 "*And the sea gave up the dead which were in it; and they were judged every man according to their works.*"

Works of the righteous from this age of mankind go into making up your fine linens, clean and white; that you will be wearing throughout eternity. However, the works from the Millennium is what you will be judge by. You will either go to hell or eternity at the end of the Millennium.

Revelation 20:14 "And death and hell were cast into the lake of fire. This is the second death" "And whosoever was not found written in the book of life was cast into the lake of fire."

This verse tells us what the Lord says about the law, it's eternal and is exactly what He meant. Although the ages of this earth will change, our [spirit] will always exist, remember the laws that govern our relationship with our Eternal Creator don't change. Sin always separates us from YHVH our Heavenly Father, whether we're living as mankind or after we're changed into our spirit bodies. It's very important that we repent and come back into righteousness with God. It's a choice every living soul has to make.

The penalty for touching the unclean in Moses and Aaron's day was, people had to bath and be separated for seven days. This is true even in the Millennium age. When one of God's Elect leave to teach out side of the Millennial Temple where Jesus is, before they can return they must bath and wait for seven days, before they are allowed to inter into the temple again. It would be very hard to go through those customs today, comprised to the way Jesus has provided for us. How merciful He is with His own.

Numbers 19:12 "*He shall purify himself with it on the third day, and on the seventh day he shall be clean; but if he purify not himself the third day, then the seventh day he shall not be clean.*"

The person that handled the ashes of the heifer or the scope goat shall be first purified by the water of separation on the third day, and then on the seventh day, he is declared by God to be clean. However if that priest or person is not purified by the water of separation on their third day, then on the seventh day he will still be declared unclean. The biblical number three is "*Divine Completeness*"; the Father, the Son, and the Holy Spirit and the number seven is "*Spiritual completeness*".

Today, every living soul born in this world has sinned and fallen short of the Glory of God. In order to wash our sins through the blood of Christ and to make ourselves right before God, is by confessing our sin to the Heavenly Father and asking for forgiveness in Jesus Christ's name. Ask Him to come into your life and fill you with His Holy Spirit who is your teacher. After you have done this, you have been cleansed before God your Heavenly Father. If people choose not to do this, then they are still unclean before God.

You may want to read Numbers 19:13-20 for yourself. However, at this point I felt it was best to skip those chapters to avoid go on through each of them in detail to keep your interest.

Numbers 19:22 *"And whatsoever the unclean person toucheth shall be unclean; and the soul that toucheth it shall be unclean until even."*

This law pertains to all types of uncleanness. When a person touched anything unclean they are unclean, which was different than when a person touched a dead body, or grave. Remember in Hebrews 9, that the "red heifer" is symbolic of the coming of Christ, and the wages of sin is death and Jesus Christ. He died for our sins and His shed blood is symbolic of purification and has saved our souls if we believed in him.

We should thank and praise God every day that we don't have to have blood sacrifices today because Jesus Christ paid the price on the cross, once and for all times. If you make your choice to accept Jesus Christ as your personal savior while your still living in Grace today you are saved for eternity. Who could ask for anything more? It's our choice.

Knowing these things, will give us greater awareness of the way things once we're before our Savior died on the cross for our sins. Although none of us are worthy of the sacrifice that Jesus made for us. His suffering on the cross has laid a deep sorrow in my soul, especially when people rejected Him when he lived, but it's worse today when people chose to reject his truth, when it's given to us with His great love. The more I read and study the more intense my heart is saddened for those millions of souls who continue to turn away from His truth. His love for them surpasses all understanding, yet my soul cries for those lost and lonely souls who know not these truths.

My prayer is that those who read and understand these chapters will be edified in their souls, and are released from the bondage of men's traditions for the first time in their lives, and are free to serve Jesus Christ our Savior. There is one Christ and one Church, and you are his living Church if you believe in Him. We're not bound by Men's Traditions any more. Amen.

CREATION
Chapter 13

Genesis, the first book of the Bible was written by Moses. In Hebrew it is called *"The Book of the Beginnings,"* however in the Greek *"Genesis"* is called *"the Book of the generations, and creation."* The book of Genesis and the book of Revelation have much more in common than most people think. Genesis is a record of the beginning of this earth age of flesh man, while the book of Revelation is a recording of prophecy regarding the end times. We learned that the destruction of this earth age is because of the corruption of mankind. Genesis records Satan's first rebellion, where as Revelation records Satan's last rebellion. In Genesis, we find where sin enters into the world in this flesh earth age of mankind and Revelation reveals it's final doom at the return of our Lord Jesus Christ.

The Book of Genesis is a key to understanding the rest of the Scriptures. When Jesus talks about the planting of *"the seed,"* and the offspring of that seed [*children*]; we saw in the chapter of the Kenites, the meaning of this as Jesus was teaching us through His parables. In fact in Matthew 13:35 Jesus revealed through His parables the secrets that were hidden from the prophets of the Old Testaments. These secrets were hidden and not understood by mankind since the foundation of the world, [Kosmos; in the Greek] until this age of flesh man.

The name *"Genesis"* is not even a Hebrew word, but a Greek rendition out of the Septuagint, which is part of the Torah. The original Hebrew name of this book was *"The Beginnings."* Today many people try to use this Word of God as the basis for placing the age of the earth at 6000 years. When they do this we know they don't understand the original Hebrew text. Its easy to document the fact that this earth is many millions of years old. However, the traces of Adam's race, and his generation, can only be traced to about the period of 6000 years. Now let's go to the Holy Scriptures and document some of these statements of the beginning of this earth age.

Genesis 1:1 *"In the beginning God created the heaven and the earth."*

There are two bodies mentioned in this verse; the heaven and the earth. It simply stated a fact and left the time factor out. The verse not only did not say when, but left it totally to our imagination, as to the eternal span of time, and how the creation took place. However, the wisdom of God came through the mouth of Solomon.

Proverbs 8:22 *"The Lord possessed me in the beginning of His ways, before the works of old."*

This is the works of the old earth age, spoken of in Revelation 12:1-6, God's *"works of old"* are the creation of this entire world, including the stars in the heavens, the sun and all the other heavenly bodies. It was in that first earth age when God created all the souls, including Satan's soul. Wisdom was with God, our Heavenly Father even before your soul and this entire universe was created. Stop and think for a moment. This is telling us that there was one point in time when every thing that is common to us and in our mind did not exist, Evolution simply could not have happened, if those elements simply did not exist.

God created our soul, and He foreordained the wisdom that you would have, before you ever existed in the flesh. It is important that each of us use the wisdom and common sense that God put into our minds. We use them in our lives and apply it to bring fourth His fruit for His Glory.

Revelation 4:11 *"Thou art worthy, O Lord, to receive glory and honour and power: for Thou hast created all things, and for Thy pleasure they are and were created."*

We must try to please and serve the Lord as we give Him our praise and glory every day.

Proverbs 8:23; *"I was set up from everlasting, from the beginning, or ever the earth was."*

This is saying that wisdom was with God, and He possessed us. *"Everlasting"* is from the moment God create our spirit bodies, and we became a living soul. Believers' will live continually through out time, until we enter eternity. However some souls will be destroyed in the lake of fire because they chose to followed Satan here on earth even after going through the 1000 years of Millennium Age. There is no time laps within the everlasting process called "erets" it will always exist. It began from the foundation of the first earth age, and goes on into the second earth age of flesh mankind. When we die in the flesh, our spirit body or soul body will live on in the Millennium age recorded in Rev. 21:1. We will all be in the "*New Jerusalem"* called the Millennium age, that Jesus revealed to us in the book of John.

Revelation 21:1 *"And I saw a new heaven and a new earth: for the first heaven and the first earth were passed away; and there was no more sea."*

This is the Millennium age. Everyone will be living in their spirit bodies like the angles have. There is no flesh in this period of time in which we are approaching today. These time periods are listed in order. *In the <u>First</u> earth age we were living in our spirit or soul bodies. *The <u>Second</u> earth age is today, we are all living in our flesh bodies and our spirit and soul bodies are living within each of us. *The <u>Third</u> earth age, called the 1000 years of the Millennium age, which is when Christ arrives and changes us from flesh bodies into our Spirit and soul bodies. *The <u>Fourth</u> is the Finial Judgment that comes. The righteous souls will go on into eternity which is everlasting life with Jesus Christ and our Heavenly Father. Those who chose to follow Satan will go into Hell fire, where they will be with Satan in the abyss. Satan and his followers will be forgotten and completely destroyed, and it will be as if they never existed.

Proverbs 8:24; *"When there were no depths, I was brought forth; when there were no fountains abounding with water."*

Before there was any need for an abyss, or pit, and the water to fill them, God's wisdom was there. Look around you, before there was anything that you can identify with your human eye, God's wisdom was here.

Proverbs 8:25; *"Before the mountains were settled, before the hills was I brought forth:"*

Before the earth even took on it's present form, with the high mountains and rolling hills, God's wisdom was there. God's wisdom played His part in the creation of this earth and all wisdom comes from God.

Proverbs 8:26; *"While as yet he had not made the earth, nor the fields, nor the high part of the [beginning] of the dust of the world."*

God was there in wisdom before that first little atom, or speck of dust of the earth was formed. Before the laws of God that control the energy forces came into being, God's wisdom was there. This entire universe is made up of the elements, and Gods wisdom make the energy forces that are part of each particle that goes into making up these building blocks of matter.

Proverbs 8:27; *"When he prepared the heavens, I was there: when he set a compass [circle] upon the face of the depth:"*

This verse allows us to know that the heavens were created before the earth that we live on was created. The *"compass"* as stated here is a perfect circle. That compass was set in place and made stable by a certain point in it's center. This is not talking about a center point of a circle, but a path that is made perfect wherein all things on this earth, plants, animals and mankind etc., exists in God's perfection. It is part of the perfect plan of God. Those that conform to that perfect plan or ways of God are part of His eternal plan. However God has allowed every soul to determine for themselves whether to be in that plan or outside of His plan. Satan chose to stay outside of God's plan.

The "depth" in the Hebrew text is the "Tehom", and it includes the teaming masses of water that are on the face of the earth. The law of God is called "gravity" it's what holds the water with in the seas, rivers and the depth of the oceans that it fills, that keeps it in bounds and away from land. It's only because of the laws of nature we live under, that we are able to predict the weather and etc..

Proverbs 8:28; *"And when established the clouds above: when he strengthened the fountains of the deep:"*

God allowed the earth to be set into a rotation so that we would have our weather patterns that allows the clouds above to water the earth below. Not only do the clouds water the earth when it rains, but the depths of the earth allow the fountains of the deep to give forth their rivers and streams of water that flows into the seas.

Proverbs 8:29; *"When He gave to the sea His decree, that the waters should not pass His commandment: when He appointed the fountains of the earth:"*

In other words, there was land, oceans, fields and lakes, thus God set His command-ment, that they should be separated through the "compass" which He set. Today it's known as "gravity". This is the force which separates all water from dry land. When the waves hit the rocks of the shoreline, they rescind back into the sea by the gravitational forces of the earth. According to scientists, at one time we had one large land mass and one body of water. However, through land drift of the continent plates, seven giant bodies of land called Continents were formed where they exist today.

The animals of the first earth age became frozen in time, in the exact place where they lived. Some were covered by volcanoes and others by ice. The evidence of a world wide catastrophe generated the course of the world that exists today. In the book "*Worlds in Upheaval*" by Immanuel Velikovsky, documents over 66 known places where such evidence is found. We know from the Scriptures that the plates of this earth has been thoroughly shaken, recorded in Genesis 1:2 bears witness to this truth. The reason for this being recorded in the Scriptures, was because of Satan's pride that caused his fall, and one third of God's children followed him.

When the fall of Satan and one third of all God's children followed him, which caused the destruction of that first earth age everyone was in spirit bodies. Then God set up of this second earth age of mankind. So that every living soul born could have eternal life, through the conception of a woman who brought fourth a child. We were first born from above, that's called "*being born again*". Every living soul was born with a free will and is able to choose for themselves whether to follow the ways of God, or follow Satan.

God allowed Job to be tested by both Satan and his fellow man, in the first thirty seven chapters of the Book of Job. However, after 37 chapters of man's nonsense, ramblings, and bad advice the people said to Job, God spoke to Job.

Job 38:1,2 *"Then the Lord answered Job out of the whirlwind, and said, Who is this that darkeneth counsel by words without knowledge?"*

Job had been tested to the point of losing His entire family, all his property, and had been inflicted by sores and sickness,

Yet, he did not curse God. When all his friends were trying to tell him he must have offended God and it was his fault that God did these things to him; Job would not accept their comments. Although Job was in bad health, and confused, he never gave up his faith in God. Yet through this entire time, Job did not curse nor blame God for his losses. All he could do was praise the Lord for His mercy. This is a lesson we should all remember in our lives.

Job 38:3 "*Gird up now thy loins like a man; for I will demand of thee, and answer thou Me."*

God told Job to straighten up and be a man, and listen to what He is about to tell him. Then God told Job how He laid out the foundations of the earth and the heaven, and all matters concerning them.

Then for the rest of Job 38 and continuing in Job 39 we can see the same wisdom we read about in Proverbs 8. God told Job how He put the universe all together. Our God is infinite in wisdom and power, and His love for His children is so great that He willingly died on the cross at Calvary for the sins of mankind. By God's great love and through His mercy, He demonstrated His love for His children. All that he went through, humbled Job before God, as it should humble each of us. However, Job fell apart in Job 40. When God, once again told Job to stand, "like a man, and give Him an answer". He made it possible for all of his children to approach God in prayer.

Let's return to Genesis 1:2 to see how God fulfilled the creation process of the earth we live on, and the universe that's around us.

Genesis 1:2 *"And the earth was without form, and void; and darkness was upon the face of the deep."*

The Spirit of God is also known as the Holy Spirit, and it is God's Spirit that moved upon the face of the waters.

In the Hebrew translation of the word, *"was,"* as used in this verse *". . . the earth was without form, . . .";* in the original text it reads, *"became without form . . .".* This same mistranslation of the word *"became"* and turning it into the word *"was"* is also present in Genesis 2:7. It should read; *". . . and man became a living soul".*

The correct Hebrew translation from the Massorah Hebrew text for the words, *"without form"* is *"tohu-va bohu"* in the Hebrew, *"Strong's Bible Dictionary".* So we see that the earth was not *"created without form"*, but it *"became [tohu] without form and void."* Let's go to *"Strong's Hebrew Dictionary"*, reference #1961 to verify the word "*was"* that we read in this verse. "Yahah, *haw-yaw; a prime root, to exit; to become, or come to pass.*" [#1961]

Now let's continue in the, *"Strong's Hebrew Dictionary"* to get the true meaning for the word *"void."* #2258, on page 36 tells us that we have to go to #2254 for the prime word means "void." #2254; "Chabal, *khaw-bal; to wind tightly as a rope, to bind, to pervert, destroy, to corrupt, spoil, travail,* "This corresponds with it's other use in # 2255, which reads; *"to ruin".*

"Tohu" of the earth, means that the total destruction had come to pass on the earth. The second *"was"* in the verse is in italics type because there is no verb *"to be"* in the Hebrew language. One of the problems in translating the Hebrew into English is that the verb, *"to be"* is not distinguished from the verb, *"to become".*

At the end of **Genesis 1:1** the first earth age ceased to exist in it's previous form. God created the earth to be inhabited, and then He destroyed it. There was an entire earth age that existed between verses one and two of Genesis. This first earth age is written about in II Peter, Jeremiah, Proverbs, and Jude. We will look into these Scripture passages and try to understand the deeper meaning of our Father's Word.

If you don't understand that there was a first earth age, you will not understand why God would say in Malachi 1:3; *"And I hated Esau . . ."*. God hated Esau even before he was born in his flesh body. Because of what he had done when he lived in the first earth age in his spirit body. Esau was living in his spirit soul body when he angered God in that first earth age. God's anger toward Esau passed on through His mother when he was born of the flesh and entered into this second earth age. Read also Romans 9:13.

This verse, proves that our earth is older than 6,000 years old. To be more exact, it's probably many millions of years old. However, no matter how old this earth is, it is the only place we can live in our flesh bodies and survive. We shouldn't worship God's creation, we are told to worship the creator, our Heavenly Father. God is in full control of all of His creation, and He destroyed all forms of life that lived upon the earth in that first earth age, written in Isaiah 45:18.

Isaiah 45:18; *"For thus saith the Lord That created the heavens; God Himself that formed the earth and made it; He hath established it He created it not in vain, He formed it to be inhabited: "I am the Lord; and there is none else."*

This is God speaking while Isaiah is writing it down, and He is telling us that when He created the earth, it was not in vain. *"Vain,"* is the same Hebrew word that we saw when God created this earth to be lived upon. In **Genesis 1:1** "God created the heaven and the earth". God created the earth to be inhabited. **Genesis 1:2**, *"And the earth was with our form, and "void";* The *"Tohu"*, the *"destruction"*, was not part of God's creation plan in verse one, but came after the fall of Satan when one third of all the souls followed Satan in the first earth age, in verse two.

We find more documentation concerning the first earth age in II Peter 3. We can read about all three earth ages, as Peter becomes a witness to this historical truth.

II Peter 3:5 *"For this they willingly are ignorant of, that by the word of God the heavens were of old, and the earth standing out of the water and in the water:"*

God said, the earth came about by *"the word of God"*. Some ministers preach that this was Noah's flood, however this was in the first earth age, known as "of old" from the time that it was recorded in Gen. 1:1, when Satan rebelled against God and he took 1/3 of all God's angles with him. That's why he was so angry with Esau when he arrived on earth.

II Peter 3:6 *"Whereby the world that then was, being overflowed with water, perished:"*

Perished means total destruction. *"The world* [age] *that then was"* ended in total ruin through another flood that was prior to Noah's day. There were no survivors of that flood; no animals, no man, no insects, nor vegetation survived in any form. Everything perished! Yet we know in Noah's time there were two life forms of *each kind saved,* and in time they replenished the earth.

When you drive out on the highway today, and look at the road cutaways, you can see the layers of earth that has formed over ages, through out eons of years. Some say this earth is 6000 years? Even a child knows better than that.

II Peter 3:7; *"But the heavens and the earth which are now, by the same word are kept in store, reserved unto fire against the day of judgment and perdition of ungodly men."*

This is the second heaven and earth age, "*earth which are now"* that we are living in. This earth age will not be destroyed until God's time of judgment upon the ungodly men of this earth age comes to a close. That time of perdition [destruction] is after the millennium, and after the judgment and then the consuming fire comes. Hebrews 12:19 tells us that our God is that consuming fire.

II Peter 3:8 *"But, beloved, be not ignorant of this one thing, that one day is with the Lord as a thousand years, and a thousand years as one day."*

One week is 7000 years, and we are coming to the Sabbath of that week very shortly. The common name for the next thousand years is "*the Millennium age.*" The Millennium age is the thousand years after the true Jesus Christ returns to earth at the seventh trumpet to establish His kingdom here on earth. All souls at that time will not be in the flesh bodies, but in another dimension. They will exist in their incorruptible bodies, spoken of in I Corinthians 15:50-54.

II Peter 3:9 *"The Lord is not slack concerning His promise, as some men count slackness but is longsuffering to us-ward, not willing that any should perish, but that all should come to repentance."*

That means that you can count on our Heavenly Father concerning His promises. God has much patience concerning His children. It isn't God's will that any soul should perish. God didn't intend for Satan to perish, recorded in Ezekiel 28, but that doesn't mean God will not bring about the destruction of souls; because it is up to every living soul to choose who they will follow, that's why we all were given a free will.

II Peter 3:10 *"But the day of the Lord will come as a thief in the night; in the which the heavens shall pass away with a great noise, and the elements shall melt with fervent heat, the earth also and the works that are therein shall be burned up."*

This quote, *"A thief in the night"* is an figure of speech meaning that Christ will come at an unexpected time. This sounds like a scary time, in the original text, however when it's translated into English it's a joy. The *"elements"* are all the *"rudiments"*; which are the evil spirits. All evil men are part of those rudiments as well as all of the various forms of idolatry. They will all burn at their appointed time. These elements are not the elements that go into making up the physical properties of this earth. This refers to the enemies' of our Heavenly Father and their evil activities. They will reap what they have sown.

So we have witnessed in II Peter 3 that there are three earth ages, and three heaven ages that correspond with the earth age meaning periods of time. We see also in Jeremiah 4 that there is another witness to the fact there are three earth ages.

Jeremiah 4:22 "*For My people is foolish, they have not known Me; they are sottish children, and they have none understanding: they are wise to do evil, but to do good they have no knowledge.*"

Today not many people fully understand God's pure Word. The Historic translators we're kind by using the word *"sottish"*, this word means *"stupid"*, or *"silly"*. The nature of mankind today is to "make money by selling trinkets and prayer cloths etc.. Today their minds are evil constantly, just as they were in the days of Noah. Truth has become void.

Jeremiah 4:23 *"I beheld the earth, and, lo it was without form, and void; and the heavens, and they had no light."*

Here we get back to the same word that we saw earlier in Genesis 1:2; The Hebrew word "*Tohu*" is "*void*". In other words, God is saying, "*I destroyed the first heaven and earth age*." There was no life form existing on this earth, at the close of that first earth age in any form.

Jeremiah 4:24 *"I beheld the mountains, and lo, they trembled, and all the hills moved lightly."*

This is why the magnetic north is 90 miles off true north, God shook the earth and everything moved from its foundations at the time the destruction "tohu" took place.

Jeremiah 4:25 *"I beheld, and, lo, there was no man, and all the birds of the heavens were fled."*

This is telling us that, No man, animals, or the birds were left alive. The earth was covered with water, and life could not exist. There were no boat floating around on the surface of the earth, because this span of time could have been for thousands of years, or a much longer.

Jeremiah 4:26 *"I beheld, and lo, the fruitful place was a wilderness, and all the cities thereof were broken down at the presence of the Lord, and by His fierce anger."*

In this flood there wasn't a tree or a blade of grass left with life in it. We know that there were cities at that time when God's the anger and fury came against Satan. A third part of God's angles followed Satan and that's what caused God to destroy the entire first earth age in Gen. 1.

That is what God meant in Hebrews 11:7 when He said, *"I shook her once and know I'll shake her again."* The only thing that will be left standing at this time, is that which is unshakeable, and it will only be those who have repented, and have Jesus Christ in their heart. They are those souls that were sealed in their minds. They did will not bow to the Antichrist, his system nor take his name, or his number. At the end of this earth age.

Jeremiah 4:27; *"For thus hath the Lord said, "The whole land shall be desolate; yet will I not make a full end."*

God allowed the waters of the first earth age to recede, and from it came a condition whereby we can live in this second earth age. Every soul, or child of God will pass through this flesh earth age once, and in this flesh life we have the choice to choose either light or darkness; Jesus Christ or Satan. When God created all living souls He gave each of us a free will when we were born into our flesh bodies. He will not nor will his followers force anyone to love God. No one can buy true love. God will only accept people who choose to love Him and are willing to serve Him with their whole hearts. It's a choice we all have to make.

We have learned from the Bible that we all have lived in our spirit bodies in that first earth age prior to this second earth age of mankind. God created that first earth age in good standing to be inhabited, written in Isaiah 45:18; then it became "*without form and void*", in the Hebrew, it was "*Tohu va bohu*".

The reason was because Satan brought sin into the world of that first earth age, and that sin was so great that one third of all God's children followed Satan, and that sin brought God's anger upon the whole world. It was then that Satan's soul was sentenced to death. This is why Satan is called the *"son of perdition"* in II Thessalonians 2:3, and John 17:12. Satan refused to repent, so God named him, "son of perdition".

Verse three starts after the first earth age, after the overthrow by Satan, "*The Chabal*", and after the total distraction of the first earth age with all life forms on it

Genesis 1:3 *"And God said, "let there be light:" and there was light."*

Almost every verse involving this creation story of Genesis one starts with the words; *"And God said".* However, the Hebrew text says; *"And the Magnificent Lord God Almighty".* The original text tells us that this is the "*full Spirit of God*" speaking.

This verse is still in the first day when the light came into being.

Genesis 1:4 *"And God saw the light, that it was good: and God divided the light from the darkness."*

Genesis 1:5 *"And God called the light Day, and the darkness He called Night. And the evening and the morning were the first day."*

The sun, moon and stars were created in this verse, however the term, *"Let there be light"* means so much more than the light of the day. It was when the Holy Spirit of God, the "*Ruach*" in the Hebrew, moved upon the face of the earth; there is *light*, for He [the Holy Spirit] is *light*. Without the Holy Spirit, there is total darkness because the Holy Spirit of God started His work on the first day.

Within the first chapter of Genesis, God reveals His entire plan. Verses three through five are not dealing with the sun and moon, they were created later. This is dealing with the presence of the Holy Spirit of God that is to be present throughout this earth age. "Ruach" or Spirit is the first and most important part of the creation, for without the Holy Spirit there is only darkness.

This also is the start of God's plan, which includes all of God's children. Every living soul must make a choice between the *"Light"*, which is the Spirit of God", and darkness. Ezekiel 28:12-19 declares Satan, *"the King of Tyrus"*, to be that darkness in the world. If anyone made their choice to follow darkness, Verse 18 declares that your destination after judgment, God said, *"I will bring thee to ashes upon the earth . . .":* this is where your soul will end up.

All prophecies in the entire Bible that refer to God's Elect, and the children of God; and those living in God's will, are called "children of light" This also applies to prophecies that are given in days, or solar years. Daniel 12:11. This has nothing to do with the people who call themselves "Children of Light" today, because there already deceivers.

In turn, all prophecies dealing with Satan, his wickedness, and his children are given in months, or moons. Satan's children, are called the "*children of darkness*", or "*of the night* ". Revelation 13:4,5, Satan is the darkness that is the negative part of God's plan. Satan was here from the beginning of this earth age, and God allowed it.

Christ was also here, He is the *"Tree of Life."* We will read about this later in the second and third chapters of Genesis, when God refers to trees, symbolic as being people.

Genesis 1:6 *"And God said, "Let there be a firmament in the midst of the waters, and let it divide the waters from the waters."*

The *"firmament*" is an "*expansion, or space*".

Genesis 1:7 *"And God made the firmament, and divided the waters which were under the firmament from the waters which were above the firmament: and it was so."*

Genesis 1:8 *"And God called the firmament Heaven. And the evening and the morning were the second day."*

Are we talking about dimensions here? What does the word *"heaven"* mean here? In the Hebrew text it is the "*high and lofty* ", or *"the upper place*." So on the second day the Spirit of God moved the waters, and divided the waters. He placed a space, or firmament in between these two bodies of water, and kept one of the bodies of water on the earth, with the other body of water above the space, or in the heavens. The waters below existed like the oceans exist today.

In the book, "*Waters Above,"* the author demonstrates how it is possible to have oceans of water in suspension above the earth, if the earth were in a perfect orbital spin. Although this condition does not exist today, however, it did at one time; as was proven by scientists in "*The Wisconsin Theory."* This study proved that the polarity of the earth changed, by their observation of the crystallization of iron particles in ancient lava flow.

To show how objects can be set stationary in the heavens, in modern day technology that most nations of the earth use today, we have satellites set in space orbit for communication. This process is so common, even third world countries have their own satellites. These physical masses use the gravity pull of the earth, balanced with an equal centripetal force that would throw the satellite out into space; to suspend these objects into a stationary place [orbit] with respect to the earth.

The book "*Waters Above*" gave the theory of how it was done, and when Voyager II space craft passed by the planet "Uranus"; we saw it become reality. How did the separations' of two bodies of water by God, placed one body of water on the earth, and the other was suspended and was floating above the earth with a space or [firmament] in-between.

Genesis 1:9 *"And God said, "Let the waters under the heaven be gathered together unto one place, and let the dry land appear: "and it was so."*

In Noah's flood, it took months for the waters to settle. However, on this third day of creation, God spoke and it happened. This is the first day that "dry land" appeared on earth in this earth age. In the eternal earth age there will be no seas or oceans as in this earth age.

Genesis 1:10 *"And God called the dry land Earth; and the gathering together of the waters called He Seas: and God saw that it was good."*

There was nothing chaotic here because everything was done in order. With the protection from the sun's rays by the *"water above"*, the dew and rain watered the earth below; and it was good.

Genesis 1:11 *"And God said, "Let the earth bring forth grass, the herb yielding seed, and the fruit tree yielding fruit after his kind, whose seed is in itself, upon the earth:" and it was so."*

Notice here that everything was created to be yielding after it's own kind. The reproducing process of every living seeds were designed to create, new generations from then on, *"after his kind"*. No genetic reproduction from a test tube nor by artificial means. Is it any wonder that crops make a good show the first year or so, then the soil has to rest for a season to prepare for new crops.

Genesis 1:12 *"And the earth brought forth grass, and herb yielding seed after his kind, and the tree yielding fruit, whose seed was in itself, after his kind: and God saw that it was good."*

Again, everything reproduces *"after it's own kind."* because God created it all and He called it good.

Genesis 1:13 *"And the evening and the morning were the third day."*

The heavens and the water separations came about on the second day, it wasn't until the third day that *"dry land appeared"*. There is simply no way that evolution can fit into in the creation of the heavens and earth. Everything that exists, whether created, man made, acting, moving, or speaking are ascribed to the Living God. There is no area that can be rendered to chance, without denial of Divine Revelation.

Man assumes he started from nothing and progressed to where he is today through evolution, which is a process of changes that takes' place through chance. This principle takes place only in human affairs: developing from a hut to a modern building; from a canoe to an ocean liner; from the spade or stick developing into the tractor, and so on.

However, birds still build their nests today as they did 6000 years ago. The moment we pass the boundary line and enter the "Divine sphere", no trace or vestige of evolution is seen. There is growth and development within each "kind". In reality there simply is no connecting between one "kind" of creature or specimen transferred to a different "kind" of creature. It is always *one "Kind after his own kind"*. That's God's law.

In fact scientists have conducted many DNA tests to prove insects a common parentage between numbers of kinds of insects. However, they proved that there was no way that these different kinds of insects could have ever come from common parentage. It is interesting how the scientific world is trying to covered up this truth. They are now trying to prove the reliability of this new scientific tool, called DNA. The "Learning Channel" ran a documentary on this particular set of DNA testing in early 1995, and the results of those tests pointed out the conflict between the tests and the evolution theory.

Each part or form of the *"theory of evolution"* is only invented to explain a partial area of the phenomena of created things. The Word of God, claims to cover all the ground through Divine inspiration of the Holy Spirit of God. Man uses the term *"higher critic"*, to give authority to those using human assumptions and reasoning; instead of using sound documentation of physical evidence and manuscripts from the Word of God.

The chaos that came after the first age is being rejuvenated into a new order of things regarding life. The grass, herbs, trees, and other vegetation kind is brought back to carry on as it did in the first age; from it's own seed. Everything after it's kind.

Genesis 1:14 *"And God said, "Let there be lights in the firmament of the heaven to divide the day from the night; and let them be for signs, and for seasons, and for days, and years: "and it was so."*

The moon and the sun are both given as signs for planting and to control tides, seasons, and the weather. We dig for clams by the position of the moon, as well as the planting of potatoes. However, there is another separation taking place, and that is the separation of day from night, and light from darkness.

On the fourth day we have a moon, sun, stars, and all the other heavenly bodies of the universe. It is on the fourth day that the earth has a constant orbit around the sun which sets the season and gives us our uniform standard, which we call time. Now we have a standard day, which is divided into years, months, days, hours, minutes and seconds in which God has created.

The other part of the universe which most of the world follows closely today, are the signs of the zodiac. These signs of the zodiac are comprised of twelve major star groupings, called constellations. These star groupings form a belt which circles the sky on a plane which follows the earth's orbit around the sun. These twelve signs of the zodiac are part of a universal language of Astronomical science. It is well known that from the earliest man, and their ancient astronomical charts will allow modern astrono-mers to pinpoint the year and the time of charting, because David wrote about it in Psalms.

Psalms 19:1-4 *"The heavens declare the glory of God; and the firmament sheweth His handy work." "Day unto day uttereth speech, and night unto night sheweth knowledge." "There is no speech nor language, where their voice is not heard." "There line is gone out through all the earth, and their words to the end of the world."*

Genesis 1:15 *"And let them be for lights in the firmament of the heaven to give light upon the earth:"*

As we look up into a clear dark night, God's handiwork comes alive. The billions of twinkling stars cover the entire sky as a blanket.

Genesis 1:16 *"And God made two great lights; the greater light to rule the day, and the lesser light to rule the night: He made the stars also."*

The sun became the pillar of our universe for all the planets to set their course around it. The sun gives us light by day, and the time of the year. Though the moon gives us light by reflection of the sun, it's gravity regulates our tides and gives us the moisture in the ground for watering the seed for our crops.

Genesis 1:17 *"And God set them in the firmament of the heaven to give light upon the earth,"*

Genesis 1:18 *"And to rule over the day and over the night, and to divide the light from the darkness: and God saw that it was good."*

The sun and the moon is doing exactly what It was designed to do, and it was good.

Genesis 1:19 *"And the evening and the morning were the forth day."*

The number "four" in the Bible means the earth. Everything about the earth is divided into four; the four quarters, the four seasons, the four points of the compass, and so on.

Genesis 1:20 *"And God said, "Let the waters bring forth abundantly the moving creature that hath life, and fowl that may fly above the earth in the open firmament of heaven . . ."*

Looking closer at the word *"Life"*, in the Hebrew text that word is *"Nephesh"*, which is *"soul"* in English. The word *"naphesh"*, though it means soul, however it's not always used as a living soul within mankind, because there are twelve classifications of the word "naphesh".

The classification form used in this sixteenth verse is the first and lowest form applied to life, and is directed only to the very lowest animal forms. Though "Nephesh" is used 754 times in the Hebrew Old Testament, it is used in the lower case form "*to lower animals"* only 22 times. It is applied to the *"soul of man"* 472 times.

Remember that on this fifth day of the creation, the first life formed were in the seas and oceans; and then came the birds of the air. God gave each of these creatures from the tiniest single cell life form, to the whale, their *"naphesh"* [Life]. In each kind of life formed, God gave the ability to do all the functions within the limits of their kind and no more. Within the DNA found in each of those animals, there was the ability to reproduce their own kind.

Genesis 1:21 *"And God created great whales, and every living creature that moveth, which the waters brought forth abundantly, after their kind, and every winged fowl after his kind: and God saw that it was good."*

Evolution just doesn't fit into the order of creation. When God created every living thing to reproduce "*after their kind,"* it eliminates the mutations through chance over a long period of time, and that is required in order to accept their own evolution theories.

Genesis 1:22 *"And God blessed them saying, "Be fruitful, and multiply, and fill the waters in the seas, and let fowl multiply in the earth."*

Genesis 1:23 *"And the evening and the morning were the fifth day."*

Make a mental note of the fact that sea and ocean life are created first and then the winged fowl. However, man has not been created yet. The creation cycle form starts with, "*And God said*". When the cycle is completed, and that part is completed, we then read; "*God blessed it*".

Genesis 1:24 "*And God said, "Let the earth bring forth the living creature after his kind, cattle, and creeping thing, and beast of the earth after his kind:" and it was so."*

Here again is the word creature, or "*nephesh*", used as a soul; as we saw in verse twenty. It is referring to the classification of lower animal life. These creatures of life forms include all insect life, wild animal forms such as the cat family, dog family, elephants, as well as all other wild beasts, of which many are extinct today.

Notice also that all animal forms of life reproduced "after his kind". In this orderly fashion, all animals followed as God has provided for each one.

Genesis 1:25 *"And God made the beast of the earth after his kind, and cattle after their kind, and every thing that creepeth upon the earth after his kind: and God saw that it was good."*

Each of these families of animals reproduced and spread throughout the earth, kind after kind, and *"each after his own kind"*;. They populated the entire earth. Each kind living in accordance to the climate, substance, and terrain God intended each of their animal forms to survive in.

Genesis 1:26 *"And God said, "Let Us make man in Our image, after Our likeness: and let them have dominion over the fish of the sea, and over the fowl of the air, and over the cattle, and over all the earth, and over every creeping thing that creepeth upon the earth."*

God set out to make man exactly the way he is. Man was then created to look like the exact image of God, and his sons; the angels. If you ever wondered what an angel form looks like? Then look into a mirror, for we are created in that image.

God created the fish first, then the fowl, and later the beasts. Following their creation, they multiplied, then God created the races of mankind. God gave mankind the dominion over all of the animal kingdom. He gave the wild animals to hunt and the cattle to provide milk etc., and fish to catch for food, as well as other domestic animals to use. Man is the highest form of all life on this earth, although many movements today act as if they don't know it when they place little or no value on their own souls and have lowered themselves to act like, the "*Naphesh*", "lower animal life".

Genesis 1:27 *"So God created man in His own image, in the image of God created He him; male and female created He them."*

On this sixth day both man and woman of all races were formed, and each after their kind. Yet all forms of mankind red, yellow, black, brown, and white were all created in the image of God.

Genesis 1:28 *"And God blessed them, and God said unto them, "Be fruitful, and multiply, and replenish the earth, and subdue it: and have dominion over the fish of the sea, and over the fowl of the air, and over every living thing that moveth upon the earth . . ."*

The intent of God was to have each race multiply "*after their kind* ". For God created all that is necessary to replenish the earth. *"Replenish"* is translated properly, and the command is to "*replenish the earth*". This earth had a population in the first earth age and it was inhabited by God's children. Satan caused one third of all God's children to fall and follow him and the result of that fall angered God. That was when *"the earth became* [tohu-vabohu] *a waste and desolation,"* as recorded in verse two.

God is now commanding the races to multiply and *"repopulate"* the earth *"after their kind."* It seems though today that the whole world is a bit color blind, or maybe they think God is out of touch with today's world. It is interesting though, following Noah's flood in **Genesis 9:1**; *"And God blessed Noah and his sons, and said unto them, "be fruitful and multiply, and replenish the earth."*

These are the only two places in the Bible where the word "replenish" is used, and both deal with the time following a destruction of the earth and mankind by causing a flood. To replenish anything, means that it had to exist once before in the same form. It is interesting that evolutionist can find animal forms dating back thousands of years prior nor any skeletons of mankind. In fact the earliest specimens of man was, carbon dated to within the limits of God's creation. It was the link that evolutionists claimed to be the link between monkey and man. However, by other testing, it turned out to be a chimp. Always remember God said, "*kind after kind*". And so it is!

God made man and all things for His pleasure. Have you given Him any pleasure lately? Have you stopped to thank Him for your blessings, or just to tell Him that you love Him. Because you are made in His image, and He has feelings just as we do. When we fall short, we should ask Him for forgiveness so He can forgive us, because He loves all of His children.

Genesis 1:29 *"And God said, "Behold, I have given you every herb bearing seed, which is upon the face of all the earth, and every tree, in the which is the fruit of a tree yielding seed; to you it shall be for meat."*

God is giving instruction here to man. He told this group of people to go and eat of the fruits of the trees, and plant life known as vegetation are for man's consumption.

Genesis 1:30 *"And to every beast of the earth, and to every fowl of the air, and to every thing that creepeth upon the earth, wherein there is life, I have given every green herb for meat:" and it was so."*

Notice that the plant life that was given for "meat" was given to both man and beast. The idea and practice of eating flesh never was ordained by God as food until after Noah's flood. This is recorded in Genesis 9:2,3.

Genesis 9:2,3 *"And the fear of you and the dread of you shall be upon every beast of the earth, and upon every fowl of the air, upon all that moveth upon the earth, and upon all the fishes of the sea; into your hand are they delivered." "Every moving thing that liveth shall be meat for you; even as the green herb have I given you all things."*

The word "Life" in this verse is translated "Naphesh" in the Hebrew text. It is classified and used in this form as applying only to "lower form animals". However, in this case it is used to show life within and not the presence of an "eternal soul", as in man.

Genesis 1:31 *"And God saw every thing that He had made, and, behold, it was very good. And the evening and the morning were the sixth day."*

At the close of the sixth day the earth and all life form's, plant and animal alike, were in existence. The condition of the earth was inhabitable and all the stars and planets were set in their places in the heavens. We know that the condition of the earth was such that God intended for mankind to have a very long life span. The age of mankind that is recorded in the Bible prior to the flood of Noah's time, was about eight to nine hundred years or more. We also must agree that it was good, for God repeated; *"and it was very good"* after the sixth days creation.

Going back in time, through the recorded generations, there are not that many, in comparison to the time evolutionist would have us believe. When we compare Joseph's father in law with Jesus father's lineage in Luke 3:23-38; we notice a continuous line from the creation of Adam to Jesus. It is interesting that there are seventy seven [77] generations from Adam to Jesus Christ. Within the Bible the number Seven represents "spiritual completeness". The double sevens gives us [77] and that would be a double witness of *"spiritual completeness*". The birth of our Lord Jesus Christ was from the white with out a doubt.

The word *"Adam"* in the Strong's Hebrew dictionary is given under #120; "Adam, *aw-dawm'; from #119, ruddy, a human being, person.*" So the prime root in the Hebrew dictionary, #119; *"Adam, aw-dam' to show blood in the face, flesh, turn rosy, be made ruddy [red]."* This race of Adam was the white race which will show ruddy [red] blood when blushing.

On the sixth day, *"male and female created He them"*. God created all the races, however, in the creation of "Adam" we will see in the next chapter that God said there was a purpose for Adam, and His intent for the Adam's race was for them *"to till the ground.*" That means that they were to be farmers.

There has developed a foolish idea that the Negro race came from a sin of Ham, "*when he looked upon his fathers nakedness.*" The meaning of the verse in Genesis.

Genesis 9:22-23 is explained in Leviticus 18:8. "*The nakedness of thy father is to lay with thy father's wife your mother."*

In Ham's case, we saw that the product of that sin relationship between Ham, and his mother, was the birth of "Canaan", Ham's son. That is why Noah cursed Canaan, and set a curse upon Canaan's children.

Both Noah's wife and Ham [Noah's son] were white, and were from the Adam's race. We are told about this in Genesis 6:9. The child Canaan was also of the same race, and simple common sense will tell us this is true. This curse on Canaan was not placed by God, but by Noah. He was angry with his son, but this curse certainly would not be the creation of a black race, or any race. All children of incest are still of the same kind as it's parents.

According to scripture, all races were created first in Gen. chapter 1, before the white Adam's race in Gen. chapter 2. It could even be a thousand years or more, however that's speculation, for there is no written documentation, The only evidence we have is the human bones found by archeologists. The records of the Adam's race located in our Bibles are very important, because through Adam's seed came the Savior Jesus Christ, of all mankind which includes all races. Through the seed of Virgin Mary, Jesus Christ the son of the living God came to earth, and is the only one who can save our Souls from eternal death. Knowing and understanding God's plan fully will set us free.

DEATH
Chapter 14

In this chapter we learn about what the bible tells us about "death". From the time of the sixth day creation, to the sounding of the seventh trumpet, all souls that were born into this earth age of flesh man will die. All except for two men: and God revealed them to us in Genesis 5:24. Elijah was the first man recorded in 2nd Kings 2:9, Enoch was the second man in seventh generation from Adam; and he prophesied by faith with Divine instruction. God took both of these men up in a whirlwind.

Genesis 5:24 *"And Enoch walked with God: and he was not; for God took him."*

Romans 10:17 *"So then faith cometh by hearing, and hearing by the Word of God."*

Enoch lived many generations before Moses and Noah. When God spoke to Enoch, he listened and obeyed all of His word. Enoch and Elijah were the only two men that never died in their flesh bodies, because God took them. All of the rest of mankind born into this earth age has either died, or will die, which is a fact of life.

When David died, his son Solomon took over the throne of Israel. He was a very young man when he went before the altar of God. Solomon asked God for wisdom and understanding to rule over God's people, and God gave granted his request. God also gave him extreme riches, and the right to build His Temple. The Scriptures point out to us that King Solomon was the wisest man that has ever lived in a flesh and blood body, except for our Lord Jesus Christ. Solomon's wrote great wisdom in three books of the Scriptures, "*Proverbs*" deals with wisdom and knowledge that only comes into our soul bodies from the our Heavenly Father, through the Spirit of God: "*The Song of Solomon*" deals with the Love of Our Heavenly Father for his bride and children: And the book of "*Ecclesiastes*" was written to "*the man that walketh under the sun*" in their flesh bodies.

Ecclesiastes is about the soul's of those who lived on this earth in these flesh bodies; and it tells also of those that follow God's word. Reading and understanding Ecclesi-astes will help us all live a happier life. Every living soul that God created must enter this second earth age of flesh mankind at conception, and be born in the flesh body, and try to live his life in happiness, regardless of what conditions they live in. When we follow the instructions that God gave to king Solomon we can live in peace and prosperity here on earth.

Every living soul (person) has two bodies. The inner spiritual soul that lives within our physical bodies. Our soul is not tied to our flesh bodies, because often times our spiritual bodies will pull against our flesh bodies. One will usually try to take control over the other. When the flesh body is in control most people will be doing things that doesn't glorify the Lord. Where as, when we're completely yielded to our Lord and we're in tune with His Word and His Ways, we strive to please Jesus Christ and glorify His name in all things. The book of "*Proverbs*" teaches us how to obtain God's wisdom so that we can allow our soul, or spiritual bodies to have control over our fleshly bodies. We learn to walk in our spirit rather than allowing our flesh bodies to control things of this fleshly world. This can only be done by yielding to the leading by the Holy Spirit of God. Wisdom comes from studying the Bible and the Holy Spirit is our teacher who gives us understanding of God's word and that is sealed in our minds if we are true followers of Jesus Christ. He is the only one who can seal His spirit within ours as we communicate with Him in prayer.

Proverbs 1:7 *"The fear of the Lord is the beginning of knowledge: But fools despise wisdom and instruction."*

The Book of Ecclesiastes gives us a guide line for happiness with purpose and reason for living. Our study of men's traditions deal with death, it begins in Ecclesiastes 12, we learn what happens to our spirit body when our silver thread of life is separated from our from our outer body, called a clay pot and known as our flesh body.

Ecclesiastes 12:1 *"Remember now thy Creator in the days of thy youth, while the evil days come not, nor the years draw nigh, when thou shalt say, `I have no pleasure in them;"*

As we grow older, it seems that the quality of life becomes a little more difficult than it was in our youth. There were far more activities that we could take part in, but as we age, the things of our youth slip's away. This verse is saying, that while you have your youth, thank the creator for the abilities that God gave to you while you're still young. This can also apply in the spiritual sense, for in the course of time, everything must come to an end.

Ecclesiastes 12:2 *"While the sun, or the light, or the moon, or the stars, be not dark-ened, nor the clouds return after the rain:"*

While the sun shines and you walk under the sun in the flesh, there is a light in everyone's life. There is also a darkness coming to this flesh body that walks and enjoys the light of the sun. The dark gathering clouds means, the end of the days of the flesh; and the end of the dispensation is, *"the dark gathering of the clouds"*. The prophet Joel discusses this day in Joel 2:1

Joel 2:1 *"Blow ye the trumpet in Zion, and sound an alarm in My holy mountain: let all the inhabitants of the land tremble: for the day of the Lord cometh, for it is nigh at hand;"*

Remember the dark clouds gathering back in Ecclesiastes 12:2.

Joel 2:2 *"A day of darkness and of gloominess, a day of clouds and of thick darkness, as the morning spread upon the mountains: a great people and a strong; there hath not been ever the like, neither shall be any more after it, even to the years of many generations."*

This is speaking about the locust army of Kenites and fallen angels that God has already allowed to come upon His people. This refers to the deception of the Antichrist, known as his *"One World Religious System"*. That's why this warning has to be sounded. When that day comes before for the coming of the true Jesus Christ our Lord, at the seventh and final trumpet, it will be the end of everyone living in their flesh body, called the flesh age.

Joel 2:3 *"A fire devoureth before them; and behind them a flame burneth: the land is as the Garden of Eden before them, and behind them a desolate wilderness; yea, and nothing shall escape them."*

No human being will escape the burning flame of deceptions that Satan, known as the Antichrist, will bring upon this earth. You will be sealed in your mind before Satan, arrives or you will be taken in by his deception. The desolate wilderness is the lack of knowing the truth of God's Word. Their desire is to follow the lies of the Antichrist and the traditions of the people who have been convinced. Even millions of Christian's will believe that Satan is the true Messiah, which is the desolate wilderness which is starting to occur today. The seal of God in the forehead of God's Elect will take place prior to the coming of Antichrist, because upon his arrival it will be too late. The sting of that scorpion will have taken place and every soul that is not sealed has already accepted Satan's mark. That makes all of God's people very sad to see their relation refuse to hear God's pure word. Those marks are seen in the man made

Rapture, Easter, Christmas etc., that is taught today in their churches that the Bible calls "*Synagogues of Satan.*" and *"It will be like the days of Sodom and Gomorrah".*

Ecclesiastes 12:3 *"In the day when the keepers of the house shall tremble, and the strong men shall bow themselves, and the grinders cease because they are few, and those that look out of the windows be darkened,"*

In the day when the people living in their house grow old, then those that were strong will be bowed over. The grinders are your teeth and may cease because most older people have false teeth. We our less active and our eyes don't see very well. The windows of our eye lids will become darkened over our eyes with cataracts'. This verse is describing older people.

Ecclesiastes 12:4 *"And the doors shall be shut in the streets, when the sound of the grinding is low, and he shall rise up at the voice of the bird, and all the daughters of music shall be brought low;"*

The *"doors"* are the "lips of your mouth", and they will be shut in the streets. When the teeth are gone, you just prefer to keep the mouth shut to hide your gums. This aged person can't hear those birds singing any more, nor the sound of those little girls singing like once before. *"Shall rise up at the voice of the bird"* means that in old age, sleep is hard to come by. There is no difference between old age to the flesh body today, for it is exactly as it was three thousand years ago in king Solomon's day. "*There is nothing new under the sun.*" When we learn from past mistakes of other's while we're young, then our fleshly lives will be a lot easier to live when we get old.

Ecclesiastes 12:5 *"Also when they shall be afraid of that which is high, and fears shall be in the way, and the almond tree shall flourish, and the grasshopper shall be a burden, and desire shall fail: (because man goeth to his long home, and the mourners go about the streets."*

In old age we get feeble. When we get in high places we become afraid that we will trip and fall. The *"almond tree"* is the gray hair that will come in masses, and even the weight of the grasshopper would be a burden to you. All your personal desires or your senses shall fail and the food changes in flavor. We eat less food and lose weight. Etc.

The "long home", in the Hebrew text, *"long"* is #5769, and from the prime root # 5956 in the Strong's Hebrew dictionary. Definition is: *"Properly concealed the vanishing point, generally time out of mind, past or future, particularly the eternity."* This is saying that once the flesh goes into this condition, it is going to stay there for an eternity. Basically, it is talking about the grave. Once the body enters the grave, your old flesh body goes back to dust. The only future for the dead flesh is decay.

When the flesh body is laid into the grave, the mourners go about the streets with a heavy heart for the loss of their loved one. Back in those day's, they even hired mourners to beat there breast, and carry the message of the loss into the streets. Most true believers' look forward to being absent from this flesh body so they can be present with the Lord. That's our hope.

Ecclesiastes 12:6 *"Or ever the silver cord be loosed, or the golden bowl be broken, or the pitcher be broken at the fountain, or the wheel broken at the cistern."*

The *"cistern"* is the clay flesh body that our soul lives in. The cistern is built to hold the water or life that is within the flesh body, but once that bowl is broken the water or life pours out of our flesh bodies. The *"silver cord"* is what holds your soul and the spirit together within our flesh body. We can call it the process of thought, which is the intellect of the mind or soul. When a person is brain dead, there is no electrical impulse within the brain, and that person is considered to be dead, even though the physical body may still be pumping blood. Life support systems are generally discontinued at this time.

When the silver cord that joins the soul body into all parts of our flesh body is broken. it instantly leaves our flesh body and death occurs. Our soul body is known as life. When our Heavenly Father want's us with him, our flesh body becomes biologically dead. Death takes place and the inner man or soul body departs from our physical body and returns to our creator, our Heavenly Father. Our flesh body will decay and return back into the dust where it came from, while all living soul's will return into it's new incorruptible body like the angels have.

In the prior chapter, "Creation", we learned that God took the dust of the earth and from those element made man and woman. He breathed life into their flesh bodies and they became living souls. God took Adam's Rib, translated in Hebrew as, *"curve"* which means *DNA* in Gen 2:21 & 22. Then in *"Strong's Concordance"* it's #6763 God from Adam and made Eve. These clay pots are called our flesh bodies and were made from the dust of the earth.

Ecclesiastes 12:7 *"Then shall the dust return to the earth as it was: and the spirit shall return unto God Who gave it."*

This was done after the silver cord breaks, when the mind is brain dead, and the body loses it's life. Then shall the flesh bodies are returned back into "*dust*" of the earth, just as it once was. For centuries food has been grown in the earth to feed millions of people though out the world. The cycle of God's master plan is astounding.

The *"spirit"* is the *"intellect of the soul" which gives us our identity,* and it lives within our flesh bodies. When the flesh body dies it goes to the grave. But our spirit and soul body returns to God who created it in heaven eons ago. This is a promise of God has given to each of us and it should be understood by all Christians as they are looking forward to, all the days of their lives

When mankind fails to understand God's promise of life after death with their creator, mankind begins to forms their own religious ideas, and neglects to teach what God's Word teaches. Many modern preachers don't put any emphasis' on these truths, that are recorded in the Holy Bible. Either they don't know what the scripture tells us, or they are all teaching from flyers provided by the "*World Council of Churches*", members of the United Nations, and "*traditions of men*".

God created the flesh body for your soul to live in at conception and God placed your spirit within your soul body. Your spirit is what gives your soul it's identity. Then, just as God gave it for a brief time of testing, He will take our soul's back to Himself instantly when our flesh body has died.

Ecclesiastes 12:8 *"Vanity of vanities, saith the preacher; all is vanity."*

This is the conclusion of the entire book, regarding the flesh body. Now we know it returns back into the form it's made of.

Ecclesiastes 12:9 *"And moreover, because the preacher was wise, he still taught the People knowledge; yea, he gave good heed, and sought out, and set in order many proverbs."*

The good preachers taught in proverbs. His teaching and knowledge was from the Word of God and His words came to life for those who hear and understand. Wisdom is, when we take something complicated and make it understandable.

Ecclesiastes 12:10 *"The Preacher sought to find out acceptable words: and that which was written was upright, even words of truth."*

In other words, the only authority for any preacher of our Heavenly Father, are the acceptable words of the truths written within God's Holy Scriptures. God is the only one who is Good and Upright. Don't study traditions of men, but rather stay within God's word, and read chapter by chapter, and verse by verse. That's how preachers should preach. Why spend your time listening to the critics and their short cuts, instead of going to the original source.

Ecclesiastes 12:11 *"The words of the wise are as goads, and as nails fastened by the masters of assemblies, which are given from one shepherd."*

A *"goad"* is a stick with a sharp point on the end that you can punch people with. Remember this verse tells us there is only one Shepherd, the Lord Jesus Christ also known as, the Living Word. The words said by Christ's should be a *"goad"* to the wise, because they are what the wise person uses when they are led by the Holy Spirit. We should keep our attention on the wisdom of God's Word.

Ecclesiastes 12:12 *"And further, by these, my son, be admonished: of making many books there is no end; and much study is a weariness of the flesh."*

By the Word of God we are to be admonished and directed in our ways. Writing books are endless, however, there is only one book that should be our focus, and that is the *King James Bible that's* recorded within "*The Companion Bible* and *Strong's Dictionary,"* with numbers.

Ecclesiastes 12:13 *"Let us hear the conclusion of the whole matter: Fear God, and keep His commandments: for this is the whole duty of man."*

To fear God, means to Reverence Him, and to love and worship Him. The only duty we have to God or man is to keep God's Commandments and conduct our life in accordance to the Word of God. When we take in all of God's Word, there isn't much time for other things if you really want to know more about God's word, rest assured it's all recorded. He has answered every question, anyone could ask about life.

Ecclesiastes 12:14 *"For God shall bring every work into judgment, with every secret thing, whether it be good, or whether it be evil."*

Every thing that we do in our flesh body is recorded in God's books in heaven, and give thanks to God that we have repentance. When we love the Lord, and do wrong, we bring it to the Lord in private, and repent to the Father in Jesus name and He has promised that by the blood of Jesus Christ, all our sins are forgiven. That is why it is important to understand the freedom that we have in Christ. Although your preacher or family would like to keep reminding people of their past sins, God says that when you have repented, put that thought out of your life, because He has not only forgiven you but He has forgotten it. Don't ever bring that old sin up again.

Your good works are important and that is the only thing that you can take with you into eternity. Each of your works that are done for the Lord are already recorded in heaven. The garment you will wear in the eternity is made up of the works you did here on earth. So it is time to start working for the Lord. Your good works are your rewards in eternity and they will always stay with you.

We studied in the chapter on the Seventh trumpet whereby there is a time coming shortly when our flesh bodies will be changed instantly, written in I Corinthians 15:50-54 and is used by most preachers when they give their funeral services. It is all part of the traditions of men to stay within their denominational teaching, which is required of them. To hear their sermon is like a make believe story, although Solomon and many other teachers within the Bible have told us not to be ignorant and Paul also wrote about this in, I Thess. 4:13.

I Thessalonians 4:13 "But I would not have you to be ignorant, brethren, concerning them which are asleep [dead], that ye sorrow not, even as other which have no hope."

This subject was also written by Solomon in Ecclesiastes, when these flesh bodies are dead, and decayed, the soul and spirit are taken by God instantly back to our Heavenly Father. To know this is to have wisdom and knowledge, However, to turn your back and pretend that a dead person is out there in a hole in the ground, is like being a heathen *"which has no hope."* Jesus Christ died and rose from the dead, and His resurrection is our hope. At death we go to where He is, in heaven at the right hand of the Father. God always repeats himself time and time again through out His word. The Bible proves it's self through out the entire Bible.

II Corinthians 5:7, 8; *"For we walk by faith, not by sight:" "We are confident, I say, and willing rather to be absent from the body, and to be present with the Lord."*

Paul is telling us, "I cannot see a spiritual body, until we have faced death". God intended our souls to return to our Heavenly Father, and that is the faith that we all must have in Him. Our hope of salvation is to return to God when our flesh bodies dies. Instantly we give up our spiritual life within. We don't have to see it, for God's eternal Word guarantees eternal life to our inner man known as our soul body. It is by faith, we know that when the (tabernacle) of our flesh body dies, then our spiritual body instantly returns to the Father who created it. Flesh and blood can not enter into the Kingdom of Heaven, however, our soul goes to heaven instantly. When the silver thread of life that joined the flesh bodies to the soul bodies are separated. We can see the eternal kingdom of God just as He has promised us.

So why would anyone in Jesus Christ be afraid to face death in the flesh, because at that very moment in time we will pass instantly into the presence of our Savior. God placed each of us here on earth for a purpose. God expects us to plant His seeds of truth, and promote the gospel of Jesus Christ. In God's given time, every soul will be removed from their physical body, and will be returned back to Him. He placed our bodies here on earth and He will retrieve our soul bodies. People who commit suicide has committed murder in the eyes of God, that's Satan's method of destroying mankind.

There are divisions in paradise, the place where the inner body goes when the flesh body dies, recorded in the parables of Jesus in Luke.

Luke 16:26 *"And beside all this, between us and you there is a great gulf fixed: so that they which would pass from hence to you cannot neither can they pass to us, that would come from thence."*

When Lazarus died, he went to the *"bosom of Abraham with God."* The rich man, on the other hand, died and went to the other side of the gulf that separated them from God and those He saved. Yes, all souls upon death return to the Father; however, for those who didn't choose God's ways in this earth age will be in a place of holding until their final time of judgment. There are two sides with a great gulf between them, for the saved and the unsaved, those under the blood of Christ and those that did not give honor to Our Father nor his son, Jesus Christ.

With passages like I Thessalonians 4:14-17 the unlearned church has created their stories of false hope through man's tradition. They actually believe that God will go against His own word. Their traditions don't allow their followers to prepare for their end time responsibilities, because of their Rapture doctrines, they have made void the subject of Paul's discussion in verse 4:13. They have inserted their own evil doctrines in verse 14-17. Where by they have been deceived by Satan.

Ezekiel 13:19-21 tells us exactly what our Lord thinks about those who teach His children to fly away, in the latter days, which is known as the Rapture Theory. God hates those Kenites and he will have His punishment upon them after the seventh trumpet sounds. That is why even in ignorance it is very serious, because it gives Christians a sense of false hope, leaving them with no reason to prepare themselves for the final days of this earth age. When the sixth trumpet sounds, God will allow Satan and his fallen angels to torment those who leave themselves open to follow Satan because of their ignorance and that is sad because, God has died for them.

Revelation 9:4,5 *"And it was commanded them that they should not hurt the grass of the earth, neither any green thing, neither any tree; but only those men which have not the seal of God in their foreheads." "And to them it was given that they should not kill them, but that they should be tormented five months: and their torment was as the torment of a scorpion, when he striketh a man."*

When a scorpion strikes a man, he is defenseless against Satan. That little bug has complete control over his victim and there is nothing that can be done for him. That's what happens if you follow the rapture doctrines, and any other doctrine of demons that goes against the Word of God. God told us to prepare ourselves by knowing these things recorded within the word of God. We must know or be sealed with His truths in our minds and put on our spiritual armor so we can be protected from deception and spiritual destruction. This is why this book was written to you.

LAST TRUMP
Chapter 15

Most Christian Churches today seem to be void of this topic. They don't want to study or discuss what this scripture is teaching us about the seventh trumpet. Every time a funeral takes place, the preacher takes I Corinthians 15:50-54 completely out of context and I Thessalonians 4:14-17 is even more off track. Yet through Paul's writings, we are given full understanding of death, and the seventh trumpet.

I Corinthians 15:50-52 *"Now I say brethren, that flesh and blood cannot inherit the kingdom of God; neither doth corruption inherit incorruption." "Behold, I shew you a mystery; We shall not all sleep, but we shall all be changed," "In a moment, in the twinkling of an eye, at the last trump: for the trumpet shall sound, and the dead shall be raised incorruptible, and we shall be changed."*

Paul spent the first 49 verses of this chapter teaching the believers the difference between the two bodies that each of us were composed of when we are born into our flesh bodies at birth. The two separate bodies are: the flesh body called the corruptible body; and the second is a soul and spirit body that lives within our flesh body is called the incorruptible body. Every one of us is made up of both corruptible and incorruptible bodies, while we're living in our flesh body. Our flesh body needs food, we can drive a car, get married and have children then as our body ages, it will die. Our spirit and soul bodies will continue to live when it returns into heaven after our flesh body dies.

Then Paul told us clearly that these flesh corruptible bodies simply can not enter the kingdom of God known as Jesus Christ's kingdom. Jesus Christ's kingdom will come to this earth when He returns to rule His kingdom in the Millennium Kingdom. There are no flesh bodies on earth because everyone has been changed into their spirit bodies until Jesus returns.

Paul is now revealing a mystery that has been hidden since the foundations of this earth age. This mystery is revealing, that there is a time coming when there will be no more death nor [sleep] on earth. There will be no death, because in an instant at God's set time, all people living in their flesh bodies, will be changed from these flesh corruptible bodies, into their soul bodies, known as their spirit bodies like the angels have. Every living person will be in their incorruptible body with full knowledge of what's right and wrong because the laws of God are implanted in their minds. Think of it, everybody will be living in the next thousand years of the Millennium and will not age one day, and there will be no sickness. Satan will be in the pit and the demons will be in their place of holding; while we will be with our loved ones for a thousand years before the *"Judgment Day"*.

Paul told us what will happen *"in a moment"*, faster than you can wink your eye. *"At the last trumpet"* When the seventh trumpet sounds, instantly at God's set time, our flesh bodies will be gone, and every living soul will be in their spiritual bodies like the angels have. This establishes the truth that Jesus Christ comes at the seventh trumpet, and everyone on the face of the earth will see him in their incorruptible bodies. So if any one claims to be Jesus Christ before the true Jesus Christ comes at the seventh trumpet and you're are still in your flesh body, you will know that he is the false Christ, known as Satan. He will come first, at the sixth trumpet, with all of his fallen angle's, and will rule the earth for 3½ months before the true Messiah arrives at the seventh trumpet.

I Corinthians 15:53,54 *"For this corruptible must put on incorruption, and this mortal must put on immortality." "So when this corruptible shall have put on incorruption, and this mortal shall have put on immortality, then shall be brought* *to pass the saying that is written, "Death is swallowed up in victory."*

The word *"mortal"* means *"liable to die"*. Simple logic tells us that in these flesh bodies, each of us will see death at some time in our life. Some die by accidents, sickness, while others will die because of their old age that's life as we know it. However, when the seventh trumpet sounds, there will be no more death, for those soul bodies are like the angels have, they will never die except on *"Judgment Day"*. Those who rejected God, will sent into hell fire with Satan. They will be destroyed for ever, never to be thought of again.

Now you know exactly what happens to those flesh bodies who followed Satan, at the sound of the sixth trumpet when Satan comes. We're told in Revelation 9:5 that Satan will be here on earth for five months, then that seventh trumpet sounds. Those who sold their soul to be with Satan will only live for 5 months. There is no rapture!

Another false tradition concerning their rapture doctrine falls apart with you including all the verses that Paul gave concerning the subject of I Thessalonians 4:13-17. The church world today likes to read verse 14, but they skip verse 13, and by changing a few words here and there, they claim to have support for their rapture doctrine.

I Thessalonians 4:1 *"But I would not have you to be ignorant, brethren, concerning them which are asleep, that ye sorrow not, even as other which have no hope."*

The next five verses lays the foundation to what is called the "Rapture theory", which is a faults doctrine. As we study this part of Father's Word, set aside your preconceived ideas regarding the rapture theory, open your eyes to see what Paul is trying to tell the Thessalonians. When you hold on to a theory for your salvation, rather than the Word of God, you have fallen into quick sand with no hope of getting out.

After Paul told these Thessalonians to live right in their community, and search their souls for sin in their lives; they were told to repent of their sins. Paul moved right into the next subject, what happens when death comes to his flesh body? This topic is important to Paul, because it is the stabilizing factor for our Christian life. It removes the fear that comes from not knowing about what happens after death. Paul gives this information for one reason is so that we're not ignorant like the heathen's are. In other words, Paul doesn't want Christians to be stupid about what happens after death occurs.

This concern is about, *"them which are asleep"* that means, passed away in death. This gives hope to the ones that are left behind when their loved one has died, and gone to be with the Lord. Paul is telling us that we should not be concerned for those Christian's who have died, for we have hope, unlike the heathen that have no hope. The heathen's fear comes from their ignorance of God's Word and His promises. The heathen have no hope, for they believe that life is over at the burial, and their body and soul is still buried in the ground.

I Thessalonians 4:14 "*For if we believe that Jesus died and rose again, even so them also which sleep in Jesus will God bring with Him.*"

Christ set the example for us when He arose after the third day, so that we would follow just as He did, by dying, and rising again. The term "*to sleep"* refers to the believers' spirit bodies that has instantly left their flesh bodies when they pass away. The Greek text is a simple language, for it's structure allows us to be more precise. The subject of this verse is; "*that ye not be ignorant as to where the dead are.*" If you are a true Christian then you believe in the death burial and resurrection of Jesus Christ and that Jesus Christ came out of the tomb after three days. If you do not believe this, Paul classifies you ignorant just like, the heathens or non-believers.

When Jesus ascended into heaven, all the souls with spiritual bodies that had passed away prier, were taken up into heaven with Jesus Christ. Their will be many souls living in their spiritual bodies, that refused the truth of God's word while they lived in their flesh bodies. They will be placed on the other side of the Gulf that separates believers from those who chose to be ignorant, they will have to wait for the time of judgment, while believers will instantly go to be with God right after their death. Those that sleep [are spiritually dead] but they are not out there in a hole in the ground, because all Christians must believe that their spiritual body will arise to be with the Father, just like Christ did. All true Christians know that those who have died in their flesh bodies are still living in their spiritual bodies with God in heaven today where as unbelievers are sent over to the other side of the Gulf.

Ecclesiastes 12:7 *"To be absent from the body [flesh body] is to be present with the Lord."*

I Thessalonians 4:15 *"For we say unto you, by the word of Our Lord, that we which are alive and remain unto the coming of the Lord shall not prevent in no wise* [precede] *them which are asleep."*

We read at the beginning of this chapter what takes place at the coming of our Lord. All flesh is done away with, and these corruptible flesh bodies are changed instantly into their new incorruptible bodies. Paul is reminding the Thessalonians and those living in our generation; that it's impossible to precede anyone into heaven that has already died, because they are already there. At death, the soul leaves the body and returns to the Father instantly. However some people cannot accept the truth, so they chose to believe in soul sleep at death. They believe that their soul and sprit bodies, are buried in the grave until the return of Christ. Only heathen's believe that, according to the scripture, in I Corinthians 15:50-54 were told that this change comes at the seventh trumpet when all flesh is done away with. That's the gospel truth.

We know that the kingdom of God is wherever Christ is. At the seventh trumpet, Christ will be here on earth with His saints, and setting up His 1000 year Millennium Kingdom. If there was such a thing as the rapture and you think you're going to go where Christ is, and that is place is right here on earth according to scripture. This is where the Millennium will take place. However, it will be in a different dimension because the things of this earth age will be gone. When the seventh trumpet sounds, it is the time for all souls to be, *"gathered back to Christ."* We will all be changed into our spiritual bodies' right here on this earth, instantly when Christ returns to earth. So there can not be a rapture!

I Thessalonians 4:16 "For the Lord Himself shall descend from heaven with a shout, with a voice of the archangel, and with the trumpet of God: and the dead in Christ shall rise first:"

The dead in Christ will rise first to be with Him because they are already with Christ. At death, they went to be with the Lord. They are the saints that are returning with Jesus for that thousand year period. Jesus made it very clear in the book of Revelation all about the events that would take place before His coming. They are all given in the gospels the night before he was taken to be crucified. Jesus let us know in Revelation 11 that He would have His two witnesses on earth during the time of Satan's rule, and that they would be killed and lay in the court yard in Jerusalem for three and a half days.

All this information was been given to us by Jesus Christ, through his disciples and prophets, to prepare us for the time that we are living in today. It shouldn't scare you, because God will protect His believers. They are saved by Grace, however, if you choose to follow the Traditions of men, then God told us in Revelation 9:5, that He will allow them to be completely ignorant of what is going on for their own protection. It will be by their works in the Millennium that they will be saved and then their name will be written in the Lamb's book of Life, however all of the true Christians who's name is written in the book of life were already saved by Grace. No one can choose for you. We all must make our own choice, either to. "*study to show our self approved unto God* "or follow the traditions of men and work it out in the Millennium. When you bow to the first Christ who comes, he is Satan the great deceiver. Millions of Christians have already made their decision to be part of the tribulation church of Revelation 17. Because no one has told them that Satan will come first.

The name, Antichrist is another name of Satan. He wants people to follow him and he will fly you wherever you want to go. He will set you up in business, fill you with pride and fame, and the best pension plan you have ever had, because Satan knows that he has only has five months to live. Remember all Satan wants is your soul.

I Thessalonians 4:17 "*Then we which are alive and remain shall be caught up together with them in the clouds, to meet the Lord in the air: and so shall we ever be with the Lord.*"

Now stop and think! If we're alive when that seventh trumpet sounds, when Jesus comes back to earth to set up His Millennium Kingdom here on earth. This *"cloud"* is a crowd of Saints who are coming with Jesus to this earth. If we are going to "*meet Him in the air*", we are going to meet him in our, "Spiritual" bodies. At Jesus' return, we will meet Him in our Incorruptible body that has been changed instantly from the corruptible flesh body into a body like the angels have.

There is no fly-away doctrine, except in the minds of those who have been deceived because they listened to false prophets. There is no way to avoid Satan when he plays the role of Jesus Christ. Jesus Christ expects His Elect and those sealed with His truth in their minds to wake up and make a stand during that time of "*The Great Tribulation*".

When Paul gave this instruction, it was to comfort one another with the fact that their loved ones that had died are with the Lord.

TWO WITNESSES IN THE LAST DAYS.

The two witnesses have a mission to perform for our Heavenly Father and they will finish their testimony against Satan, and the beast from the bottomless pit. These two witnesses are called the *"Two Olive Trees,"* as well as the *"Two Candle Sticks,"* and they will let their light shine in this wicked world during that time of *"The Great Deception"* for that entire time. God will protect each of them and if anyone will try to harm them, fire will come out of their mouth, and will kill those that would plot against them. These two witnesses will shut up the heavens so that it could not rain during their time of prophecy and they will bring plagues down upon the earth whenever it is necessary for their protection.

Think about it, the things that everybody expects Satan to do, these two witnesses will be doing, and the things that people think the witnesses will do, is being done by Satan. If you follow the traditional thought of the church world today, they both will play the opposite role, rather than what is being taught in most church houses.

Revelation 11:7,8 *"And when they shall have finished their testimony, the beast that ascendeth out of the bottomless pit shall make war against them, and shall overcome them, and kill them." "And their dead bodies shall lie in the street of the great city, which spiritually is called Sodom and Egypt, where also our Lord was crucified."*

The entire world will rejoice over the death of these two witnesses. The location of this is in Jerusalem that is, *"where our Lord was crucified."*

Satan and his fallen angels are the seven thousand that were released from the bottomless pit, and when Satan takes the credit for killing God's witnesses, the people of all nations, tongues and races will praise him and worship him as God.

Revelation 11:9 *"And they of the people and kindreds and tongues and nations shall see their dead bodies three days and an half, and shall not suffer their dead bodies to be put in graves."*

According to the scripture, God's two wittiness' has to be Enoch and Elisha because they are the only two men of God that has never died in their flesh bodies. We know that Moses' body was buried because God himself buried his body and took his spirit into heave. These two men will have the power to pull fire down form heaven, and doing many other spiritual acts. Most people hated them for spreading the truth of God's word, and displaying the wrath of Almighty God where ever they went. While most of the people were worshiping Satan as their God, because he was giving them wealth and prosperity, and God's two witnesses were showing God's anger about it all. The two witnesses stood on the corners of the earth and insulted those fallen Christian's who called Satan their messiah while the entire world worshipped Satan.

Revelation 11:10,11 *"And they that dwell upon the earth shall rejoice over them, and make merry, and shall send gifts one to another; because these two prophets tormented them that dwelt on the earth." "And after three and an half* [days] *the spirit* [breath] *of life from God entered into them, and they stood upon their feet; and great fear fell upon them which saw them."*

If you' re not one of the Elect and sealed in your mind with the truth, you will be one of those who will be celebrating at this time. Most Christians will actually look upon God's two witnesses as their enemies. Remember their minds are closed to the truth, and they will not be opened until after Christ has returned at the seventh trumpet. That time will be very short lived, because 3½ days later, life comes back into these two witnesses, and immediately a paralyzing fear will come over everyone who saw it.

Remember after this world event in Jerusalem takes place, when God's two witness' that all the whole world hates, were dead for three and a half days, then life entered their dead bodies. That is instant that God ends this second earth age of mankind.

Revelation 11:12,13 *"And they heard a great voice from heaven saying unto them [the two witnesses], Come up hither. And they ascended up to heaven in a cloud; and their enemies beheld them." "And the same hour was there a great earthquake, and the tenth part of the city fell, and in the earthquake were slain of men seven thousand: and the remnant were affrighted, and gave glory to the God of heaven."*

Just like child birth, the pangs are one right after the other. That's how quickly the events will be when these witnesses are ascending into heaven. Seven thousand fallen angels that Satan brought with him out of the bottomless pit will be gone instantly into the pit along with Satan. That instant before the seventh trumpet sounds and mankind is changed from their flesh bodies into their spiritual incorruptible bodies, and people will know exactly what is taking place.

Revelation 11:14,15 *"The second woe is past; and behold, the third woe cometh quickly." "And the seventh angel sounded; and there were great voices in heaven, saying. The Kingdoms of the world are become the kingdoms of our Lord, and of His Christ; and He shall reign for ever and ever."*

As the world is in fear, the Elect of God [the remnant] will see all this as a day of rejoicing. Think of it, faster than you can wink your eye, you will be in your spiritual incorruptible body and rejoicing and giving God the glory along with the rest of the saints that came with Jesus. What we have just discussed here, is given many times in the Scripture, and this is why you must be aware of what is going to happen at the sixth and seventh trumpet. Once you become aware that there is no rapture, then that is the time to prepare your self by knowing *"The Seven Seals"* in your minds.

That is your protection when the seventh trumpet sounds. Those seals are given in the order of importance, as the trumpets are sounded giving the command to carry out the order from God. Each event that happens will happen at God's set time, and not one moment before. This is why Paul warned us in Thessalonians.

II Thessalonians 2:1,2 *"Now we beseech you, brethren, by the coming of our Lord Jesus Christ, and by our gathering together unto him," "That ye be not soon shaken in mind, or be troubled, neither by spirit, nor by letter as from us, as that the day of Christ is at hand."*

Paul did not want any of the Elect to misunderstand the order that these events would take place. When you see these things taking place, you will know exactly when Jesus Christ will return! Because It's all part of the plan of God and He is in full control. Don't be worried about it all. We are in the last generation and many of us will be part of what we are writing about.

II Thessalonians 2:3,4 *"Let no man deceive you by any means: for that day shall not come, except there come a falling away first, and the man of sin be revealed, the son of perdition." "Who opposeth and exalteth himself above all that is called God, or that is worshipped; so that he* [Satan] *as God sitteth in the temple of God, shewing himself that he is God."*

Satan is known as *"the son of perdition"* he will be sitting on his throne in Jerusalem just before the seventh trumpet sounds. He will kill God's two witnesses and declared himself to be God, and then the entire Christian Church world will have committed the *"abomination of desolation"* because the *"Communion Table"* has been removed from the churches and their active followers will think that our Lord Jesus Christ is here with them. *"The Great Deception"* is going on today as they are setting up new laws in order to receive Satan as their God, which will be the false Jesus Christ. We're fighting a spiritual war fare today, and most people know something is wrong, but they don't know what the bible tells us about it. That's why this book has be written this book, so you will know God's truth.

Once the seventh trumpet sounds, then all seven vials are poured out upon the earth at the same time. These seven vials of Revelation 16 are the cup of God's wrath coming upon the earth instantly as this second earth age of mankind ends, is when the seventh trump sounds. As you read through these seven vials that these seven angels bring, each vial is part of God's cup of wrath that Jesus spoke of when He was in the Garden of Gethsemane the night before His crucifixion.

Matthew 26:39 *"And he went a little further, and fell on his face, and prayed, saying, O my Father, if it be possible, let this cup pass from me: nevertheless not as I will, but as thou wilt.*

Jesus came into this world to fulfill the will of our Heavenly Father, and Redeem lost souls back to the Father. The choice of receiving the gift of Salvation is up to each individual. Yet right up to the very last instant in time, the Lord's clock is set, and right up to this last pouring out of the vials of the cup of wrath onto the earth, every single event will occur right at God's set time. He has written this letter to us, called the Bible and has revealed every event that will happen to us. It is up to us to study to show ourselves approved unto God and rightly divide the Word of God. Our references are listed in the back of this book.

Aaron and his sons went into the holy place of the Sanctuary, and this book of Numbers tells us what those assigned duties were. This is talking about the first Vail in the main Sanctuary, and about the second Vail, leading into the Holy of holies.

Hebrews 9:7 *"But into the second [Holy of holies] went the high priest alone once every year, not without blood, which he offered for himself, and for the errors of the People."*

The High Priest went into the Holy of holies once each year to sacrifice first for his own sins, and then for the sins of the people. When the High Priest entered into the Holy of holies he entered with the blood of goats and calves that was to be the sacrifice. This blood was temporary because it was an example of the blood of our Lord Jesus Christ that became the perfect and unblemished sacrifice, when He died on the cross for our sins, much later.

Hebrews 9:8,9 *"The Holy Ghost this signifying, that the way into the Holiest of all was not yet made manifest, while as the first tabernacle was yet standing:" "Which was a figure for the time then present, in which were offered both gifts and sacrifices, that could not make him that did the service perfect, as pertaining to the conscience;"*

When we come under the blood of Christ through our repentance in Jesus name, we enter into the Holy of holies, into the place where we are in the presents of our Heavenly Father. The Holy Spirit has taught us the way that we can approach the holiest of all places that wasn't made known in the time of Moses. It was not known until the death and resurrection of our Lord Jesus Christ. When that first tabernacle was still in place, the only way to approach the Father was under the first covenant, through animal sacrifices made by the High Priest. However, with the coming of Christ, His body became our inner tabernacle. Only through the workings of Jesus Christ, the Holy Spirit, and faith, believing in repentance can take the guilt from your conscience, through the blood of Jesus Christ.

Hebrews 9:10 *"Which stood only in meats and drinks, and divers washings, and carnal ordinances, imposed on them until the time of reformation."*

Only though those rites and ceremonies of those meat and drink offerings, and the washings, could these coverings for sin be practiced; until the time of Christ's crucifixion and resurrection.

Hebrews 9:11,12 *"But Christ being come an High Priest of good things to come, by a greater and more perfect tabernacle, not made with hands, that is to say, not of this building;" "Neither by the blood of goats and calves, but by His own blood He entered in once into the holy place, having obtained eternal redemption for us."*

It was through the blood of Christ at the cross that changed the ways of the Old Covenant to the Way of the New Covenant. Jesus Christ became our High Priest once and for all times. The Vail leading into the Holy of holies was rent in two, and each of us could now approach the throne of God directly, when we place ourselves under the blood of Christ. Our New Tabernacle is now in heaven at the right hand of the Father; and we can enter that tabernacle today. You don't have to wait until Christ comes again. We can enjoy the *"mansions"* of our Heavenly Father's house right here on earth today. However, we are told in Hebrews 9:13:

Hebrews 9:13 *"For if the blood of bulls and of goats, and the ashes of an heifer sprinkling the unclean, sanctifieth to the purifying of the flesh:"*

This is the ordinance statutes of the red heifer that is spoken of in Numbers 19:2. If that sprinkling of the blood of the red heifer could make someone clean back in Moses day; this cleansing lasted for only one year.

Hebrews 9:14 *"How much more shall the blood of Christ, Who through the eternal Spirit offered Himself without spot to God, purge your conscience from dead works to serve the living God?"*

Jesus Christ is the God of the Living, and as we study of the red heifer in Numbers, it is all about the blood of Christ that will be spotless and without blemish. This red heifer was the only way that a person could enter into the Holy of holies for the sin offering in Moses day. The blood of Christ was not offered to the people at the time of Moses, nor in the Old Testament times.

Hebrews 9:15 *"And for this cause He is the Mediator of the new testament, that by means of death, for the redemption of the transgressions that were under the first testament, they which are called might receive the promise of eternal inheritance."*

Our Lord Jesus Christ became the sacrifice by his Precious blood, which was without spot or blemish.

I Peter 1:19-21 *"But with the precious blood of Christ as of a Lamb without blemish and without spot:" "Who verily was foreordained before the foundation of the world, but was manifest in these last times for you," "Who by Him do believe in God, That raised Him up from the dead, and gave Him glory; that your faith and hope might be in God."*

Today we have an antidote that cleanses us from all sin, and our covering for all of our sins is the precious blood of Jesus Christ. The whole purpose of our studies is to allow each of us to understand why we are living here on earth, and where we fit into God's perfect plan. There is work for us to do while we're here on earth, and there is a time when Christ will return and the work of this flesh and blood earth age will be over.

John 14:1-3 *"Let not your heart be troubled; ye believe in God, believe also in Me." "In My Father's house are many mansions: if it were not so, I would have told you. I go to prepare a place for you." "And if I go and prepare a place for you, I will come again and receive you unto Myself; that where I am, there ye may be also."*

The first time Jesus came, He lived a spotless and unblemished life and he was the only perfect sacrifice, but the next time Jesus comes, He will receive all of His believers unto Himself. That is a promise that He gave to those of us who believe in Him. The way in Moses' day was through the sacrifices at the altar, and within the Holy of holies. However, when Jesus died on the cross, that old way was replaced by, and a new way into heaven was established by God. The New Covenant through His Son Jesus Christ. was made for mankind to return to the Father. No man can inter into the presents of the Creator YHVH, except through Jesus Christ.

John 14:12 *"Verily, verily, I say unto you, He that believeth on Me, the works that I do shall he do also; and greater works than these shall he do; because I go unto My Father."*

When Jesus died and rose from the dead, He went directly to set at that right hand of the Father as our advocate; but as He is there with the Father, Jesus told you personally that you can ask anything in His Name [Jesus' Name] and He will give it to you. His third promise from John 14 was that when He goes to the Father, a Comforter would come to warm our hearts, comfort and give us direction to our souls. This comfort and direction comes through the Holy Spirit so that our minds are open to His Word. He not only gave us His promises, but also the understanding of the events of this world age that are in, which is the plan of God. God's Spirit gives us "*peace of mind*" when we come to know God's plan and how we fit into His plan.

John 14:13 *"And whatsoever ye shall ask in My name, that will I do, that the Father may be glorified in the Son."*

This verse is a continuation of the prior verse, whereby Jesus promised us that we shall do greater works after He has gone to be at the right hand of the Father. It's up to us whether we have the peace of mind that only our Savior can give through His Holy Spirit. We don't have to wait on the High priest today to enter into the Holy of holies, because we can live in the mansion God promised today. That mansion is having a peace of mind in Our Heavenly Father and the Lord Jesus Christ. We were given Grace, when the Vail was rent in two at Christ's death, the way was opened for us to have direct access to the throne of God in heaven through prayer.

Stop and think of what a wonderful Father we have, and loving Savior we have in our Lord Jesus Christ. He is there for each of us the moment that we ask Him for help, but those things that are done in Our Lord Jesus' name, are done for us so that Our Heavenly Father will be glorified through Jesus Christ. Keep this in mind as we continue in Volume two of Numbers. Those Old Testament methods of salvation just don't work any more, for the blood of dead animals is not the way. The "Way" the truth and the "Life" that is offered today is only through our Lord Jesus Christ. We don't look to a dead and cremated heifer for our comfort to be released from our sin, because we have our living Savior who has set us free in Him.

As we continue in Numbers 19, and remembering that what we are about to study is an example of God's warning to all of us living in these end times.

Numbers 19:3 *"And ye shall give her* [the red heifer] *unto Eleazar the priest, that he may bring her forth without the camp, and one shall slay her before his face:"*

The word *"her"* that is spoken of here is that old female *"red heifer"* that was to be used as the animal sacrifice. Normally "sin offering" were all done by the High priests. However, because of the limits set on the High priest in Leviticus 21, the High priest were not allowed to approach a dead body of man, animal, nor his own immediate family. Eleazar was not a high priest but was, a priest and the son of Aaron who was chosen to give this sacrifice outside of the camp. Remember that sin offerings, as written in verse seventeen of this chapter, would have been offered in the area of the sanctuary following the customs and instructions for that sin offering.

This female *"red heifer"* was not allowed to be sacrificed in the camp site, and this is to be an ensample for us, because our Lord Jesus Christ was also taken out side the city limits of Jerusalem to the hill of Calvary, and slain there. Notice the parallel running through the scriptures between the Old and New Covenant.

Numbers 19:4 *"And Eleazar the priest shall take of her blood with his finger, and sprinkle of her blood directly before the tabernacle of the congregation seven times:"*

Keep in mind that this sacrifice was outside the camp, yet the blood would be taken on Eleazar's finger and then he would sprinkle blood seven times toward the tabernacle.

Numbers 19:5 *"And one shall burn the* [red] *heifer in his sight; her skin, and her flesh, and her blood, with her dung, shall he burn:"*

This sacrificial burning would not have included all these parts of the animal if the sacrifice was back at the altar of burnt offerings at the tabernacle. Remember that this female, the "red heifer sacrifice" was once used for "the purification of death, or sin". However, our antidote for sin and death today, is through the blood of Christ, for when Jesus blood was shed on the cross, that old Vail was rent in two giving us access directly to the Father today.

Numbers 19:6 *"And the priest shall take cedar wood, and hyssop, and scarlet, and cast it into the midst of the burning of the heifer."*

When you added the cedar wood, the Hyssop and the scarlet in the living water, it would make up *"the water of separation"*. This is what was used to purify one from the uncleanness of death. The *"Cedar wood"* is symbolic of the incorruptible continuance of life. The *"Hyssop"* had many purifying qualities about it, and the "scarlet" was the strongest strength of life, and the scarlet represented the blood of our Lord Jesus Christ.

Numbers 19:7 *"Then the priest shall wash his clothes, and he shall bathe his flesh in water, and afterward he shall come into the camp, and the priest shall be unclean until the even."*

So after Eleazar the priest came in contact with the sin offering, he had to bathe and wash his clothes completely before he was allowed to enter back into the camp.

On the tenth day of the seventh month of each year, the High Priest would enter into the Holy of Holies and make the offering for atonement for the sins of himself and for the people. It was a national holiday. A bullock was offered for the sins of the High Priest first, and then two goats were also selected, one to be sacrificed, and the other to be turned loose into the wilderness. One goat was taken by lot for God, and the other to represent the scapegoat, *"Azazel"* in the Hebrew. This is discussed in Leviticus 16:9-22.

Leviticus 16:9,10 *"And Aaron shall bring the goat upon which the Lord's lot fell, and offer him for a sin offering."* "*But the goat, on which the lot fell to be the scapegoat, shall be* *presented alive before the Lord, to make an atonement with him, and to let him go for a scapegoat into the wilderness."*

"Azazel" is another name for Satan, so you have one goat for the Lord, and one goat for Satan. So the person that would take that scapegoat, the goat that the lot fell on to be released, was laying the sins of the whole congregation on the head of that goat. Then the man would take that sin *"ladened goat"* into the wilderness and left him there far away from the congregation. Symbolically, this act would separate all the sins of the Israelites from the camp and leaving them in the wilderness. So the man that lead the goat into the wilderness was unclean, and had to be bathed and his clothes cleaned. Eleazar became unclean after witnessing the sacrifice of the red heifer, and placing the cedar wood, Hyssop, and Scarlet to the water, to make the water of separation, and placing it on the burnings.

Numbers 19:8 *"And he that burneth her shall wash his clothes in water, and bathe his flesh in water, and shall be clean until the even."*

So the priest, Eleazar, that burneth the red heifer, or anyone that came in contact with the ashes or any part of this sacrifice was to bathe and wash his clothes, and that evening he shall be considered clean again. This act is symbolic of death, but now we will see an example of this next verse nine.

Numbers 19:9 *"And the man that is clean shall gather up the ashes of the* red *heifer, and lay them up without the camp in a clean place, and it shall be kept for the congregation of the children of Israel for a water of separation: it is a purification for sin."*

Keep in mind that the red *"heifer"* was an "antitype" for Jesus Christ. However, who claimed the body of Jesus Christ after His blood was shed and He was taken down off the cross? Remember, these ashes of the red heifer were a type of the blood of Christ.

Joseph of Arimathea was the one who declared himself to have the right to claim the body of Christ. Because Joseph of Arimathea was the rich uncle of Jesus that went to Pilate, and as next of kin, demanded and was given the body of Jesus to prepare for burial. By Roman law, only the next of kin could claim and recover a dead man's body. Joseph of Arimathea was a voting member of the Sanhedrin, and a follower of Christ, and was a very rich uncle of our Lord Jesus Christ. Recorded in Matthew 27:57-60, Luke 23:50-53 and in John 19

This *"water of separation"* that was a "*purification for sin*" from the death sacrifice of the female red heifer is basically a sin offering. It was for the purification for not only death but also for "Sin" because there both are tied together, *for "the wages of sin is death*".

Numbers 19:10 *"And he that gathereth the ashes of the heifer shall wash his clothes, and be unclean until the even: and it shall be unto the children of Israel, and unto the stranger that sojourneth among them, for a statute for ever."*

So this burning of the female red heifer, that was called a *"law statute"* in verse two of this chapter, applied not only to the children of Israel, but to those that were living amongst them at the time that the sacrifice was made.

Numbers 19:11 *"He that toucheth the dead body of any man shall be unclean seven days."*

This is how the "*water of sacrifice or separation*" was to be used when anyone came in contact with the dead. Anyone that touches a dead body of man or animal shall be unclean for seven days. Remember that this law is eternal, even into the Millennium age, after the return of Christ at the seventh trumpet. Ezekiel reminds us of this law even after flesh and blood corruptible bodies are done away with, so this is dealing with the spiritually dead.

Ezekiel 44:25 *"And they shall come at no dead person to defile themselves: but for father, or for mother, or for son, or for daughter, for brother, or for sister that hath had no husband, they may defile themselves."*

This is applied to the Zadok, those who did not bow a knee to Satan as the Christ at the sixth trumpet as they were not Satan's bride. The Just or Zadok knew the truth; they were the Elect that did not bow a knee to Satan. Their family members ran to Satan asking him to save their loved ones. Of course it was all done in ignorance. However, their choice still left their souls spiritually dead at the seven trumpet known as the last trumpet at the coming of Christ. This verse is in the Millennium, when the "Elect" or Zadok are allowed to go to see their loved ones that did not except the truth in the time of Grace. In this age of flesh man we can accept by faith through repentance in Jesus wonderful name. But not when we're in the Millennium age when we're in our Spiritual bodies, because it's too late. The Elect can urge their relatives to pay attention and follow their works according to the ways God has planed for them to do.

Ezekiel 44:26 *"And after he is cleansed, they shall reckon unto him seven days."*

After the Zadok came into contact with their unclean relatives, they can not enter back into the tabernacle of God where Jesus is for seven days. In this new Millennium age we're in our Spiritual bodies, and those who rejected Jesus Christ will have another chance to change their minds. The Elect will teach them and help their relatives to accept Jesus Christ as their personal savior, in hopes to save their souls.

Ezekiel 44:27 *"And in the day that he goeth into the sanctuary, unto the inner court, to minister in the sanctuary, he shall offer his sin offering, saith the Lord God."*

Remember that the blood of lambs and goats was done away with when Christ's died on the cross. Our sin offering then became our belief and acceptance in the new way. That New Way, is our acceptance through repentance in Jesus Name, for when we pray in Jesus Name, we are telling God that Jesus is the only begotten Son of the YHVH our Heavenly Father and that Jesus was perfect with unblemished blood who became the sacrifice for our sins.

So in the Millennium age of Jesus Christ's Kingdom here on earth, all the things of this earth age of flesh man is over and done away with. They simply don't exist here on earth or in the minds of mankind. Because all Souls will be changed back into their incorruptible bodies like the angels have, yet many will still have mortal, or liable to die soul bodies. In this thousand years of testing, all souls will know the truths from God's Word and exactly what is expected of them. Then at the close of this thousand year Millennium age, comes the "G*reat White Throne Judgment*".

Revelation 20:11,12 *"And I saw a great white throne, and Him that sat on it, from whose face the earth and the heaven fled away; and there was found no place for them." "And I saw the dead, small and great, stand before God; and the books were opened: and another book was opened, which is the book of life: and the dead were judged out of those things which were written in the books, according to their works."*

At the close of the Millennium age, when the dead, are those souls in their incorruptible bodies, that lived through the Millennium that were not part of the first resurrection of the coming of Christ at the seventh trumpet will stand before God. Each of their acts from the Millennium age will be recorded in either "*the book of life, or the books."*

Revelation 20:13 *"And the sea gave up the dead which were in it; and death and hell delivered up the dead which* *were in them: and they were judged every man according to their works."*

Works of righteousness from this age of flesh man go to make up your fine linens, clean and white that you will be wearing throughout eternity. However, the works of the souls through out the Millennium age, will be in the final Judgment, their souls will either go to hell or eternity at that time.

Revelation 20:14 *"And death and hell were cast into the lake of fire. This is the second death." "And whosoever was not found written in the book of life was cast into the lake of fire."*

Although we have strayed somewhat from Numbers, it's time to emphasize that when our Lord says that a law is eternal, that is exactly what He meant. Even though this second earth will change, and the form that our souls will exist in, remember the laws that govern our relationships with our Eternal Creator do not change. Sin separates YHVH our Heavenly Father from mankind even when they have been changed into spirit bodies, it is important that we come back into righteousness with God.

The penalty for touching the unclean in Moses and Aaron's day was bathing and separation for seven days. This applies to God's elect even in the Millennium age, where God's elect would not be able to go back into the Millennial Temple where Jesus is, until they have bathed, and waited for seven days.

Numbers 19:12 *"He shall purify himself with it on the third day, and on the seventh day he shall be clean: but if he purify not himself the third day, then the seventh day he shall not be clean."*

This person that handled the ashes of the heifer or the scapegoat shall be first purified by the water of separation on the third day, and then on the seventh day, he is declared by God to be clean. However, if that priest or person is not purified by this water of separation on their third day, then even on the seventh day he still shall be declared unclean. Three in biblical numeric is for "*Divine Completeness*"; the Father, the Son, and the Holy Spirit. Seven is "*Spiritual Completeness*".

Numbers 19:13 *"Whosoever toucheth the dead body of any man that is dead, and purifieth not himself, defileth the tabernacle of the Lord; and that soul shall be cut off from Israel: because the water of separation was not sprinkled upon him, he shall be unclean; his uncleaness is yet upon him."*

This sacrifice was absolute in Moses' day, and the only way that we can be purified today from death and sin is through the blood of our Lord Jesus Christ. Whether out here in the wilderness with the children of Israel, or today in our church houses, or in the Millennium tabernacle of the age to come of Christ's Kingdom here on earth; no man can defile the tabernacle of the Lord and be part of the children of God. We have got to respect the ways that God has set up for us to approach Him. All other ways will end in death, spiritual death and separation. The Tabernacle of the Lord is where our Lord dwells. At this point in time, God is dwelling with man from the Ark of the Covenant; in the Holy of holies, and in a tent called the tabernacle. If someone of the priesthood did not cleanse themselves by this method, then they were not fit to approach the tabernacle and their presence would have defiled the sanctuary of God.

Our Lord is Holy death and anything related to death is sin. This red heifer was the means whereby a person could be purified. Today our means for purification is to approach the Father through the blood of our Lord Jesus Christ. Being cut off from Israel is just as severe as being cut off from fellowship with the many members of the body of our Lord Jesus and His Church. No, we don't have to go through all the ritual that Moses and the Israelites had to go through for repentance, for we can go directly to the Father, under the blood of Christ for repentance and fellowship with our Lord. Once we repent of our sins, we are clean at that moment in time and we can come into His presence in heaven.

However, when you do not repent, it is the same thing as when these early Israelites refused to bathe themselves in the water of separation. It is an act of choosing; you bathe or you do not bathe; you repent in Jesus Name, or you do not repent in His name.

There is only one way to reach God the Father, that is under the blood of Jesus Christ.

God's Way is under the blood of Jesus Christ, in the name of Jesus.

Numbers 19:17 *"And for an unclean person they shall take of the ashes of the burnt heifer of purification for sin, and running water shall be put thereto in a vessel:"*

So if any person has come in contact with the dead, they must take the ashes of the Burnt heifer of purification from sin, and these ashes and fresh running water shall be put into this clean vessel. The Living Water today is our Lord Jesus Christ, and His blood is the covering for our sins, just as these burnt ashes of the red heifer were used for the covering for mankind's sin's. This Living Water is also specified in Leviticus 14:8,9 and was used for the purification for Leprosy.

Exodus 12:22 *"And ye shall take a bunch of Hyssop, and dip it in the blood that is in the bason, and stike the lintel and the two side posts with the blood that is in the bason; and none of you shall go out at the door of his house until the morning."*

That night when the death angel passed over Egypt, those firstborn that were in their homes, and under the blood that was dipped by this Hyssop, were not slain. Hyssop was a very important part of the purification process in that first Passover, as they dipped the Hyssop into the blood bason, and painted blood over the top of the door and on the sides of the door post of their homes so that the death angle of the Lord could pass over God's people. Read more about *Hyssop*, see page 259 of *"Smith's Bible Dictionary"*.

The death angel passed over the firstborn at the first Passover, and Christ defeated death and became our Passover when He shed His blood at the cross. Today we celebrate Passover when we take the bread and wine of the communion table, "In remembrance of His body and blood." We do it because God's told his disciples and followers to do it in remembrance of Him, until He comes at the seventh trumpet. His is one of the most sacred day of the year, and Easter the sun goddess has nothing to do with it.

Numbers 19:19 *"And the clean person shall sprinkle upon the unclean on the third day, and on the seventh day: and on the seventh day he shall purify himself, and wash his clothes, and bathe himself in water, and shall be clean at even."*

If they were unclean, they would be kept outside the camp because it would defile the camp. The Lord resided with the people inside the tabernacle. So again, after the purification process took place for the sins of the people, and the person that was involved with the sacrifice process had bathed and been clean for seven days, he could enter the camp as a clean person that evening. Modern Churches should remember this when they invite the heathen goddess into their church on this Holy day.

Numbers 19:20 *"But the man that shall be unclean, and shall not purify himself, that soul shall be cut off from among the congregation, because he hath defiled the sanctuary of the Lord: the water of separation hath not been sprinkled upon him; he is unclean."*

The sanctuary today is in heaven, for where ever the Lord is, there the sanctuary is also. Today we are to wash our sins in the blood of Christ, and those that have not washed their sins in the blood of Christ is unclean before God. That soul is spiritual dead when their sins remain in them. It is very important to tend to our spiritual matters while there is time to take those sins, and wash them through repentance in Jesus Name. The Holy Spirit is here with us now and the Word of God is open to those that will seek the truths from it. However there is a time coming shortly when you can seek the truth and you just will not find it. You may wonder why the answer is written in Amos 8:11**.**

Amos 8:*11* *"Behold, the days come, saith the Lord God, that I will send a famine in the land, not a famine of bread, nor a thirst for water, but of hearing the word of the Lord:"*

Amos 8:12 *"And they shall wander from sea to sea, and from the north even to the east, they shall run to and fro to seek the word of the Lord, and shall not fine it."*

Now is the time to seek the truth and accept Jesus Christ as your personal Savior, and wash your sins away under the blood of Christ, and receive eternal life. In the eons and ages of time, our life of 70 years is less that a wink of the eye in time compared to eternity. To discard this eternal bliss for a few things of this flesh life is complete ignorance.

Numbers 19:21 *"And it shall be a perpetual statute unto them, that he that sprinkleth the water of separation shall wash his clothes; and he that toucheth the water of separation shall be unclean until even."*

This verse then is a perpetual statute to all those that have sinned, have touched the dead and things pertaining to the dead. When you have sinned, the way to reclaim your righteousness before God and become clean was through the offering of this water of separation, bathing and washing of your clothes; and if you choose not to do those things you were unclean before God and His people.

We have all sinned and come short of the glory of God, and to wash our sins through the blood of Christ is to make ourselves right before God, and when a person refuses to do so, than that person shall be unclean before God,

Numbers 19:22 *"And whatsoever the unclean person toucheth shall be unclean; and the soul that toucheth it shall be unclean until even."*

This law pertains to all types of uncleanness. When a person touches anything unclean they are unclean, which was different than when a person touch a dead body, or grave. So here in chapter nineteen the *"red heifer"* was the type for the coming Christ, and the fact that the wages of sin is death, and the antidote for sin at that time, was in the ashes of the red heifer, and the water of purification. Today we have a better antidote than the blood of any animal, and we read this in Hebrews 9 that the blood of our Lord Jesus Christ was not for just a year, but for eternity. With God's own blood, He paid the price on the cross once and for all times. If you except Jesus Christ as your personal savior while your living in Grace, your soul is saved for eternity.

MILLENNIUM AGE
Chapter 16

When we enter into the Millennium age, there will be no flesh bodies according to I Corinthians 15:50-54. *When the seventh trumpet sounds, Satan and the fallen an*gels are confined to the pit where they will be waiting for their final destruction. Armageddon and Magog will never happen. Because when the Seventh Trumpet sounds, they will end instantly as all flesh bodies are changed into spirit bodies. The evil ones will go into the pit with Satan instantly and those who worshipped our Lord Jesus Christ will enter the New Millennium age, where many things are going to change.

Ezekiel chapters 40-43 gives us details and measurements of Jerusalem and the temple that will exist at that time. The lands that will be allotted to each tribe as well as the Gentile nations. Every living soul will be in their incorruptible body, like angels. Then God will place within everyone's mind, the laws that He expects His children to follow. Those that were deceived by Satan during the sixth trumpet and took his name and number will be assigned their lots and each person will do the work that is assigned to them.

Revelation 20:11-15 tells us that at the "*Great white throne judgment*" occurs following the thousand year Millennium, Satan will be released for a brief season, just like in this earth age and will go out to deceive many. Most preachers today stay away from teaching the Millennium Kingdom of our Lord Jesus Christ. Much of the word is cloudy to them because Traditions of Men have covered up the truths written in the Word of God.

This chapter teach us what the different types of *"over comers,"* will be doing in the Millennium age.

The <u>first</u> ones are those who fell short of Christ's mark, because they didn't study to obtain the knowledge of the Word of God in their minds, which left them in ignorance. They chased after the Antichrist and took his name and number. They will be discipline and taught for 1000 years in the Millennium age.

The <u>second</u> are the priests, or ministers that ultimately came into the truth, but it is too late for them because the Millennium age had already come to pass. There will be discipline and taught for 1000 years in the Millennium age.

The <u>third</u> are those who stood against the Antichrist, and his system they will be allowed to approach our Lord in the Millennium. They are called the elect or Zadok and are already in God's Eternal family, Ezekiel, 42-48. They will serve Jesus Christ in the Temple of God. They will be able to leave the temple to minister God's word to their relation, however, once they leave the presents of Christ. They will have to be cleansed for seven days before they can go back into the presents of Jesus Christ in the temple of God. They are not allowed to touch any of those living out side of the temple.

The <u>fourth</u> are Christian's with free will who lived and died in the flesh age of Grace, before the antichrist comes at the sixth trumpet. When they died in the flesh they knew instantly all of God's plan. They are not in the Millennium age, because they and are locked up in heaven and everyone is in their spiritual, or incorruptible bodies.

The Millennium age is only for those who need to be taught and those who will be teaching. All people living during the time of the Antichrist; who stood against Satan, as well as those who were deceived will be present in the Millennium. We will be there along with Jesus Christ the Messiah, the true Son of the Living God; and the Prince King David.

We will see that God's *"Elect"* the *Zadok* are those who stood against Satan in the first earth age, as well as making their stand in *"The Great Tribulation"*. These Elect that were not deceived by the Antichrist in this flesh age will also be discussed in this chapter. The time that this Millennium period begins is spoken of by Paul in I Corinthians 15:50-54. That moment in time is when all flesh will be done away with and people will be changed from their flesh bodies into their incorruptible bodies for a thousand years. This change will be "*in the twinkling of an eye*". Ezekiel 44 begins after our Lord Jesus Christ has arrived on earth, and sets His feet down on the Mount of Olives.

Ezekiel 44:1 *"Then he brought me back the way of the gate of the outward sanctuary which looketh toward the east; and it was shut."*

When our Lord Jesus Christ arrives on the Mount of Olives and walks through the east gate into the Sanctuary; the gate will be shut and locked after His entry.

Ezekiel 44:2 *"Then said the LORD unto me; "This gate shall be shut, it shall not be opened, and no man shall enter in by it; because the LORD, the God of Israel, hath entered in by it, therefore it shall be shut."*

The east gate is closed. We are not talking about eternity. Were talking about the east gate of the Millennium Temple in this verse.

Ezekiel 44:3 *"It is for the prince; the prince, he shall sit in it to eat bread before the LORD; he shall enter by the way of the porch of that gate, and shall go out by the way of the same."*

This east gate is for the Prince of Israel, and his identification is given by Ezekiel. In Ezekiel 34:24; this Prince is King David. David is the only Prince that can use the east gate.

Ezekiel 44:4 *"Then brought he me the way of the north gate before the house: and I looked, and, behold, the glory* *of the LORD filled the house of the LORD, and I fell on my face."*

Our Lord Jesus Christ's place is on the North side and this is why Satan chose to be on the North side when he arrives to deceive the whole world, as written in Isaiah 14:13.

Ezekiel 44:5 *"And the LORD said unto me, "Son of man, mark well, and behold with thine eyes, and hear with thine ears all that I say unto thee concerning all the ordinances of the house of the LORD, and all the laws thereof; and mark well the entering in of the house, with every going forth of the sanctuary."*

"Mark well" means to *"write it down"*; our Lord Jesus is telling Ezekiel twice so it will be remembered.

The ordinances will be enforced during the Millennium, yet not as they were in this earth age. The ordinances will be a form of discipline that will be strictly followed according to the law and during this time, we will have the Messiah with us. All of His laws will be followed at that time. These laws are God's laws of love and unselfishness. Remember this is the Millennium age. Don't mix it up with the age of Grace we are now living in. The needs of those souls living in the Millennium age will not be as they are in this flesh age, because there will be no sickness, and no need to satisfy a physical body, because everyone will be in their spiritual bodies.

Ezekiel 44:6 *"And thou shalt say to the rebellious, even to the house of Israel, Thus saith the Lord God: O ye house of Israel, let it suffice you of all your abominations,"*

Our Lord Jesus Christ is drawing our attention to the failure and laziness of *the house of Israel,* which are the Christian nations and all those who called themselves a Christian. Can you imagine how our Lord Jesus Christ will feel when He returns to earth to find His *"bride" known as,* Christians that has become a bunch of spiritual whores? They have allowed themselves to follow the lies of their false teachers, such as the rapture doctrine. Many preachers, today have been taken in by Satan's tricks and supernatural activities. Jesus makes it clear that His coming is after the Antichrist has come. It is at the sixth trumpet when Satan has deceived the whole earth. In ignorance, the Christian world continues to follow their false shepherds blindly and they will be lead right into the Antichrist's camp.

God is not happy with His people, called the House of Israel known as the Christian people. This falling away from Christ, is Satan's *"abomination"* that's spoken of here.

Ezekiel 44:7 *"In that ye have brought into My sanctuary strangers, uncircumcised in heart, and uncircumcised in flesh, to be in My sanctuary, to pollute it, even My house, when ye offer My bread, the fat and the blood, and they have broken My covenant because of all your abominations."*

Remember in II Thessalonians 2:3-4, where Paul is saying that he wants to talk to you about us "returning to Jesus Christ". Paul said that it shall not happen until that *"stranger"*, the "*son of perdition"* will stand in the Sanctuary of God, claiming himself to be God. This is the "*abomination of Desolation"* spoken of by Daniel in Daniel 9:27 and all denominations will be part of that abomination. All their false shepherds had led their flocks into this abomination.

The churches of today are bringing in *"strangers"*, with their strange doctrines [doctrines of demons] and the Christian churches are accepting false doctrine in ignorance. This is happening today on a massive scale. Even the Sodomites want their part in God's Sanctuary, and Christians are allowing them to play their wicked role. The *"Kenites",* the offspring of Satan through Cain, want to lead the Christian World into accepting the idea of joining Christianity into Judaism, and other false religions where by mixing God's love and Salvation with their false standards. This is flourishing today.

In Daniels 70th week, in the middle of that week, the bread and the wine of the Holy Communion will be removed from all of the churches by the Antichrist when he arrives. Christians will become an active part in Satan's abominations as they give themselves over to his lies. This is what our Lord is speaking of here.

Ezekiel 44:8 *"And ye have not kept the charge of Mine holy things: but ye have set keepers of My charge in My sanctuary for yourselves."*

The men of God are not teaching the Word of God, but the doctrines of men that "*strangers*" called the Kenites who are bringing them in. They are placing these *"strangers"* as hirelings over their churches. Their strangers or *"keepers"* are the sons of Satan, through Cain, through the offspring of Eve and Satan from the Garden of Eden. Many pastors today would rather teach fairy tales and apples, rather than the truth of God's Word. They allow strangers to keep pour their poisonous doctrines into minds of their followers. As they sit in the Sanctuary mocking God and His pure word, to keep from offending anyone there.

Ezekiel 44:9 *"Thus saith the Lord GOD; 'No stranger, uncircumcised in heart, nor uncircumcised in flesh, shall enter into My sanctuary, of any stranger that is among the children of Israel."*

It is just like it was in Ezra and Nehemiah's day when the sanctuary was filled with the heathen Nethinims [Kenites] that were hired to do the liturgical duties, such as the rites for public worship. Satan's children, the Kenites took over, even to the point of becoming the scribes and the keeper's of the records. Their names are listed in Chronicles and not one Levite name is listed, Kenites took full charge of the sanctuary. However

Almighty God gave the Levites the duties of taking care of His Sanctuary.

I Chronicles 2:55 *"And the families of the scribes which dwelt at Jabez [Jerusalem], The Tirathites, the Shimeathites, and Suchathites. These are the Kenites that came of Hemath, the father of the house of Rechab."*

These Kenites are not of Judah, nor of the lineage of Abraham, Noah or Adam. They are of their father Cain, the son of Satan from the Garden of Eden, through the lineage of Rechab. They have no right to be sitting in the seat of Moses, yet the house of Judah has given the Levites duties over to them. Even to this day they are in control over most of the Christian world. These are the same people that sought to murder Christ when he walked on the earth in the flesh, and continued their murderous acts.

When Ezra was on his way back to Jerusalem, he stopped to count the number of Levite priests, and there was not one single Levite with them. They were all Babylonian *"Kenite"* [Nethinims]. In fact over half of the people returning were not even Hebrew. We know by the recorded listing of their family names.

Ezra 3:15 *"And I gathered them together to the river that runneth to Ahava; and there abode we in tents three days: and I viewed the People, and the priests, and found there none of the sons of Levi."*

Today most Christians and Pastors have no idea about this fact at all. They read it as though it was all true, in the fact they have returned to Jerusalem and they don't even see the abominations that took place on that day. They are ignorant and blind to the truth, that this was an abomination before the Lord, because they don't know the Word of the Living God.

Just as those events in Ezra's day were an abomination to the Lord, it is also an abomination today within the Sanctuaries of God, that we call the modern Christian Churches. Christians are letting all these heathen traditions into their Sanctuaries to teach their false doctrines and prepare Christians for the coming of the false Christ, Satan. Someone should send the warning to them. My prayer is that pastors will wake up.

The *"Levite priest"* of today is the man of God who is filled with the Holy Spirit and teaches the entire Word of God, rather then heathen doctrines and philosophies. This verse nine has come to pass today, and many have gotten into the Sanctuary, claiming to be of God, when in fact they are not.

The teaching that the "*circumcision of these times*", is the *"circumcision of the heart*" that was taught by Jesus Christ while He was on the earth.

Ezekiel 44:10 *"And the Levites that are gone away far from Me, when Israel went astray, which went astray away from Me after their idols; they shall even bear their iniquity."*

Remember, we are in the Millennium here, and Jesus is speaking to Ezekiel about the Levites leaving their spiritual posts way back in the early days. It was the Levites that allowed the Israelites of both houses to go astray. The tribe of the Levites were scattered amongst all tribes to fulfill their duties before God.

In the final days of this earth age, it is also the 144,000 scattered amongst all tribes, 12,000 from each tribe will be saved when they hear the Elect open their mouths and the Holy Spirit of God speaking through them. These are the Levites that went astray and will be saved to full fill their Levities duties in the Millennium. They will hear the words, and the Holy Spirit will make it come alive to them. This is through the *"tongues"* spoken of by Joel in Joel 2:28-32, and Peter in Acts 2:16-21.

Not like the unknown tongues in the churches today. Because there is no such thing as unknown tongues in the Bible.

Ezekiel 44:11 *"Yet they shall be ministers in My sanctuary, having charge at the gates of the house, and ministering to the house: they shall slay the burnt offering and the sacrifice for the people, and they shall stand before them to minister unto them."*

Even though they went astray, they will be ministers in Jesus Christ's Millennium Sanctuary. These 144,000 thousand are of the virgin bride also, because they came out before they were changed into their incorruptible bodies. Recorded in I Corinthians 15:50-52. These 144,000 will be the preachers in the Millennium age. They will teach those who were deceived.

The *"daily oblation"* means that every knee will be bowing to Christ.

Ezekiel 44:12 *"Because they ministered unto them before their idols, and caused the house of Israel to fall into iniquity; therefore have I lifted up Mine hand against them, saith the Lord GOD, and they shall bear their iniquity."*

Because these preachers didn't teach the truths of God's Word, the people were allowed to fall into the iniquity of worshipping Satan in the role of the Antichrist. These Millennium priests were saved out of the Antichrist's system, they are not allowed to approach the Messiah because they ministered before idols. They are saved, but they will pay for their crimes for bowing to Satan in this flesh age.

Ezekiel 44:13 *"And they shall not come near unto Me, to do the office of the "Priest unto Me, nor to come near to any of My holy things, in the most holy place: but they shall bear their most holy place: but they shall bear their shame, and their abominations which they have committed."*

Jesus is telling them, yes you are saved, but get out of my sight. Your job is teaching sinners, so do your job. Since you peddled your rapture doctrine, and played games with the enemy; God's word tells us unless you repent, you can spend the next thousand year's correcting your ways. Just don't come near me, and my holy things. They may be saved, and their flocks will be taught, but there will be a thousand years that they will not be able to even look upon our Lord Jesus Christ.

Ezekiel 44:14 *"But I will make them keepers of the charge of the house, for all the service thereof, and for all that shall be done therein."*

To put it in military terms, they are going to be on work detail for a thousand years. They will do all the dirty work for having allowed their flocks to follow the rapture theory into Satan's camp. Does the rapture theory still sound good to you? God will judge those preachers first, as we saw in Ezekiel 34:1-16, and the dignified lives they lived in this age will be turned into a different life style in the next age. It's time to stop playing games, humble your selves and get into God's Holy Word. Ezekiel is talking about the 144,000 who let the *"Kenites"* do their thinking for them, and they will learn a lesson.

Ezekiel 44:15 *"But the priests the Levites, the sons of Zadok, that kept the charge of My sanctuary when the children of Israel went astray from Me, they shall come near to Me to minister unto Me, and they shall stand before Me to offer unto Me the fat and the blood, saith the Lord God:"*

These priests are the ministers who were not deceived by Satan the Antichrist, and it is they that shall stand before Me to offer unto Me the "*fat and the blood offering*," however, there is no flesh in the Millennium, so this is the gifts and sacrifices of the millennium time. God's "Elect" are the "*Zadok*", in Hebrew means *"the just."* They will serve God, and be in His presence.

If you think when the Millennium comes you can run up to Jesus and be buddy-buddy, you're wrong. There will be so few that will be in this final generation that will be in the first resurrection, and only those will be allowed to personally serve our Lord. The reason for the deception, is because of the false doctrines that have become part of the Church. If you can't accept it now you will accept it after it happens.

Ezekiel 44:16 *"They shall enter into My sanctuary, and they shall come near to My table, to minister unto Me, and they shall keep My charge."*

These Zadok, or Elect are still watchman that will watch over His command. It is only the Zadok that our Lord Jesus Christ will allow to come near Him at this time of the Millennium age. They will be the personal representatives, and the ones doing the work and judging over all the people for our Lord. They will be the only ones that Jesus Christ gives unconditional controls, for they have been tried by the Antichrist in this earth age, and found to be true and steadfast. There will not be only a few in this position. Most of those living today that call themselves Christian's simply do not have the time to prepare themselves for the battle of deception that is coming upon the earth. It is easier to follow false doctrine, because these false doctrines are designed to be appealing to them rather than using common sense.

Ezekiel 44:17 *"And it shall come to pass, that when they shall be clothed with linen garments; and no wool shall come upon them, whiles they minister in the gates of the inner court, and within."*

This *"linen"* is the *"righteous garments"* that we will have in the Millennium age, and on into eternity. That garment is made up of your righteous acts according to Revelation 19:8. Our righteous works goes into making up the material for your heavenly garments, so that we will not appear to be naked. The Elect will not put any man spun garments, such as wool, next to them. These elect are treated differently than the 144,000 priests, for they will be in the very presence of the Lord within the inner court.

There is a deeper meaning to the term *"no wool shall come upon them"*. The Christians of this earth age are referred to as Christ's sheep and Jesus said in John. All reference to Christ and His true followers are given in terms of the Shepherd and His sheep.

John 10:27-28; *"My sheep hear my voice, and I know them, and they follow me: And I give unto them eternal life; and they shall never perish, neither shall any man pluck them out of my hand."*

In most church denominations today, the Minister or preacher calls himself a shepherd of Christ's flock but they are nothing more than a *"hireling."* He is in it for the money, or whatever drove him into that occupation. He cares very little for each individual sheep that God has in trusted to him. Because he doesn't take the time to search the Scriptures for the truth to warn his flock. Most of these religious systems are out to fleece every last strand of wool off of the sheep of Christ. In short they rip them off and then put them in bondage, that God did not tell them to do. Then when they see the wolves coming with their false doctrines, they pack up and leave. God is telling Ezekiel that each person's righteous acts will be their own. It will not be something that has been taken from others. It will be righteous acts of their own doing.

Ezekiel 44:18 *"They shall have linen bonnets upon their heads, and shall have linen breeches upon their loins; they shall not gird themselves with any thing that causeth sweat."*

The Elect or [Zadok] couldn't ware anything that would cause them to sweat. Jesus knows His Elect by the special garments he prepared for them. The Elects' own works or efforts, and no other clothing is allowed at Jesus' table. It's like the man at the wedding wearing the wrong garment or someone who is not one of the Elect of God being there.

Ezekiel 44:19 *"And when they go forth into the utter court, even into the utter court, even to the People, they shall put off their garments wherein they ministered, and lay them in the holy chambers, and they shall put on other garments; and they shall not sanctify the People with their garments."*

Their holy garments are only worn in the presence of Jesus Christ in the inner court. In the outside world, they will not wear that clothing in front of the commoners to be scoffed at. They will have work clothes because their work is to govern and teach. Those who have fallen short in this earth age are not worthy to see those garments at this time. This is why those compartments existed in the Sanctuary for the Priests of the Zadok. These compartments are for storing the Elect's holy garments. Not only will the people not see Jesus Christ in the Millennium age, but they won't even see the righteous acts preformed by the Zadok before our Lord.

Their teaching in the Millennium will not be for learning God's Word, because all the people will know and understand the entire word and what is required of them. The teaching is to enforce that which is known and has been taught and that will require discipline.

Ezekiel 44:20 *"Neither shall they shave their heads, or suffer their locks to grow long; they shall only poll their heads."*

The Elect will be neat in appearance. Remember you are not in the flesh age, but in spiritual, incorruptible bodies here. This is not in this earth age, but in God's Millennium Kingdom age. Although the spiritual bodies don't age in their incorruptible stage, those who are not part of the first fruits of the first resurrection will remain in their mortal stage. They are mortal, liable to die because they have not overcome yet, they are not first fruits who accepted God's truth in the Grace period. This will not happen in the presence of Christ.

Ezekiel 44:21 *"Neither shall any priest drink wine, when they enter into the inner court."*

This will not happen in the presence of the Jesus Christ.

Ezekiel 44:22 *"Neither shall they take for their wives a widow, nor her that is put away: but they shall take maidens of the seed of the house of Israel, or a widow that had a priest before."*

What does, *"take wives"* mean? It is a wedding taking place even here. It is not the marriage of the lamb, it will be another wedding, and this is in reference to that other wedding. There will be another marriage after the final judgment and all those souls that are saved out of the Millennium age, that have earned their names to be written in the book by their works they did in the Millennium. They become part of the bride at this wedding. This is recorded in the *"Lamb's book of life"*, spoken of in Revelation 21:27.

Those who are part of Jesus Christ's bride will be taken because they have proven themselves to be worthy to be Christ's bride. They will have earned it the hard way. Keep in mind this is not the flesh earth age where we become saved by our faith in Jesus Christ, rather than the sacrifice that Jesus gave when he died on the cross of Calvary. We, being raised with Him through our acceptance of Jesus Christ, with our hope being in our faith that He will do exactly as God promised He would do in His holy Word. The bride of the Millennium becomes a bride only because of their works that were written down at that time.

Ezekiel 44:23 *"And they shall teach My People the difference between the holy and profane, and cause them to discern between the unclean and the clean."*

The Elect will teach the difference between the holy and the profane, through the true Christ and not Satan [the false Christ]. The truth will be taught. Christ is on earth with all people in their spiritual bodies and everyone will know the difference between right and wrong, clean and unclean. There will be no shades of truth because only truth will exist. They will understand perfectly. All the people will go through a boot camp that they will never forget. They will be taught what to do and what not to do. They will be drilled and drilled until they fully understand.

Not everyone will see Christ. Those who bowed to the Antichrist and those who were deceived will not want to stand before the Savior until they are worthy, after the judgment following the Millennium age and on into eternity. You can be one of those who will stand before our Lord, by studying the truth and being able to identify the Antichrist [Satan] at his arrival. Then the Antichrist will not be tempting to you.

Ezekiel 44:24 *"And in controversy they shall stand in judgment; and they shall judge it according to My judgments: and they shall keep My laws and My statutes in all Mine assemblies; and they shall hallow My Sabbaths."*

The judges in the Millennium age will be the Elect of God. They will be fair and just. The judgments will not be bought, coerced, bartered with or sold. The rights, standards, and punishments will all be justified, because they are set by the Lord.

Everyone will be obedient to all of the feast days, Sabbaths, laws, and ordinances. They will all have incorruptible bodies with full understanding and will know all of the Lord's requirements.

Ezekiel 44:25 *"And they shall come at no dead person to defile themselves: but for father, or for mother, or for son, or for* *daughter, for brother, or for sister that hath had no husband, they may defile themselves."*

This is the same dead that are spoken of in Revelation 20:5. They are mortals, meaning they are liable to die. All flesh is already done away with. In other words, it is your loved ones who were deceived when they entered the Millennium age in a fallen state. You cannot touch them, but you will be able to recognize your family and loved ones and help them by speaking to them with encouragement and righteous indignation. Very few will get this opportunity, because this is one of the promises given to those who stood against the Antichrist.

We will all be able to recognize each other in the Millennium age. Our friends and loved ones will know each other and we will be able to communicate with them.

Ezekiel 44:26 *"And after he is cleansed, they shall reckon unto him seven days."*

After they are cleansed, the priesthood of the Zadok, will be able to reckon, see and talk to their family members while they are in a defiled state. They can warn his family members and encourage them so their soul won't go into the lake of fire. We are talking about the soul bodies that are living in the Millennium. If your one of the Zadok's you will be able to teach them one on one, to support them, show your love for them, but you will pay a price for it. Christ does not want them near Him, which are those who did not come by Grace. They are mortal [liable to die] spiritual bodies. Nor does He want you near Him after you have talked to them. It will be like visiting a leper colony; they can see, talk, and help them, but can not touch them, but if do they have defiled themselves.

When you return from your visit with your family, there is a seven day waiting period before you can put on your linen garments and come back into the presence of Jesus Christ.

This tells you what Jesus thinks of those who have allowed themselves to be contaminated with Margaret McDonald's 1830 *"rapture theory"*. they have left them-selves open to the Antichrist.

Many who are sleeping today can't see the truth because God has put blinders on them. It is impossible for them to know, for in their minds, the truth of God's written word is not important to them. That is why Jesus said we are to plant the seed, and it is by the Holy Spirit of God that makes the seed of truth grow. Only God can make people understand his word through his angels as they perpair the harvest.

Without compassion and love for God's people it's impossible for the elect to please God. We must want to share God's word and help others to serve Him. He want's us to have the desire to be a comfort to all of the children of the Almighty God. One of the traits of God's elect is they have compassion for God's children.

Ezekiel 44:27 *"And in the day that he goeth into the sanctuary, unto the inner court, to minister in the sanctuary, he shall offer his sin offering, saith the Lord God."*

You will pay a price to teach and be in the presence of your family and friends in this earth age of flesh man and also in the Millennium age. The sin offering is given because some one had actually touched a mortal or person who is likely to die, even though they are in their incorruptible or spiritual body. Christ will even love you for it, but you still have to pay the sin offering, for the salvation of their soul.

Ezekiel 44:28 *"And it shall be unto them for an inheritance: I am their inheritance: and ye shall give them no possession in Israel: I am their possession."*

The elect will not receive one thing in Israel, for God is their possession. When you are a possession of God and joint heirs with Jesus Christ, then you are part owner of everything. God owns it all, thus it is your inheritance. When a farmer owns a farm and leaves that farm to his son for an inheritance, that son has ownership and all rights that his father had to the farm.

The inheritance of the elect is Israel, given by our Heavenly Father. Will the elect take ownership in this inheritance? No, because God's elect are more interested in the position God has placed them in, by teaching and helping their families than in a temporary gain. The heart of God's elect is to give to others at their own expense, not to gain worldly possessions.

Ezekiel 44:29 *"They shall eat the meat offering, and the sin offering, and the trespass offering; and every dedicated thing in Israel shall be theirs."*

Ezekiel 44:30 *"And the first of all the first fruits of all things, and every oblation of all, of every sort of your oblations, shall be the priest's: ye shall also give unto the priest the first of your dough, that he may cause the blessing to rest in thine house."*

What ever you give to God is to the priest, even in this age. When you give him the first of your offerings, it causes a blessing upon you because it is to serve Almighty God.

Ezekiel 44:31 *"The priests shall not eat of any thing that is dead of itself, or torn, whether it be fowl or beast."*

This is in reference to Leviticus 22:8; *"That which dieth of itself, or is torn with beasts, he shall not eat to defile himself therewith: I am the Lord."*

In this age of the Millennium Kingdom, things will be different. The land will be restored and the new Millennium Temple will not be the same as the Temple that was in this earth age. The land on earth will have changed and been restored for this period prior to the "*Great White Throne Judgment*", with each tribe and nation getting it's fair portion. The Levites will have their portion and the priests will have theirs.

Ezekiel 45:9,10 *"Thus saith the Lord God; `Let it suffice you, O prince of Israel: remove violence and spoil, and execute judgment and justice, take away your exactions from My People, saith the Lord God." "Ye shall have just balances, and a just epah, and a just bath."*

Those that rule over the tribes of Israel will be required to give an accurate account of their deeds and actions. It will not be like today, where untold millions of dollars of our land simply disappears out of the government system. Payoffs under the table and special deals to those that give favors, will not be allowed. Remember that our Lord Jesus Christ will be with us, and He knows the thoughts and intents of our hearts.

Although the things of value in this earth age will not apply in the next earth age; every thing that is done will be honest and this applies not only to weights, balances, and in judgments between neighbors and nations. There will be no taxes to private governmental systems because there is only one Government system that will exist, that is the Kingdom of our Lord and Savior, Jesus Christ. God will have His portion, and there will be no unfairness in the oblations or offerings that are given to support His ministers.

Ezekiel 45:16,17 *"All the People of the land shall give this oblation for the prince in Israel." "And it shall be the prince's part to give burnt offerings, and meat offerings, and drink offerings, in feasts, and in new moons, and in Sabbaths, in all solemnities of the house of Israel: he shall prepare the sin offerings, and the meat offerings, and the burnt offering, and the peace offerings, to make reconciliation for the house of Israel."*

Remember from I Corinthians 15:50-51 that flesh and blood cannot enter into the kingdom of God nor the kingdom of the Millennium age. Jesus Christ is reigning here on earth and all flesh bodies has returned to dust. At this time that we are living in our spirit bodies in the Millennium age, we are told to be obedient toward holy things that still applies. We will have complete understanding and knowledge of what our Lord expects of us. We will serve and obey our Savior in our spiritual bodies for eternity for that's the will of Our Heavenly Father.

The prince of Israel is required to be fulfilled in the blood of Christ. These offerings and oblations were required to bring God's people closer to Him and to remove the separation barrier between God and man. The Prince of Israel will have his respect from the people and his duty is to oversee and take care of his people. Remember this is a time of learning, but mostly discipline that is put into action and every one will know what is right or wrong according to the Word of God.

Then at the close of this thousand year time of discipline, comes the "*Great White Throne Judgment*". However, before that happens, God will release Satan from his pit for a very short season and he will go out to deceive the entire world once again. This will determine the fate of those who will be part of the second resurrection. Let's discuss the two resurrections.

"*The first resurrection*" happens at the seventh trumpet when the Elect that were saved and under the blood of Christ did not follow Satan. The Elect did not take his name, number, or mark in their minds, nor service through their hands. The Elect shall reign with Him for a thousand years.

Revelation 20:4,5 "*And I saw thrones, and they sat upon them, and judgment was given unto them; and I saw the souls of them that were beheaded for the witness of Jesus, and for the Word of God, and which had not worshipped the beast, neither his image, neither had received his mark upon their foreheads, or in their hands; and they lived and reigned with Christ a thousand years*" "*But the rest of the dead lived not* *again until the thousand years were finished. This is the first resurrection.*"

Although a person who was living in the flesh followed Satan and is changed into their new incorruptible body, that body is still mortal and liable to die at the close of the Millennium age. The Elect of God were sealed with the truth in their minds with God's Holy Word and did not find any part of Satan tempting. However, those people that were in their dream world with the traditions of men didn't study to prepare themselves, followed Satan ways and were deceived. Satan spoke through the preacher's as they chased after Satan's unknown tongues, rapture, Easter, Christmas etc.. Doctrines of demons took over their lives. They didn't wait patiently for our Lord's coming. Yes we have all be deceived for centuries, according to the Word of the living God. It's all recorded.

Revelation 20:6 "*Blessed and holy is he that hath part in the first resurrection: on such the second death hath no power, but they shall be priests of God and of Christ, and shall reign with Him a thousand years.*"

This identifies those of the Elect that made their stand and were sealed with the truth, and did not take part in Satan's gifts. Their rewards were as the priests of the Millennium age. All mankind will be in their spiritual bodies in the Millennium, yet only these that held true to Christ and were not deceived have their eternal body and the mark or stain of mortality removed from their spiritual body.

THE MILLENNIUM AGE IS THE REAL TIME OF TESTING.

Revelation 20:7,8 "*And when the thousand years are expired, Satan shall be loosed out of his prison* [the pit]," "*And shall go out to deceive the nations which are in the four quarters of the earth, God and Magog, to gather them together to battle: the number of whom is as the sand of the sea.*"

In this Millennium thousand year period, all races and nations, that have lived for that thousand years under an honest, just and peaceful government, will receive their final time of testing. God placed the wisdom of His Word and law into their minds and yet they still went against what they knew to be true. As this army comes against God's people, it will be quick and over in a very short season. Satan will be released from the pit and allowed to go back in the midst of those same people he deceived in this earth age and most of them will believe those same lies just as they will do when he comes at the sounding of the sixth trumpet.

Even today people look to superstars like movie stars, singers, musicians, and all kind of sports and players are made into modern idols which makes Satan very happy. Satan was created in the full pattern of wisdom and beauty, he was not a god, but he had supernatural strength and wisdom. Satan was to stand watch over the altar of God, yet he defiled it and went out to present himself as a god to the sons of God. One third of God's children followed him and those same souls will follow him joyfully right into the pits of hell fire. Rather than destroy His people, God allowed two other times of testing for His children, to see if they would follow Him, or turn as they did to Satan in that first earth age. This is Almighty God's mercy for his people.

If Satan sounds good to you when he comes into this earth age, think of the joy you will receive when he comes out of the pit at the end of the Millennium. If you are so lazy that you allowed him to buy your soul the first time; you will really sell yourself short this second time. All the nations of this entire earth are going to join in with this man of sin, known as "*the son of perdition*", and will come against God's people in Israel. The tribes and priests of Christ will be living safely in their allotted lands, as this massive armed force comes against them.

Revelation 20:9,10 "*And they went up on the breadth of the earth, and compassed the camp of the saints about, and the* *beloved city: and fire came about, and the beloved city: and fire came down from God out of heaven, and devoured them."* *"And the devil that deceived them was cast into the lake of fire and brimstone, where the beast and the false prophet are, and shall be tormented day and night for ever and ever."*

God allowed Satan to be kept in the pit for the thousand years, but the beast and the false prophet were sent to their eternal damnation at the seventh trumpet. God is complete and quick in His judgments. At the close of this earth age, Satan will kill the two prophets; when the three and a half days are over the seventh trumpet sounds instantly and all souls will be changed from their fleshly bodies into their incorruptible bodies. When this massive army of Satan comes against Jerusalem and Israel, God will pour out his wrath and put an end to Satan quickly ". . . *fire came down from God, and devoured them*". Just as the people realized who Satan was when he was placed in the pit; God sends Satan into hell fire, the people will see their leader's final end and it is all over. Then comes the finial, "*Great White Throne Judgment*" of God Almighty.

FINAL JUDGMENT
Chapter 17

When the Millennium age has come to an end, Satan will be released for that short time and the people living in their incorruptible bodies will act just as they did at the close of this earth age. When Satan declared himself God and killed the two witnesses, the bodies of the two witnesses lay in the streets to be observed for three and a half days. People started their gift giving and celebrations for three and a half days. It didn't end until life comes back into the bodies of God's two witnesses, and the seventh trumpet sounded which ended this earth age of flesh mankind.

In the Millennium age, Satan will present himself again to the people of that age and most of them will do just as they did in this flesh earth age. That including many that call themselves Christians today, will become part of Satan's army. As Satan sweeps the earth, devouring nations and bring millions of Christians into his camp. They will come to an end when Satan's army is on the doorstep of Jerusalem. The land allotted to God's children are the tribes of Israel. When Satan and the people of the sea come close to Jerusalem God puts a stop to it all, as we move on into the final stages of this earth ages, and on into the Millennium age toward the "Great White Throne Judgment".

Revelation 20:9,10 ". . . *And fire came down from God out of heaven, and devoured them.*" "*And the devil that deceived them was cast into the lake of fire and brimstone, where the beast and the false prophet are, and shall be tormented day and night.*"

As far as Satan is concerned, this is the finial death of Satan, as he is put into the lake of fire, and is turned into ashes.

This sets the stage for the final act of God just before we enter eternity, we will see the "*Great White Throne Judgment*".

GREAT WHITE THRONE JUDGMENT

Revelation 20:11 "*And I saw a great white throne, and Him That sat on it, from Whose face the earth and the heaven fled away; and there was found no place for them.*"

There is no hiding from this point at the judgment seat of God. All souls will be in their incorruptible bodies or they simply will not exist. Satan and the false prophet, as well as his beast's system has already gone into hell fire and now it's time to separate those faithful servants of our Lord and Heavenly Father.

Revelation 20:12,13 "*And I saw the dead, small and great, stand before God; and the books were opened: and another book was opened, which is the book of life: and the dead were judged out of those things which were written in the books, according to their works.*" "*And the sea gave up the dead which were in it; and death and hell delivered up the dead which were in them: and they were judged every man according to their works.*"

Remember that the Elect are also known as the wife of Christ which were judged in the first earth age because they stood against Satan. They received their rewards at the seventh and last trumpet. The people of the free will that chose to follow Christ are the bride of Christ who received their rewards at the return of Christ to this earth. The rewards to both the Elect and the bride of Christ are equal, because they are the only ones that have their names written in the Lamb's book of life. God separates two kinds of people. Those who's names are written in the book of life and those that are written in the books, which were those that the judging of the dead came from.

We are saved by Grace in this earth age by the blood of our Lord Jesus Christ through His death and resurrection. You have no works recorded in this book, because all our hope and glory is done for the glory of our Lord and Savior Jesus. If anyone thinks that they are a Christians when they are serving Satan in their ignorance, they're wrong. God does not forgive you for becoming a religious whore in the service of Satan; Christian or not. This judgment is for those who didn't make it through the great tribulation, but gave themselves over to Satan willingly. It is also for all those in this earth age who rejected God's gift of Salvation through Jesus Christ. That gift is offered to each and every living soul born in the flesh, Israelites, Gentiles, Kenites, and sinners alike. All a person has to do is repent and ask forgiveness in Jesus Christ's name, then seek the Lord with all their hearts and accept His word as they live one day at a time.

There is no escape from this judgment, and no attorney to defend you, or judge that can be bought off, like in our present court system. God knows it all, and it is all written down for the moment of judgment. Every soul will be judged out of these books according to your works. This is not referring to those who's names are already written in the book of Life.

Revelation 20:14,15 *"And death and hell were cast into the lake of fire.* This is the second death." "And whosoever was not found written in the book of life was cast into the lake of fire."

From the first moment that Satan was filled with pride he wanted to be worshiped as God. He will come to earth and declared himself as Jesus Christ; in the last few months of this earth age of mankind. All of the evil and wickedness that will follow him is cast into the lake of fire with Satan. There is no more chances after the second death, for the first death is the death of these flesh bodies, and the second death is the death of their soul and spirit bodies. If you were judged by your works in the Millennium age, your works of this earth age did not apply, because you were given the full knowledge of what you were doing and yet millions of souls will choose to follow Satan. If you followed the rules and commandments during that thousand year period while serving God and met your obligations, then your name will be added into the book of life. From this point on, all these souls are saved and will move on into the new heaven here on earth.

PEOPLE ON THE NEW EARTH.

As we consider Revelation 21, we must bear in mind that Satan, all unsaved Kenites, all of Satan's demonic angelic forces and all men and women who have lived in this earth age and refused our Lord Jesus Christ's blood for their atonement for sin, will have perished. Their flesh bodies were lifeless at the sounding of the seventh trumpet when Jesus Christ returned to set up His kingdom. Read I Corinthians 15:50-52.

All living souls, good and bad, will enter into the Millennium age for 1,000 years in their incorruptible (spirit) body. Those saints who did not take the *"mark of the beast"*, by not following the Antichrist as the true Christ, nor tried to win others over into Satan's camp. They will put on their immortal soul bodies, and will never to die. However, those who were unfaithful in the tribulation, and in ignorance followed the Antichrist will be in their mortal soul bodies that could die. However, by overcoming in the Millennium age, they will be judged by their works, and will be given immortality (never to die) at the "Great White Throne Judgment", when the books are opened.

Praise God, because from here on there is only happiness, joy, in the presence of our Lord Jesus Christ for all the over comer's.

Revelation 21:1 *"And I saw a new heaven and a new earth: for the first heaven and the first earth were passed away; and there was no more sea."*

At the close of Revelation 20, the fire of hell that consumed Satan and all his followers will not exist. They will never again return in any form, and in their place will be a rejuvenated earth. This will be a perfect place right here on earth, not on some far off planet.

We see in II Peter 3:10,11 that the existence of this present earth age will be changed with all the physical elements and all of the evil rudiments are done away with, on the *"day of our Lord"*. Then in II Peter 3:12, at the end of the Millennium age, the evil souls are turned to ashes. This is called the *"day of God."*

II Peter 3:13 *"Nevertheless we, according to his promise, look for new heavens and a new earth, wherein dwelleth righteousness."*

This new Heaven and New earth is a promise given by God to the earliest prophets and we have seen throughout the Holy Scriptures that God keeps all of his promises.

II Peter 3:14 *"Wherefore, beloved, seeing that ye look for such things, be diligent that ye may be found of him in peace, without spot, and blameless."*

Revelation 21:2 *"And I John saw the holy city, new Jerusalem, coming down from God out of heaven, prepared as a bride adorned for her husband."*

God allowed John to see in his vision this new city, the New Jerusalem; coming down to earth dressed in all it's beauty. Christ made this New Jerusalem just as He would adorn it for His first love [the Elect], and His bride. The New Jerusalem is for those of us who are His bride, that makes up His church. Praise God for His Love for us.

Revelation 21:3 *"And I heard a great voice out of heaven saying, Behold, the tabernacle of God is with men, and he will* *dwell with them, and they shall be his people, and God himself shall be with them, and be their God."*

The Hebrew text reads, "*the throne"* instead *"of heaven*", and that great voice is the voice of God, our Heavenly Father.

The word *"Behold"* in the Greek is *"idou"*, and is the imperative *"eidon*". It is calling attention to a subject other than himself, which is, *"the tabernacle of God*".

Hebrews 9:11 *"But Christ being come an high priest of good things to come, by a greater and more perfect tabernacle, not made with hands, that is to say, not of this building;"*

Hebrews 9:12 *"Neither by the blood of goats and calves, but by his own blood he entered in once into the holy place, having obtained eternal redemption for us."*

We do not need the blood of sheep and goats anymore, for Jesus Christ is our sacrifice and tabernacle.

Hebrews 9:13,14 *"For if the blood of bulls and of goats, and the ashes of an [red] heifer sprinkling the unclean, sanctifieth to the purifying of the flesh:" "How much more shall the blood of Christ, who through the eternal Spirit offered himself without spot to God, purge your conscience from dead works to serve the living God?"*

Hebrews 9:15 *"And for this cause he is the mediator of the new testament, that by means of death, for the redemption of the transgressions that were under the first testament, they which are called might receive the promise of eternal inheritance."*

We don't serve a dead God, but a living Savior. He is our loving and living God. Here in verse 15 we see it is Jesus Christ who is our mediator, our tabernacle, which allows us to approach God. Almighty God is saying in verse Revelation 21:3

that this tabernacle (Jesus Christ) is going to be with men from here on throughout all eternally. Jesus Christ will be with us and leading us, because we are His people who have accepted Him as our personal savior.

Not only will we have our Lord Jesus Christ by our side in the New Jerusalem, but the Heavenly Father will be dwelling on earth also. It would be hard to fully imagine in our minds the splendor of these next three verses.

Revelation 21:4 *"And God shall wipe away all tears from their eyes; and there shall be no more death, neither sorrow, nor crying, neither shall there be any more pain: for the former things are passed away."*

The new soul body that each of us will be in, is an incorruptible body, which will never grow old. There is no pain or sorrow in that body, for all sin and guilt are blotted out of our memories by the blood of Christ. Some may say, "What about our loved ones which lay burning in hell fire?" Those souls were burned to ashes and all thought of them will be blotted out from our memory. It will be as if that loved one had never existed.

All *"former things"* [Strong's #4413, #4453] in the Greek dictionary says; *"protos", best previous, formerly, of root #4453; "poleo", to be busy, to trade, to peddle, to be sold."*

We will not be creating or selling anything to earn a living, but tending to the rewards of a joyous life God has for us. The problems we face in this life will not be there. Work and backbiting won't exist. The problems of poor health and the handicap will be gone and our nourishment will flow from the eternal fountain of God. Think of this glorious time, then stop and consider the few problems that we have in this flesh life. All of those problems will never come back to haunt us again it's as if they never existed.

Revelation 21:5 *"And he that sat upon the throne said, Behold, I make all things new. And he said unto me, Write: for these words are true and faithful."*

This is our Heavenly Father talking to John here, and He told John to *"write"*. These words John writes are about Our Lord Jesus Christ, His son. This we know for in Revelation 19:11, Jesus Christ is named *"true and faithful."*

Revelation 21:6 *"And he said unto me, It is done. I am Alpha and Omega, the beginning and the end. I will give unto him that is athirst of the fountain of the water of life freely."*

All the wrath of God that was ever to be poured out upon the earth, was because of the wickedness of man, Satan, and his fallen angels. The workers that came as the seventh angel poured out his vile upon the earth in Revelation 16:17 is God's finial wrath is fulfilled, *"It is done"*.

God's plan will be completed and all of the disobedient children of God are gone forever. We see God's name, *"I am"*, and the reference to His eternal existence in *"Alpha" and "Omega"* (Greek), *"the beginning and the end."* God promises life to all who accept Christ, for that life is given to us only through the resurrection of Jesus Christ, by God our Heavenly Father.

We see this in these three verses, as well as many more: I John 5:12, Romans 6:10, II Corinthians 13:4. It's well worth your study time to look them up, and claim them for God's promise to you. God deserves our praise because He is the "*fountain of living water"* that flow's freely to everyone who asks. Our Eternal life has been paid for by Jesus' blood on the cross. Though it is free to us, it was the ultimate price ever given in the universe by God's own begotten Son. As people grow complacent toward salvation, there is not one thing anyone can do to earn any part of God's gift. Even if your works in the Millennium age allow you to pass over judgment and receive an immortal soul, it is still only by Jesus Christ's blood that your immortality has been given to you. That's what we call love for there is no greater love than His love for each of us.

Revelation 21:7 *"He that overcometh shall inherit all things; and I will be his God, and he shall be my son."*

To inherit, means we are to possess a share of the Heavenly Kingdom; that beautiful New Jerusalem that has been prepared for those who wait on the true Christ and do not follow the Antichrist.

Romans 8:17 *"And if children, then heirs; heirs of God, and joint-heirs with Christ; if so be that we suffer with him that we may be also glorified together."*

Revelation 21:8 *"But the fearful, and unbelieving, and the abominable, and murder-ers, and whore-mongers, and sorcerers, and idolaters, and all liars, shall have their part in the lake which burneth with fire and brimstone: which is the second death."*

Once again we see those who will not have an inheritance in the New Jerusalem. They will be destroyed in the hell fire, prior to the coming of the New Jerusalem.

We know that all sins ever committed can be covered by the blood of Christ, except the sin of not, allowing the Holy Spirit to speak through you, when you are delivered up before the synagogues of Satan, as written in Mark 13:11. That is the unforgivable sin. We must have a repentant heart when we confess our sins to the Lord in prayer.

Revelation 21:9 *"And there came unto me one of the seven angels which had the seven vials full of the seven last plagues, and talked with me, saying, Come hither, I will shew thee the bride, the Lamb's wife."*

This is one of the seven angels we read about in Revelation 15:1,6,7. They were the angels that poured out the wrath of God upon the earth. John is going to be shown the bride of Christ by him.

John is now taken in the spirit by this angel of the seven vials to visit the new Jerusalem. This was a time in the far distant future (beyond the Millennium age) when we occupy that city of joy.

Revelation 21:10 *"And he carried me away in the spirit to a great and high mountain, and shewed me that great city, the holy Jerusalem, descending out of heaven from God."*

We know that the *"great and high mountain"* represents a place where all the saints of God are. These are the heirs of the New Jerusalem. John was there and is telling us what it was like, as we will see this place in person when our eternal home "descends out of heaven from God".

Revelation 21:11 *"Having the glory of God; and her light was like unto a stone most precious, even like a jasper stone, clear as crystal;"*

This New Jerusalem, the place where John is taken in the spirit, is receiving its light by the Heavenly Fathers own glory shining forth. This *"light"* giving forth, as recorded in the Greek text is called "*phoster.*" Used in the term of a "*light bearer or giver.*" It is also used in Genesis 1:14, 16.

The light in the New Jerusalem will be a clear pure light and it's light will be eternal in God's New City that was prepared for His saints.

Revelation 21:12 *"And had a wall great and high, and had twelve gates, and at the gates twelve angels, and names written thereon, which are the names of the twelve tribes of the children of Israel:"*

We have a double witness to these great walls of the New Jerusalem, for both John and Ezekiel wrote as they were moved by the Holy Spirit. Read Ezekiel's vision in Ezekiel 48:31-34.

Revelation 21:13 *"On the east three gates; on the north three gates; on the south three gates; and on the west three gates."*

Revelation 21:14 *"And the wall of the city had twelve foundations, and in them the name of the twelve apostles of the Lamb."*

We see that the New Jerusalem will have each gate marked with the names of the twelve tribes of Jacob (Israel). These twelve tribes, we are told, were the *"foundation"* of the saints of God. Though many today think "it is the Jew who is the chosen of God", and they think the other ten tribes were lost in a desert to both God and themselves. This is nothing but one of Satan's deceptions. Because the Bible tells us that the twelve tribes of Jacob called Israel, were never lost. They are all the Christian Nations of the world. They are England, USA, Canada, Alaska, Norway, Ireland, Sweden just to name a few and these nations have never been lost.

The minor prophet Hosea, in his first 13 chapters issues a warning to Israel that God would divorce one of His wives, the "House of Israel", because of their idolatry. Yet He would not divorce the "House of Judah". Then we see in the 14th chapter how Israel repents and God takes Israel back. This is possible because, following the death of our Lord Jesus Christ on the cross as recorded in Isaiah 54, not only Israel but all Gentile peoples including the Kenites have access through Christ's death and resurrection to have salvation and eternal life.

In Ezekiel 37:1, Ezekiel is told to prophecy to these *"dry dead bones of the House of Israel."* As he does, flesh comes upon them and life comes back into them. Who are they? "*The whole House of Israel."* That nation is the one which Hosea, the prophet, said God had divorced them and then he brought back to himself following Christ's death.

In Ezekiel 37:16-19, God told Ezekiel to take two sticks and write on one "*Israel*" and on the other "*Judah*". God then tells Ezekiel to put the two sticks together in one hand. This was to represent how God would deal with Israel and Judah (Jews)—all twelve tribes—as one.

As we relate to these two separate nations; the ten-tribes of the "House of Israel" and the two tribes of the "House of Judah" (Jews), we see all the tribes have become the "foundations" of the gates of entry into God's new and holy city, "Holy Jerusalem".

We see also the names of the twelve apostles written upon these foundations. These were the twelve men Jesus personally taught and commissioned to carry the message of the gospel with God's authority. It is upon them and Paul that Jesus built his church.

Revelation 21:15 *"And he that talked with me had a golden reed to measure the city, and the gates thereof, and the wall thereof."*

Revelation 1:16 *"And the city lieth foursquare, and the length is as large as the breadth: and he measured the city with the reed, twelve thousand furlongs. The length and the breadth and the height of it are equal."*

Revelation 21:17 *"And he measured the wall thereof, an hundred and forty and four cubits. According to the measure of a man, that is, of the angel."*

John is given the dimensions of the four square city of God, the "New Jerusalem". The dimensions are given in units of a reed, furlongs, and cubits. To bring this to units of measurement we can understand, a "reed" is about 31/2 yards. A "furlong" is approxi-mately 220 yards, and a "cubit" is the length of an arm, about 21-25 inches in length.

When we compare God's "Holy City" to the "holy of holies", we see they were both cubes and proportionate. The "Holy City" is a cube of 12,000 furlongs to a side. The "Holy of Holies" being 20 cubits to a side.

Revelation 21:18 *"And the building of the wall of it was of jasper: and the city was pure gold, like unto clear glass."*

The stone *"of jasper"* is held as the most precious. In Exodus 28:20 we see that it was the stone in the high priest's breastplate as a symbol of purity, like *"a crystal."* The jasper stone is the most precious of all the gem stones which are used in Revelation 21:19-21, representing the twelve tribes of Israel. The jasper in the wall shows the importance our Lord held for His disciples, who were at His side when He walked, taught, died and arose while He walked upon the earth, in the flesh.

Revelation 21:19 *"And the foundations of the wall of the city were garnished with all manner of precious stones. The first foundation was jasper; the second, sapphire; the third, a chalcedony; the fourth, and emerald;"*

Revelation 21:20 *"The fifth, sardonyx; the sixth, sardius; the seventh, chrysolite the eighth, beryl; the ninth, a topaz; the tenth, a chrysoprasus; the eleventh, a jacinth; the twelfth, an amethyst."*

Revelation 21:21 *"And the twelve gates were twelve pearls; every several gate was of one pearl: and the street of the city was pure gold, as it were transparent glass."*

What a city: streets of pure gold! In describing the streets, John could not relate the actual material element and referred to as being similar to pure gold. There will be many surprises of pure splendor in this city which John saw.

Revelation 21:22 *"And I saw no temple therein: for the Lord God Almighty and the Lamb are the temple of it."*

The temple is a place of worship, and atonement for sin. We see this New Jerusalem will not have a temple. The temple of the Millennium, where Jesus Christ sets up His reign for the 1,000 years is done. There is no more sin, tears, sorrow, flesh, death, and all thought of them are void. There is no need for atonement for all of these things are either blotted out as if they never existed or burned to hell fire.

The only need for a temple is for a place of worship. We will be walking the streets of the New Jerusalem with our Heavenly Father, and the "Lamb", our Lord Jesus Christ. There will be no need for a temple and that is why John saw no temple there.

Revelation 21:23 *"And the city had no need of the sun, neither of the moon, to shine in it: for the glory of God did lighten it, and the Lamb is the light thereof."*

Isaiah 60:19 *"The sun shall be no more thy light by day; neither for brightness shall the moon give light unto thee: but the Lord shall be unto thee and everlasting light, and thy God thy glory."*

Isaiah 60:20 "*Thy sun shall no more go down; neither shall thy moon withdraw itself: for the Lord shall be thine everlasting light, and the days of thy mourning shall be ended."*

Revelation 21:24 *"And the nations of them which are saved shall walk in the light of it: and the kings of the earth do bring their glory and honour into it."*

Revelation 21:25 *"And the gates of it shall not be shut at all by day: for there shall be no night there."*

Revelation 21:26 *"And they shall bring the glory and honour of the nations into it."*

All peoples of every ethnic background which were saved in this earth age, or the Millennium shall be in that great city of God. They will all know why they are there, and will give our Lord Jesus Christ the praise. All those who do not except Christ, simply will not exist and not even the memory of them.

All who are there as citizens of that city, and God's kingdom, are children of the Heavenly Father and joint heirs with Christ Jesus (the Lamb). You will go in and out of that city freely, just as you would do in your own home.

There will be no night or darkness in the New Jerusalem. There will be no need for rest nor recuperation in the eternal kingdom because our bodies will be eternal and incorruptible. Our bodies will not have pain nor need of rest because our bodies are immortal at this time.

The kings and their nations spoken of in verse 24 are the "sheep" nations of His right hand during the Millennium reign recorded in Matthew 25:31-46. Each of these kings and nations will contribute to the glory and honor of God's beautiful "New Jerusalem".

Revelation 21:27 *"And there shall in no wise enter into it any thing that defileth, neither whatsoever worketh abomination, or maketh a lie: but they which are written in the Lamb's book of life."*

Why do we know that no sin or defiling thing will be allowed in the eternal city? Because all who followed Satan and who bowed to idols have been destroyed prior to the *"New Holy City of God"* coming down out of heaven. The only persons entering eternity are those whose names are recorded in the *"Lamb's Book of Life"*, who have their sins covered and blotted out by Jesus Christ's shed blood. In Revelation 20:15.

It's not worth taking chances in this life, for not paying attention to the warnings given to us by Our Lord Jesus Christ.

After reading Revelation 21, and John 3:16-17 our commitment to our Lord Jesus Christ and His Word makes much more sense.

John 3:16 *"For God so loved the world that he gave his only begotten Son, that whosoever believeth in him should not perish, but have everlasting life."*

John 3:17 *"For God sent not his Son into the world to condemn the world; but that the world through him might be saved."*

The offer of eternal life is ours for the asking. Our Lord is a God of love, for he knows our weakness and our sins; and the only way to reach Him is by confessing our sins, and asking him for forgiveness in Jesus Name. Ask Jesus for faith in the name of Jesus Christ who is the son of God. Only through the name of Jesus Christ can we obtain our credentials to enter into the throne of God. Its no harder than seeking help from a friend. His love and rewards cannot be compared to anything in this life.

ETERNAL KINGDOM
Chapter 18

This chapter allows us to get a glimpse of the eternal city and life within the New Jerusalem, as John is being escorted into that period of time by a messenger of God. When this new city is presented for the bride of Christ, no other person, or angel, in any form will be in existence other than those who were saved under the blood of Lord Jesus Christ.

God has set the standard for worshipping Him and having our sins forgiven. When Jesus Christ shed His blood on the cross, and came out of the tomb victorious over death, the price was paid for all of the sins of mankind who will repent of their sins.

Revelation 22:1 *"And he shewed me a pure river of water of life, clear as crystal, proceeding out of the throne of God and of the Lamb."*

The *"pure river of water of life"* is more of a rainy substance as seen in *Strong's Greek Dictionary* #5204, *"Hudatos"* (as if rainy). The *"water of life"*, or *"Zoe"* #2222 in *Strong's Greek Dictionary*, takes us to the root of word #5590 meaning *"psyche"*, which is merely *"vitality"*. This vitality is extended even into plant life; and extends into the human heart, life, mind, and every living soul.

This substance is eternal and came from the throne of God and the Lamb. The Lamb is our Lord Jesus Christ, who became the perfect sacrifice for our sins, through His sinless life, and shed blood on the cross. These thrones of our Heavenly Father and His Son will be in our midst as we spend all eternity with them.

God is a loving God who has the ability far beyond what any human mind can comprehend. He gave us repentance and salvation to any one who will hear His word, confess their sins, and ask Him for forgiveness. He even set up a kingdom on earth, for 1,000 years, for teaching and testing, just so every living soul can have a fair opportunity to understand and choose Him for their savior. If anyone perishes in hell, that soul chose it of their own free will, no one else made their choice for them.

Revelation 22:2 *"In the midst of the street of it, and on either side of the river was there the tree of life, which bare twelve manner of fruit; and yielded her fruit every month: and the leaves of the tree were for the healing of the nations."*

"In" in the Greek text, *"en"* governs only the case (the dative) and denotes being and remaining within to give rest on a continuance. It is about a place and space as in Matthew 10:16 and a sphere of action in Romans 1:5,8. It also denotes a continuance in time as in Matthew 2:1 and John 11:10.

The *"tree of life"* is our Lord Jesus Christ, who we read about in Genesis 2:9. Well, how can that be? Remember in Revelation 21:6, he said, *". . . I am [always was] Alpha and Omega . . ."*. Jesus existed prior to becoming a baby in the manger in Bethlehem. However, this *"tree of life"* is a certain tree, providing not only fruit for enjoyment, but its leaves give a divine provision for preserving and restoring health, specifically for the nations.

Ezekiel 47:12 *"And by the river upon the bank thereof, on this side and on that side, shall grow all trees for meat, whose leaf shall not fade, neither shall the fruit thereof be consumed: it shall bring forth new fruit according to his months, because their waters they issued out of the sanctuary: and the fruit thereof shall be for meat, and the leaf thereof for medicine."*

As we saw in **Revelation 21:4**, all former things are passed away, and there will be no sickness or sorrow.

Revelation 22:3 *"And there shall be no more curse: but the throne of God and of the Lamb shall be in it; and his servants shall serve him:"*

Revelation 22:4 *"And they shall see his face; and his name shall be in their foreheads."*

There will no longer be any cursed things in peoples' souls because all evil forces against God are turned into ashes. Even the memory of them are gone. The only thing on the minds of God's children will be to love and serve God with praise to Our Lord Jesus Christ. Whatever questions you will have about the trinity, eternity, or any other subject will be understood at this time, because there will be no confusion.

In verse 4, It will be the same way with, marking in your forehead as it was following the Millennium age and the "Great White Throne Judgment". This marking will not allow you to worship Antichrist, because Satan will not have any part in the eternal age. The marking in your forehead is in your mind. You will know Jesus Christ comes at the seventh trumpet following Satan's reign on earth, and that no flesh can go into Christ's Kingdom. God has given us His truths that is recorded in His word our Holy Bible, and all of God's children will know Him because it's all sealed in their memory.

Revelation 22:5 *"And there shall be no night there; and they need no candle, neither light of the sun; for the Lord God giveth them light: and they shall reign for ever and ever."*

That's right, the light in eternity will come from Our Heavenly Father. We know it will not be from the sun that we now get our light from today. This source of light is provided by God. It will be an eternal light source, from God's reign that will have no end.

Revelation 22:6 *"And he said unto me, These sayings are faithful and true: and the Lord God of the holy prophets sent his angel to shew unto his servants the things which must shortly be done."*

"He" is the angel showing John the Holy City. The angel is telling John that the *"Words"*, or Holy Bible you are now studying is *"faithful and true"*. You can trust in it.

It was the Lord God that personally sent His messengers to His holy prophets, to give us their recorded truth. And He allowed His messengers the angels to speak to His servants, such as John, Paul, Ezekiel, and in all of the other writings of the Bible. They give us a glimpse of what is to come.

If you have *"The Companion Bible"* & *"Strong's Concordance" with numbers*, to understand it, you have no excuse for being ignorant in this final generation. Call on the Lord and pray that the Holy Spirit of God will open your mind, and He will. See a list of the tools we are using in the back of this book.

In this, the final generation, you may never die in the flesh, but you will be changed as we saw in I Corinthians15:50-54. Once you're changed into your incorruptible bodies and immortal soul, you are as you will be for all eternity. Your soul receives immortality when Christ comes into you heart. Then, at the sounding of the seventh trumpet, which may be measured in months, or at the most, a few years, you will reign eternally as joint heirs with Christ.

Revelation 22:7 *"Behold, I come quickly: blessed is he that keepeth the sayings of the prophecy of this book."*

Jesus is saying, *"Behold, I come quickly: . . ."*. Though it be quickly, we can still watch the happenings on the news and see the world around us, to know this one world system will collapse with no political credibility. When the world sees the United Nations is used only to advance a few Kenites and their international banking for their industrial-commercial families' interest, their political beast will fall. The mortal wound to the head of a government means it ceases as a governing unit. The dollar dies and money is worthless paper. Advanced technology will run the lives of mankind.

Once the Antichrist comes on the scene, Satan proceeds to do his work and takes full control. His deception is overwhelming, thousands of Christians will believe Satan is the true Christ who has returned. He will rule for the next five months preceding, the seventh trumpet that sounds and then the true Jesus Christ arrives. see Revelation 9:5 "*Blessed is he that keepeth the sayings . .* " of the Bible, for you will be an over comer. You will know the prophecies, and be a watchman. Jesus said in Matthew 24:32-25 to learn these prophecies so you won't be deceived, because the Antichrist will come first.

Revelation 22:8 *"And I John saw these things, and heard them. And when I had heard and seen, I fell down to worship before the feet of the angel which shewed me these things."*

After John had been allowed to see and hear all that we have studied in this Book of Revelation, he was going to fall down and worship this angel. Sort of like many people today, ready to worship anything or anyone that performs wonders for them.

Revelation 22:9 *"Then saith he unto me, See thou do it not: for I am thy fellow servant, and of thy brethren the prophets, and of them which keep the sayings of this book: worship God."*

This messenger that showed John around in Revelation 22, in the New Jerusalem let John know that he was also a fellow-servant and prophet, like John. However He doesn't say who it is.

Remember the first commandment of God is, *"Though shalt have no other Gods before me"*. We are to worship the one and only living God the Father.

Revelation 22:10 *"And he saith unto me, Seal not the sayings of the prophecy of this book: for the time is at hand."*

The angel warned John not to seal up the prophecies of Revelation because they are about to happen especially to our generations, who are living today. We are to learn them, and seal them in our minds so that we're not deceived.

Revelation 22:11 *"He that is unjust, let him be unjust still: and he which is filthy, let him be filthy still: and he that is righteous, let him be righteous still: and he that is holy, let him be holy still."*

God is telling John through the angel not to be concerned, about the deception coming upon the world, but to learn and know in your own mind so that we are not deceived. It's an individual message given to the end time believers'. We must learn the complete plan of God so our minds are prepared and we're not deceived by Satan nor His fallen angles.

Revelation 22:12 *"And, behold, I come quickly; and my reward is with me, to give every man according as his work shall be."*

Revelation 22:13 *"I am Alpha and Omega, the beginning and the end, the first and the last."*

God is giving us a second warning of His soon return, and the rewards He has prepared for His adopted sons and daughters. He is telling us about His power and glory, which is eternal.

Revelation 22:14 *"Blessed are they that do his commandments, that they may have right to the tree of life, and may enter in through the gates into the city."*

Revelation 22:15 *"For without are dogs, and sorcerers, and whoremongers, and murderers, and idolaters, and whosoever loveth and maketh a lie."*

The messenger is repeating for us, so that the rewards and eternal life will be our's when we accept Jesus Christ and keep His commandments. He compares those who violate His words as dogs, and gives them the same ranking as all those who will be destroyed in hell fire, and will never see the "New Jerusalem".

Revelation 22:16 *"I Jesus have sent mine angel to testify unto you these things in the churches. I am the root and the offspring of David, and the bright and morning star."*

Our Lord Jesus Christ now speaks to John, and there can be no mistake why He allowed John to see and witness all that is about to happen. It was so that we can know what is to come and that knowledge will keep us from being deceived. This should be taught in our churches. That we may know our Savior is the promised messiah, and our redeemer, and that we know the prophecies concerning His birth, and resurrection is true but that's as far as they have studied.

If you have eyes to see and ears to hear, you will understand, for it is by the work of the Holy Spirit that His Word is made clear to us.

Revelation 22:17 *"And the Spirit and the bride say, Come. And let him that heareth say, Come. And let him that is athirst come. And whosoever will, let him take the water of life freely."*

The Holy Spirit and the church are drawing you to Christ. To be part of the bride of Christ means we will be partakers in the beautiful eternal New Jerusalem. The only one holding you back is yourself. However, there is only one way, and that is through the blood of Jesus Christ, who has paid the full price with His blood. We receive the forgiveness of our sin by asking for it, through repentance to God for all our sins were forgiven as if we never committed them. Then He will lead us and change our lives as you study His living word, in the "*King James Bible*".

Revelation 22:18 *"For I testify unto every man that heareth the words of the prophecy of this book, If any man shall add unto these things, God shall add unto him the plagues that are written in this book:"*

Revelation 22:19 *"And if any man shall take away from the words of the book of this prophecy, God shall take away his part out of the book of life, and out of the holy city, and from the things which are written in this book."*

God's prophets wrote the scripture to all of us. If any one tells us something, we should always check it out in the Bible, for ourselves and verify what they said. First we must see if it's written in the Bible. It is our responsibility to make sure it is accurate according to the "*King James Bible*".

Revelation 22:20 *"He which testifieth these things saith, Surely I come quickly. Amen'. Even so, come, Lord Jesus."*

Revelation 22:21 "*The grace of our Lord Jesus Christ be with you all. Amen'.*"

It is God, and Our Lord Jesus Christ that testifies of the promises and prophecies. This is the seventh and last testimony that Jesus Christ said, "*Behold, I come Quickly.*"

Grace is given to *"you all,"* meaning *"all the saints"* Grace is the riches, and the unmerited favor of God given to you freely for accepting it, and claiming those promises from God's Word which gives us our salvation.

SALVATION
Chapter 19

Salvation, as presented from church to church, and in each different denomination seems to change; one church puts one requirement on you, and another demands a membership or something else. Ask a person; Are you saved? and the answer will probably giving you is the name of the church they attend. So, what is "Salvation" and why is it necessary that we understand what salvation is all about? In the prior chapters of this book, we have seen many different topics from the creation of our souls, to the final destination where all living souls will be rewarded: Some will have eternal bliss and eternal life with our Lord and Our Heavenly Father, while others will have eternal judgment and the lake of fire.

The best way to define Salvation is to review the Salvation chapter of the Book of John, and allow our Lord Jesus Christ to present this Way of Life to us. The details of that first earth age are given in other chapters of this book, also the fall of Satan, and when one third of all souls chose to follow Satan. This second earth age is the time when every soul will come into this earth age of flesh man innocent of the events of that first earth age that once was. Each soul must be born of woman and will be given the free will or right to choose God's Way or follow Satan's path to destruction. Instead of attacking what different churches hold dear, the intent of this book is to see what the Scriptures say about the subject, so we can be guided by the living Word of God. In this case, Nicodemus is the one coming to Jesus, and asking Jesus to explain what is meant by Salvation and what it means. Being *"born from above", is* also called *"Born Again"*.

JESUS QUESTIONED BY NICODEMUS

John 3:1 *"There was a man of the Pharisees, named Nicodemus, a ruler of the Jews:"*

Nicodemus was a member of the Sanhedrin, and according to secular writings of Rabbinical tradition, he was one of the three richest men in Jerusalem [*Light foot, Vol. xii, page 252*] when Christ walked the earth. The word *"Nicodemus"* means *"conqueror of the people"*. Nicodemus will later become a disciple of Christ, and he will be with Joseph of Arimethea when the body of Christ is claimed in Pilate's court, and he will also be part of the group that prepares and anoints the body of Christ for burial.

Though Nicodemus was a member of the high court, the Sanhedrin, he was a believer in Christ, and truth that is based on fact. Nicodemus had the eyes to see by the Holy Spirit, and God allowed Nicodemus to see and understand Christ's teachings.

John 3:2 *"The same came to Jesus by night, and said unto Him, "Rabbi, we know that Thou art a teacher come from God: for no man can do these miracles that thou doest, except God be with him."*

Nicodemus came to Jesus in the night to ask Jesus some questions of Him. *"Rabbi"* in the Hebrew tongue means teacher or Master, and Nicodemus was a well educated man who was in a position of seeking out the truth in all events. He was one of the men at the top of the religious order in the Temple, and he was the one sending these scribes, Pharisees, and chief priests out to witness what Jesus was saying and doing. Nicodemus was a wise man, with sound logic.

When Nicodemus saw and heard of the miracles done by Jesus Christ, he knew that no human being could do such miracles. Nicodemus knew that the words that Jesus spoke had to came from God. When Nicodemus came at night to Jesus, he was careful because of the position in the religious community that he held. It was not a popular thing to be seen with Jesus because that was tarring down the traditions of men that the Jewish Kenites religious order had built up.

John 3:3 "Jesus answered and said unto him, "Verily, verily, I say unto thee, except a man be born again, he cannot see the kingdom of God."

This is a very interesting statement, and in most King James Bibles the margin reads *"again"* means "from above." In Strong's Greek dictionary, #509, the word is "Anothen," "from above." You will never understand this statement that Jesus made unless you understand what it means to be *"born from above."* In a later verse it was documented that you must be "*born from above*" or your soul will be lost for eternity.

The church world has their sayings and songs that "*Ye must be born again,*" and yet these verses that they sing miss the mark, because they don't understand that it means to be "*born from above*", also means [*born again*]. This is part of God's plan that every living soul must to be born of woman, which also means "*born from above*". Recorded the Book of Jude, where it's written about the fallen angels that left their place of habitation. Angels were required to inhabit heaven or paradise, however at this time of the second earth age, they were not to enter into the flesh age except when sent by God for a mission.

Jude 1:6 *"And the angels which kept not their first estate, but left their own habitation, He hath reserved in everlasting chains under darkness unto the judgment of the great day."*

Angels are not to be on the earth in the flesh age, except on a special mission by God Himself. These fallen angels that are bound in chains are held for destruction. They left the heavens without the permission of God, and as it is written in Genesis

6, were not born from above, but came from above. They were not born of woman, but observed woman and made playmates out of the daughters of men.

Genesis 6:1,2; *"And it came to pass, when men began to multiply on the face of the earth, and daughters were born unto them," "That the sons of God saw the daughters of men that they were fair; and they took them wives of all which they chose."*

These fallen angles mingled with women, and the offspring of this weird relationship between these fallen angels and women were called *"geber"* which is to say "giants." They were the misfits that roamed the earth. These fallen angels brought with them the knowledge of that first earth age, and this was contrary to God's plan for this age. It was in this genetic way that Satan and his tribe of fallen angels hoped to destroy the daughters of Adam, whereby there would not be a women fit to bring forth the promised Messiah, the Christ child. Satan had brought the Adam's human race to the point of extinction; In Satan's plan the only human life left would only be Satanic, angelic hybrids which would be a mixture of man and angel. This is why the flood of Noah's day had to came to pass.

Genesis 6:4 *"There were giants in the earth in those days; and also after that, when the sons of God [the angels] came in unto the daughters of men, and they bare (children) [the word children is not in the text] to them, the same (became) [not in the text] mighty men which were of* old, men of renown."

This inbreeding with these defiant fallen angels caused the entire population of Adam's family to be contaminated, and to be worthless for God's plan. These offspring of the wicked angels had the mind of their parents, *"and wickedness was great upon the earth"*. The children of these angels were as wicked as their fathers, which were the fallen angels.

Genesis 6:8,9 *"But Noah found grace in the eyes of the Lord." "These are the Generations of Noah; Noah was a just man and perfect in his generations, and Noah walked with God."*

Notice the phrase, "perfect in his generations". The word, *"Perfect"* is from the Hebrew word, *"tamin"* means *"without blemish as to breed or pedigree."* This perfection is talking about a blood line. This blood line or pedigree refers to Noah and his family. There was only one of Adam's family left on the face of the earth that was perfect in that generation, who had not mixed with the fallen angels. So God destroyed the earth, and all the wicked ones in the flood. They were destroyed, and their souls as recorded in Jude 6 are being held for destruction.

John 3; tells us that this *"death"* was to going contrary to God's plan. These people did, because it was essential that one be *"born from above".* Your soul comes from above, from God, for we were with God in that first earth age, and upon death Ecclesiastes 12:7 tells us that our souls will return immediately to God.

God's plan required that all souls must be born innocent because of what happened in the first earth age. God's plan requires that every soul must come into this world age through it's mother's womb with the free will to make it's own mind up whether that soul will follow God or Satan. That freedom gives us the right to choose the final destination of our own soul. Each soul is born innocent of what happened in that first earth age, and the result of that first overthrow by Satan's downfall, is recorded in Genesis 1:2, when *"the earth became void."*

Jesus Christ is giving the very basics of salvation to Nicodemus.

John 3:4 *"Nicodemus saith unto Him, "How can a man be born when he is old? can he enter the second time into his mother's womb, and be born?"*

Nicodemus still did not understand what Jesus was saying, because he could only see the flesh realm and the law. He was looking only at the flesh.

John 3:5 *"Jesus answered, "Verily, verily, I say unto thee, Except a man be born of water and of the spirit, he cannot enter into the kingdom of God."*

"Verily, verily" means, *"truly, truly".* Jesus is telling him that there must be two births necessary; the birth of the water and of the Spirit. Many people teach that *"born of the water,"* means to be baptized, and this is not what is being talked about here. To be "*born from above"* means to be born through the "*womb of your mother".* Every child born is carried in a bag of water and when the bag breaking the child is born. And God put's it first breath of life, called Spirit in every new born baby and it becomes a living soul. So we see in this that everyone must be born of woman, in innocence, and then *"be born of the Spirit".*

Born of the spirit means to accept the Spirit of Christ: Every soul must choose by their free will, in order of have the Spirit of Christ live within them. That is what the marriage of Christ is all about; to become one in Christ.

This is why most people simply do not know what being *"born from above means,"* when they disregard what happened in the book of Genesis, and in that first earth age. They overlook all of Satan's attempts to destroy the womb of woman, and God's plan to send us His Son so that we might have redemption. God intervened in Satan attempt, as He will always do. This is why the book of Jude is so important.

John 3:6 *"That which is born of the flesh is flesh; and that which is born of the Spirit is spirit."*

To understand this, read **I Corinthians 15:50**; *"Now this I say, brethren, that flesh and blood cannot inherit the kingdom of God; neither doth corruption inherit incorruption."*

No soul in their flesh and blood body can enter the Kingdom of Heaven. The Kingdom of Heaven is where ever God is, and for the soul to enter that Kingdom, it must first die or be changed. The soul must be separated from the flesh first before that soul returns to the Father that created it. This is the basic principle of the plan of our Heavenly Father. Remember back in Ecclesiastes when God told us what happens to the soul and the flesh when the flesh body dies.

Ecclesiastes 12:7; *"Then shall the dust return to the earth as it was: and the spirit shall return unto God Who gave it."*

Our flesh bodies are the accumulation of all the elements of the earth that we consume which is food. Upon death our body goes through process of decaying then returns back to those elements. Our soul and spirit came from God, and it will return to God when this flesh body dies. Every one of our souls, will return to the Father, to be judged for destruction or eternal life. Jesus is teaching Nicodemus here, and Jesus knew that Nicodemus should have understood, but he didn't.

John 3:7 "Marvel not that I said unto thee, Ye must be born again."

"Ye must be born again," as we have seen, *"ye must be born from above."* If you are not born from above, that is to say, *"born of woman,"* then you would be either a demonic spirit, or from a fallen angel that has entered into the realm of this age of flesh man. This is against God's law and the plan of God.

John 3:8 *"The wind bloweth where it listenth, and thou hearest the sound thereof, but canst not tell from whence it cometh, and whither it goeth: so is every one that is born of the Spirit."*

Jesus is using an analogy here. He is saying that you can hear the wind, but you can't see it. You can see the objects that are blown about in the wind, but the flow of the air itself you can not see. When man's spirit separates from the flesh body, the soul's spirit goes where ever the soul goes. Man's spirit is the intellect of his soul which is the part of him that controls his soul and tells him what to do. The soul and the spirit are as one. The spirit is where your emotions come from and it gives you the ability to know right from wrong. It is from your spirit that your conscience gives you directions.

Jesus is telling Nicodemus that you cannot see where your spirit goes, for it is like the wind to our flesh senses, when it ascends to the Father. When you are with a loved one at the moment of death, you will not see the soul and spirit departs from the physical body at the moment of death. But if you are familiar with that soul, your spirit will know when that soul has departed. Many times it has been reported that when a person died they have spoken and talked to a loved one that had passed on; just prior to giving up their spirit of life. God will send an angel to accompany the departing soul, back to the Father who created it.

Each soul must enter into an embryo once, be born and live in the human form as a flesh man or women only once. Every person has the free will to choose who they will follow God, or Satan. Our flesh body is discarded at death and the soul departs from the body, and returns to the Father who created it. There is no transmigration of souls, as is taught by the eastern religions, there is only one soul that enters one body and lives within that body until God appoints that soul to return home to be with Him, in heaven.

What you do in this body is important, for your works follow you, and on judgment day that is what you will be judged by. That is why it's so important to repent and believe in Jesus Christ when we can. He is the only one who can give us salvation for our soul He removes our sins before judgment day. Paul addresses this in Hebrews

Hebrews 9:27,28; *"And as it is appointed unto men once to die, but after this the judgment:" "So Christ was once offered to bear the sins of many; and unto them that look for Him shall He appear the second time without sin, unto salvation."*

When this happens you will not see the transfer of the soul and spirit body when it returns back to our Heavenly Father. For eons this activity has been reality, however we cannot see these thing happen with our eyes, although we know it happens.

John 3:9 *"Nicodemus answered and said unto Him, "How can these things be?"*

When you do not understand the spiritual realm, then this is a normal question. Nicodemus had seen Jesus perform miracles enough to know that those miracles did not come from the physical realm so they must have come from God. Nicodemus is opening his mind up to Jesus for understanding.

JESUS ANSWERS NICODEMUS

John 3:10 *"Jesus answered and said unto him, "Art thou a master of Israel, and knowest not these things?"*

Jesus then reverses the question back to Nicodemus; *"Are you not a teacher to Israel and you do not know these things?"* This is the same reason so many fall short in their teaching even today. There are many that claim to be teachers of God's Word, yet they peddle their wears of false teaching for many different reasons. If you have the understanding of God's Word, that is a gift from God, then that knowledge belongs to God. Jesus is telling Nicodemus, you claim to be a teacher, and you don't even know this?

Nicodemus didn't know the Word because he didn't study the word. Nicodemus studied the traditions of the Kenite's which are of mankind that were accepted by the religious community of that day. In fact, he was one of the spiritual leaders of his religious community.

John 3:11 *"Verily, Verily, I say unto thee, We speak that we do know, and testify that we have seen; and ye receive not our witness."*

"Truly, Truly" Jesus is saying to him, I'm sharing these things that I know to be true, and it appears that you are questioning our witness to those words.

John 3:12 *"If I have told you earthly things, and ye believe not, how shall ye believe, if I tell you of heavenly things?"*

Jesus is telling Nicodemus, now that I have told you where and how the soul has come into the flesh and departs to the Father; these things that are fleshly and you still can not understand. There is no way that you can understand the revelation that Christ brought from the spiritual realm without the Spirit of God. It is impossible.

SALVATION

John 3:13 *"And no man hath ascended up to heaven, but He That came down from heaven, even the Son of man which is in heaven."*

Here now is the second witness to those things given, as to how you must be born from above. There is no way that you can make baptism out of this verse. It sums up the whole matter of being born from above.

No man, can go up into heaven, unless he has first been created from above. Every living soul was created by God and must be born of women, when the soul entered the womb at conception. Then when the flesh body dies it is returned to the Father. There isn't a living soul on this earth that did not come down from the Father first, and at death shall return to the Father.

This doesn't mean that they are all going to have eternal life, yet heaven is where the Father is, and that is where judgment takes place. This is in reference to obtaining salvation for their soul, into eternal life. All souls return to the Father, however many of those that return will be condemned to destruction. The finial judgment takes place at the time of the *"Great White Throne Judgment"*. Until that time, those sinning souls will stay right there in paradise where there is a great gulf between God and the sinning soul, this is stated in the parable of the rich man, in Luke 16. So far there has never been a soul destroyed since the beginning of time.

This thirteenth verse is talking about being born again. It means that you must be born from above. You can't be as those fallen angels nor take short cuts through this earth age, yet it must be done according to God's plan of salvation.

John 3:14 *"And as Moses lifted up the serpent in the wilderness, even so must the Son of man be lifted up:"*

Numbers 21:9 *"And Moses made a serpent of brass, and put it upon a pole: and it shall come to pass, that every one that is bitten, when he looketh upon it, shall live."*

The children of Israel had left Egypt and were starting their wandering in the wilder-ness. God feed them manna and quail, they had a fire to warm them at night and a cloud to shade them from the hot sun in the day time. After a while the Israelites were tired of the easy life and they started complaining to Moses.

Because of their grumbling, God brought fiery serpents that killed thousands of the Israelites. Then God gave Moses a sample of the type of Christ, He told Moses to put a serpent on a pole, which was symbolic of Jesus Christ on the cross.

Then God told Moses to tell the people to look upon it and their lives will be saved from the serpent bites. Did the serpent on the pole save the person that had been bit? No.

Jesus Christ is telling John that it was because of their belief and their faith in Him, that saved them. Jesus is telling Nicodemus that if you believe in Jesus Christ, and His death on the cross, just as those Israelites when they looked upon that pole. They saw the serpent hanging on it and their lives were saved. This is symbolic of the fact that believers' will also be saved by faith. Jesus had not died at this point in time, yet the death of a promised Messiah was well known to Nicodemus.

John 3:15 "*That whosoever believeth in Him should not perish, but have eternal life.*"

To "*perish*" means to turn your soul into ashes, and eliminate all memory of you after the lake of fire, following the *"Great White Throne Judgment ".*

John 3:16 *"For God so loved the world, that He gave His only begotten Son, that whosoever believeth in Him should not perish, but have everlasting life."*

The condition required on our part is to prevent our soul from perishing, is that they we must, *"believeth in Him"* who is the Lord Jesus Christ. All those that believe in Jesus Christ will not be turned to ashes on judgment day, because, they will have everlasting life. The word "*everlasting"* is better translated from the Greek text, *"eternal,"* because eternal means "from the very beginning of the creation of each soul, lives on into eons "*Aion*" of infinity and there is no break in time."

This is saying that the person's soul will not die, but will live from the time that their soul was created in that first earth age, in the distant past, all through this earth age and on into eternity. There will never be any spots of void in the life of their living souls. This eliminates the pagan worship of *"soul sleep"*, such as those who teach that when you die, your soul stays in the ground until a so-called rapture. This is a tradition that will lead them into the camp of the Antichrist before long.

When you take the word "*everlasting*" as used in John 3:16, and go to Strong's Greek dictionary, #166, we find, *"Aion"*, *"Perpetual, of past time, present and future, eternal, from beginning without end."* If you believe in Jesus Christ, you will never see the death of your soul body, which is your spirit body, yet your flesh body will decay. The truth is, there is no such thing as soul sleep.

The serpent that Moses placed on the pole was an example to the Israelites to obey God and they would be given life for believing and obeying His word. Jesus is telling us that this is exactly as it is with eternal life. The pole that we look to is the cross that Jesus Christ shed His blood on, and when we look to Him and accept His shed blood for our forgiveness, through repentance, we have eternal life. When Nicodemus was talking with Jesus here, the crucifixion had not taken place, but Nicodemus would be one of the men that would prepare Christ's body for burial.

It is nice to be baptized because Christ was, but that is not what gives us eternal life. There are memberships in the church's, with all the other dos and don'ts but they have nothing to do with our eternal salvation. What is important is that we look to the cross that God's only begotten Son died upon, and believe on His only begotten Son, and that is where eternal life comes from.

Don't let people rob you of the simplicity of God's Word, the simple truth is that those who believe in Him and repented in Jesus name shall not perish, but have eternal life.

John 3:17 *"For God sent not His Son into the world to condemn the world; but that the world through Him might be saved."*

God sent His only begotten Son into the world for the sole purpose of being crucified, in fulfillment of His Word. When He died on the cross, God didn't condemn the world for their actions against His Son. Because this was the only way that God could draw people back to Himself. Christ's death on the cross paid the full price for every sin that people committed, because of His death, Our Heavenly Father is offering us eternal life for our souls, also the inheritance we share with His Son, Jesus Christ. That is something all the wealth of this world can't buy, it is offered to us, and all we have to do is accept it. Remember God loves you, and you can come to Him by repenting and believing in Jesus Christ.

CONDEMNATION

John 3:18 "He that believeth on Him is not condemned: but he that believeth not is condemned already, because he hath not believed in the name of the only begotten Son of God."

Because if you don't have eternal life, then you are already condemned and sentenced to death. It is cut and dried, you either believe or you don't. There is only one *"begotten Son of God"* and His name is Jesus Christ. This is why we are to pray all of our prayers "in Jesus name", for that identifies you before our Heavenly Father as one of His redeemed Children. In Jesus name you have the right to come to the Father with your petition, for at Christ's death on the cross, the vial or barrier into the Holy of Holies was rent in two.

John 3:19 *"And this is the condemnation, that light is come into the world, and men loved darkness rather than light, because their deeds were evil."*

If we're following the ways of this world, we are following the ways of Satan. He is the evil prince of this earth age of flesh man.

John 3:20 *"For every one that doeth evil hateth the light, neither cometh to the light, lest his deeds should be reproved."*

This is saying is that if you are going to be a thief, a murderer, or do any of the other acts of evil, you will flee toward the darkness. You want those acts to be hidden not only from God, but for those around you. You will not seek the light, but you will choose to operate in the darkness, and keep your wicked deeds hidden.

John 3:21 *"But he that doeth truth cometh to the light, that his deeds may be made manifest that they are wrought in God."*

When you believe in Jesus Christ, you become a member of the body of Christ. As a member of the body of Christ, God will give you gifts to serve Him, and those gifts are to be used in the light. You are to use those gifts to draw others to the light, and the more you use them, the more the world can see God in you. God's Word is simple and it's the truth, His message to the world is that God loves you so much that He sent His only Son to die for all your sins. When you believe in Jesus Christ you are brought into the light, and are given eternal life.

Once you understand what happens at death, then the fear of death is removed, and God's will is done. Believers know that our eternal home is with Him, and this life of the flesh age is but a vapor in time and world pleasures can not be compared to what our Heavenly Father has in store for each of us.

BAPTISM

John 3:22 *"After these things came Jesus and His disciples into the land of Judaea; and there He tarried with them, and baptized."*

The translation here is off a little, for Christ never helped baptize anyone. The way that He becomes part of some ones baptism is that He paid the price, and we were all baptized in His name. Jesus Christ took away the sins of the world for all those who willingly repented and believe upon Him. When we are submerged in baptism, it is in His name. He is the Messiah and our personal Savior. "He took the stripes and we were healed."

It is not important which man performs the baptism, for the baptism is strictly between the person being baptized and his [her] looking to the throne of God, with Christ there. Baptism identifies you as a believer in the Virgin birth of Christ, in his ministry, crucifixion and resurrection of our Lord Jesus Christ. If you did not believe in Christ, why in the world would you ever want to be baptized?

John 3:*23* *"And John also was baptizing in AEnon near to Salim, because there was much water there: and they came, and were baptized."*

Jesus along with His disciples came to this place AEnon where John the Baptist was baptizing, and many were baptized there by John. *"Disciple"* means "one disciplined," and that is why we must be baptized, because it is part of the discipline a Christian and all followers of the Lord obey because it's His will.

John 3:24 *"For John was not yet cast into prison . . ."*

So we see that the disciples were being baptized in one place in Judaea, and just a little ways away down stream at AEnon where John was baptizing. While this is going on, we will see these Kenite Jews, scribes and Pharisees came to John and tried to turn John against Jesus' disciples. This is how the Kenites work and it is very similar to how they work today, by turning one ministry against another, and trying to set up conflicts within the Christian community. However, there is no difference between those of the elect regardless what the different groups call themselves.

When you truly accept Jesus from the heart and believe in Jesus name, and have repented of your sins, there is no difference regardless of the physical world around you. We all must be saved the same way, our inheritance is laid out the same, and all Christians love the same Lord. Jesus is pointing out here that all Christians are in the same family of God, and these family ties are eternal, so it is time to understand this in our minds.

John 3:25 *"Then there arose a question between some of John's disciples and the Jews about purifying."*

Here, John's followers were met and challenged by men sent from the religious leaders regarding purifying. These Jews were sent there to argue and create conflict. This bickering and arguing is also going on in the churches today if the pastors allow it to happen. John has not been put in prison yet, but it will happen shortly.

John 3:26 *"And they came unto John, and said unto him "Rabbi, He That was with thee beyond Jordan, to whom thou barest witness, behold, the same baptizeth, and all men come to Him."*

This Kenite tribe of religious misfits is calling attention to John, that Jesus, the one that he had baptized in the Jordan river. They had a much bigger crowd on down the river a ways. These men are trying to make trouble. They are comparing one ministry with another, and the comparison is on the basis of their number of members in their churches. This can cause jealousy and strife amongst some Christians, and discourage a ministry that is not geared to large numbers for profit. Some ministries are for evangelism of large numbers, while others are for teaching as pastors.

When you set forth to use the gifts that God has given you, each gift is to fill the part that God has equipped you to perform for Him. When this truth came to John's attention, it did not disturb him, for he knew that he had a mission and a duty to perform his service for God, and he knew where all gifts came from.

If God has given you a great gift, then He expects a great service from you. He expects you to develop the gifts and talents that you have, and for you to give one hundred percent of that talent to Him. We should each thank the Lord for what we have, and pray for our fellow Christians as they strive to use their talents for the glory of God.

When John baptized Jesus, he saw the Holy Spirit descending like a dove and landing on Jesus, and then John heard God speaking from heaven.

Matthew 3:16,17 *"And Jesus, when He was baptized, went up straightway out of the water: and, lo, the heavens were opened unto Him, and He saw the Spirit of God descending like a dove, and lighting upon Him:" "And lo a voice from heaven, saying," "This is My beloved Son, in Whom I am well pleased.*"

John knew that Jesus was truly the Son of God, so these Kenite Jews could never cause a conflict between Jesus and his disciples, John and his followers.

John 3:27 *"John answered and said, "A man can receive nothing, except it be given him from heaven."*

We must be on guard when we see a power play such as this and identify it for what it is. Remember, earlier in this chapter when Jesus told Nicodemus that every man must be born from above. Everything that comes to this earth comes from God, and that includes your soul and spirit as well as your gifts and all of the blessings and wealth that we enjoy.

John is telling these Jews that there is no exception to this rule, for a man can receive nothing except it be given by God from heaven.

We receive our heavenly rewards from the works and services that we give to Him, according to our ability. God even places those souls before us to witness to, and helps when they are in need. Then He watches to see how we use the gifts that He has given us, and He rewards us. God knows the thoughts and intents of our heart and mind. That is what these rewards are based on in regard to what we do with what we have.

John 3:28 *"Ye yourselves bear me witness, that I said, I am not the Christ, but that I am sent before Him."*

John is calling attention again to these same religious leaders, reminding them that he was not the Christ. This was recorded back in **John 19-23.**

John 1:19-23 *"John the Baptist told these same men from the temple;" "I am the voice of one crying in the wilderness, `Make straight the way of the Lord,' as said the prophet Esaias."*

John answered these men with the Word of God, as that prophecy was taking place right before their eyes.

John 3:29 *"He that hath the bride is the bridegroom: but the friend of the bridegroom, which standeth and heareth him, rejoiceth greatly because of the bride-groom's voice: this my joy therefore is fulfilled."*

John is telling these Kenite scribes and Pharisees that it is for this reason that I was sent, to prepare the way for the one that would come later. John is telling them, don't try to make me jealous of Jesus, for that is why I was sent in the first place.

From this quote, *"He that hath the bride is the bridegroom;"* many teach that the bride is Israel and the bridegroom is Jesus. However Revelation 19:6-9 tells us that Jesus, the Lamb of the world had both a wife and a bride. This has to do with the Election and free will. The Elect and the Free looks back to what happened in that first earth age, and the judgment that took place and was also recorded in Ephesians 1:4-5.

Jesus is the bridegroom, and those in the service of Christ are not in competition with each other. Those that hear and preach the Word of God are not all on the same level of understanding, and any person who is a friend of the bridegroom can only find joy for themselves, when the bridegrooms finds joy. John is saying, I am the bride-groom's friend. I came to announce that Jesus Christ is coming for His bride or believers'. How can I be jealous when His bride is going to Him in multitudes and are being baptized by His disciples. I see this happening and I rejoice as my joy is fulfilled. John accomplished a good work, and he paid a price. However, seeing the success of His work gave John much joy.

There are many that will try to do this to you because of the work you do for the Lord. They will put your work with another work, drawing many more souls, and by this method try to downgrade. All the work we do for the Lord is important. If you only reach one soul that requires 100% of your talents, then you are just as successful as the ministry that has reached thousands. God requires you to take the responsibility for what He has given you, and you're not required to answer for another person's talents. When God's work succeeds, that is a cause for all Christians to rejoice.

John 3:30 *"He must increase, but I must decrease."*

To determine if your ministry is successful, see If Christ has increased your ministry, and outsider's are drawn to Jesus Christ, then your ministry is of God and the ministry is fulfilled. If your ministry is focused on a certain person who is preaching, or the size of the congregation has increased or decreased it may be because of the reputation of the preacher is on him rather then on Jesus Christ, then it's time to look at the goal of the that church.

If there are pie socials, fund raisers, baby sitting, ball games, entertainment activities, garage seals, stage shows or singing programs for entertainment. etc. It is not God's House of Prayer any more. The Bible tells us, the Lord God calls his church a House of Prayer. Remember the day that Lord came into the tabernacle and tipped over the tables in a state of anger toward the Pharisee's for what they were doing in His house of prayer. Are we any different today?

John 3:31 *"He That cometh from above is above all: he that is of the earth is earthly, and speaketh of the earth: He That cometh from heaven is above all."*

Christ is the Anointed One that comes from above and is above all men. The thing to consider here is that all of mankind that comes through the womb is flesh and their physical end will be their physical decay that will go back into the elements. Those demonic fallen angels, or "sons of God," as spoken in Jude 6, refused to come through woman are judged and condemned already. There is a move going on today to clone the human embryo and bypass the birthing process, that is not part of the plan of God. They use names that are tricky and deceiving so people will accept it. The word "Cloning" is referred to by different names. The reasons for doing this is because it's all part of Satan's work, just as bringing those fallen angels into this earth age to destroy the seed of Adam. If God had not interceded, the prophecy of the Messiah in Genesis 3:15 would not have taken place. That prophecy foretold about the nail that would be driven into the heel of Jesus by the Kenite's, and the actions of Satan's own son's will condemn their father Satan to his final destruction.

However, Jesus Christ did not come like all other men came to this earth, because his father was the Spirit of God who conceived the Christ child in the Virgin Mary's womb, and this was the fulfillment of the promises of the word of God, for all ages. Jesus Christ was God in the flesh, He was conceived by God.

John is telling those Kenite religious leaders that Jesus Christ came from above and could never compare with earthly man, for God is the Father and creator of them all. The creation can never be above the creator of it. Even Satan is a created being, and as such can never be compared to the one that created him. Jesus is God, and in John 10:30 Jesus told this to the Jews; *"I and My Father are one."* When the Jews heard Him, they took up stones to kill Him.

There is no way that any human being can understand the total revelation that Christ would bring in the New Testament. And naturally, the more man knows about Christ, all the more John will decrease as Christ is increased through heavenly revelations.

John 3:32 *"And what He hath seen and heard, that He testifieth; and no man receiveth His testimony."*

A human being can only testify as to what he has seen and heard, and this is why it is not possible to understand the mind of God.

John 3:33 *"He that hath received His testimony hath set to his seal that God is true."*

If you can understand the testimony or teachings of Christ, then you have set God's seal in your mind. Not only is that seal in your mind, but you know the Word that Jesus brought is true. This isn't a theory because it becomes reality to ever believer. Religion is formed by man for man. However, the truths that Jesus Christ spoke is reality.

Religion today is no different than it was in Athens when Paul stood there on Mars hill. The people didn't know who to worship so they built a statute to all the gods. Because none of the gods satisfied them, so they thought that there must be an unknown god, so they built a statute to their unknown god.

Acts 17:22-26 *"Then Paul stood in the midst of Mars' hill, and said, "Ye men of Athens, I perceive that in all things ye are too superstitious." "For as I passed by, and beheld your devotions, I found an altar with this inscription, TO THE UNKNOWN GOD. Whom therefore ye ignorantly worship, Him declare I unto you . . ."*

We read Paul's declaration in Acts.17.

Acts 17:24& 26 *"God That made the world and all things therein, seeing that He is Lord of heaven and earth, dwelled not in temples made with hands;" "And hath made of one blood all nations of men for to dwell on all the face of the earth, and hath determined the times before appointed, and the bounds of their habitation;"*

God has total control over all the events in history and happenings on earth, as well as the universe. We have the "higher critics" who are still active in our day. They claim to know all about God's Word, yet they are unbelievers; however, there are some exceptions to this rule. The "higher critics" are the ones who makes an effort to study the ancient manuscripts for the sole purpose of destroying truth of God's word. Yet many who do so are converted and become believers. Through striving to disprove truths, God allows the light of His word to shine on their hearts [minds], and they no longer continue as "higher critics", but were changed into believers.

John 3:34 *"For He Whom God hath sent speaketh the Words of God: for God giveth not the Spirit by measure unto Him."*

John is comparing the Messiah with himself. He said that God sent this one [himself] with the Word of God, for God gives the Spirit by full measure to human beings according to God's will. The reason for this is that it would be impossible for any human being to receive the full measure of understanding like Jesus had. Jesus is God, and man is limited by his created body with limited understanding. Jesus Christ was very special, for in the flesh body, he experienced the emotions, experiences and temptations that we have, yet He was God. He remained perfect and innocent to stand in our place because He paid the price on the cross.

Keep in mind that the subject that is running through the last part of this chapter, is the wedge that the Jews were trying to drive between John the Baptist and Jesus and His disciples. The Jews were telling John that he was the one that started the ministry, and Jesus and His disciples are the ones that are getting the crowds. John in turn is telling them, that's what I came for. I'm happy and I can't be compared to Jesus.

John 3:35 *"The Father loveth the Son, and hath given all things into His hand."*

God did not give man the full measure and He did not give John the full measure, but God gave His Son, Jesus Christ the full measure of all authority into His hand. Jesus Christ now sits at the right hand of the Father until all things are put under His feet.

John 3:36 *"He that believeth on the Son hath everlasting life: and he that believeth not the Son shall not see life; but the wrath of God abideth on him."*

"He that believeth on the Son [Jesus Christ] *hath everlasting life."* Even a small child can understand this statement. He that believeth not in the Son of God shall not see everlasting life. You either see, or you don't; and if you understand that eternal life is given to you by faith you will have eternal live, yet if you

don't want to believe that Jesus died for you, your soul is under the condemnation of judgment.

There are no qualifications to this statement nor requirements or any other things to be performed. The price has already been paid for our eternal life and the inheritance that each of us will receive has been done by Jesus Christ our Savior. To receive your gift, just reach out and take it by faith then repent for our sins in Jesus name. If we confess our sins and ask forgiveness in Jesus name, while we're living in our flesh bodies our soul body, will not go to hell nor will it be destroyed. The final judgment comes after the "*Great White Throne Judgment*".

Revelation 20:15; *"And whosoever was not found written in the book of life was cast into the lake of fire."*

God's wrath at the end of the flesh age is to correct His children, and bring them back into His fold with love and understanding. God doesn't want to correct anyone, for that is why He gave each of us a free will. Even though we fall short, when we repentance to God in Jesus name, it is though we were perfect just as Jesus was perfect, when our sins are removed from us, our names are written in the "Lamb's book of life."

There is no church to join nor oath to take, and there is no money to pay nor any ridged guideline to follow. The only requirement is we must believe in Jesus name, and we do that by confessing our sins to Him, and telling Him that we love Him. We express our love to Him by studying His Word, and allowing His Spirit to work in our lives. The Bible reveal's the *"Will and Testament of God",* and when we study His word, God's Holy Spirit will open our minds teach us what we should know and our spirit or conscience will guide us all through our lives everyday that we prey to him. He will never leave you or forsake you, because he died for the entire human race, and He wants us to know how much He loves each of us.

REFERENCE LIST

* *"Great Massorah Text",* known as the Old Testament. All of these authors and their teams, have translated from the original *"Great Massroah Text."* They all knew the old Hebrew, Greek, Chadian and English languages. The original *"Great Massroah Text"* is now in the museum in London England.

* *"The Interlinear Bible",* was coded with *Strong's Concordance* number system and was printed by the Trinitarian Bible Society in London England, written by J.P. Greens, Sr., and his team. There are IIII Volumes. Our research was taken from *"The Interlinear Bible" copyright 1985 by Jay P. Green Sr. Published by Sovereign Grace Publishers P. O. Box 4998, Lafayette, In. 47903 All rights reserved.*

* *"The Companion Bible"* uses the *"King James Bible"* with foot notes and 198 appendixes and was written by D.W. Bullinger and his team in the late 1800's through early 1900's. They worked together on this publication between 1822-1894. This book is the only Bible you will ever need. Our research came from *"The Companion Bible" With the King James Bible", version 1611.copyright 1990 by E. W. Bullinger. Published by Kregel Publications, Grand Rapids, Mi. Used by permission of the publisher. All rights reserved.*

* *"The New Strong's Exhaustive Concordance of the Bible".* James Strong and his team compiled and provided their cross references with numbers, used as a guide for their understanding of the original Hebrew, Chadian, and Greek languages which is known as the first five books of the Bible. *"Smith Dictionary" was written by* William Smith, *Sr.,* and his team. This publication provides history, photos and descriptions of various biblical periods of time. *"The New Strong's Exhaustive Concordance of the Bible." "Published by*

Kregel Publication", Grand Rapids, MI. Used by permission of the publisher.

* "*Smith Bible Dictionary*" was written by William Smith, Sr. and his team, 1813-1893. This publication provides many old etchings that illustrate various biblical artifacts, people, places, plants, and other things. Our research was taken from, *"Smith Bible Dictionary" 1813-1893. Revised and edited by F. N. and M. A. Peloubet, and Published by Thomas Nelson in 1986 Publishers, Nashville, Camden, New York.*

CPSIA information can be obtained at www.ICGtesting.com
Printed in the USA
LVOW050152280812

296185LV00001B/29/P